PROTESTANT BIBLICAL
INTERPRETATION

PROTESTANT BIBLICAL INTERPRETATION

*A Textbook of Hermeneutics for
Conservative Protestants*

BY

BERNARD RAMM, B.D., Ph.D.

COMPLETE REVISED EDITION

W. A. WILDE COMPANY
Publishers   *Boston*

Made in the United States of America

DEDICATION

This volume is dedicated with Christian affection to Dean Earl Kalland of the Conservative Baptist Seminary of Denver, Colorado; a friend, scholar, and Christian.

ACKNOWLEDGMENTS

The author wishes to express his gratitude to the following publishing houses for permission to quote from their publications:

James Nisbet & Co.: *Types of Modern Theology*, by H. R. Mackintosh.

The Macmillan Company: *The Bible in the Church* (copyright, 1948), by R. W. Grant.

The Presbyterian Guardian: *The Infallible Word*.

Charles Scribner's Sons: *Faith and History*, by R. Niebuhr.

E. P. Dutton & Co.: *Apologia pro vita sua*, by Newman.

AUTHOR'S PROLOGUE

The author has endeavored to present that system of hermeneutics which most generally characterizes conservative Protestantism. In pursuit of this goal we have not defended any specific school of thought within Protestantism.

The material has been, therefore, kept general, and individual instructors may make their own emphases. Some writers on hermeneutics devote considerable space to detailed exposition or illustrations. We have tried to restrict our illustrations to a minimum, leaving that part of hermeneutics to the teacher to supply. Other writers defend distinctive doctrines that a literal method leads to, e.g., hyperdispensationalism, dispensationalism, or premillennialism. In our view of hermeneutics these are different conclusions that men have come to following the same general method of interpretation.[1] They are the result of the interpreter's skill or art, or lack of the same. It is our purpose to lay bare the essential features of the literal system. If we commence defending specific doctrines, we confuse hermeneutics with exegesis.

Greek and Hebrew words have been put in italics. Those who know the languages may resort to them, and those not

---

[1] For example Graber definitely claims that dispensationalism and ultradispensationalism do *not differ in their respective hermeneutical systems*. The difference is in exegesis of various passages of Scripture. John B. Graber, *Ultradispensationalism* (unpublished doctoral dissertation, Dallas Theological Seminary, 1949), p. 1.

familiar with them will not be too confused by the presence in the script of the original languages.

The word 'literal' is offensive to some even within the conservative circle. In subsequent definitions, however, we make clear what the word means in our system of hermeneutics. The reader may turn to our citation in Chapter III in which E. R. Craven so clearly defines what is meant by 'literal.' There is no other word that can serve our purposes except possibly 'normal.' But the use of that word has its limitations and problems.

A special word of gratitude is to be extended to Dr. Gleason Archer for linguistic help; Dr. Edward Carnell for assistance in the chapter dealing with neo-orthodoxy; Dr. Wilbur Smith for many valuable suggestions throughout the book; Dr. Charles Feinberg for correcting the manuscript and giving valuable assistance in every way; Professor Walter Wessel for reading parts of the manuscript; Miss Inez McGahey for reading the manuscript for grammatical matters; Miss Barbara Pietsch for typing the manuscript; and to my wife for help on literary and grammatical matters.

We are grateful to God that this book in its first edition has been used in Christian schools literally around the entire world. Since the first edition we have rethought some problems, and read wider in hermeneutical literature. We have rewritten much of the book and changed the order of it in certain places.

The preaching and pulpit teaching in our land is not as yet sufficiently guided by a sound hermeneutics. One saying of Alexander Carson has stayed with us during most of this revision and could well be the theme of this revised edition:

"No man has a right to say, as some are in the habit of saying, The Spirit tells me that such or such is the meaning of such a passage. How is he assured that it is the Holy Spirit, and that it is not a spirit of delusion, except from the evidence that the interpretation is the legitimate meaning of the words?" (*Examination of the Principles of Biblical Interpretation*, p. 23.)

PREFACE

St. Luke, in his record of what has been called by some the most beautiful chapter in all the Bible, the account of the walk of the risen Lord with the two disciples on the way to Emmaus, tells us that Jesus, "beginning from Moses, and from all the prophets, interpreted to them in all the scriptures the things concerning himself." The word here translated *interpreted* is the Greek word *diermeneuo*. If we take away the two first letters, the prefix, and give a rough breathing to that initial letter "e" we have exactly the word from which our word *hermeneutics* is derived, meaning, then, the science of interpretation. (In the New Testament this word, in its various forms, may be found, e.g., in Matt. 1:23; Mark 5:41; 15:22,34; John 1:8,38; 9:7; Acts 4:36; 9:36; 13:8; I Cor. 12:10; 14:28; Heb. 7:2.) Hardly any study in the whole vast realm of intellectual life could be more important than the science of hermeneutics as applied to the Word of God, that which gives us an understanding of the eternal revelation of God to men. When such is absent not only have men misinterpreted the word, but they have taken falsehood out of the truth, and thus have deceived many when they should have led them out of darkness into light.

Half a century ago the great London preacher, Dr. Joseph Parker, delivered a sermon on the phrase, "which being interpreted is," which he entitled "The Interpreter."

Perchance most of the readers of this book have not seen a copy of this sermon, I would like in this preface to confront this generation of Bible students once again with the opening and closing paragraphs, from the heart and

mind of him who did so much to awaken new interest in the
Word of God in the London of another generation:

" 'Which being interpreted,"—that is what we need: a man to
tell us the meaning of hard words and difficult things and mysteries which press too heavily upon our staggering faith. The
interpretation comes to us as a lamp, we instantly feel the comfort and the liberty of illumination. When we heard that word
Emmanuel we were staggered; it was a foreign word to us, it
brought with it no home associations, it did not speak to anything that was within us; but when the interpreter came, when
he placed his finger upon the word and said to us. The meaning
of this word is God with us, then we came into the liberty and
into the wealth of a new possession.

"So we need the interpreter. We shall always need him. The
great reader will always have his day, come and go who may.
We want men who can turn foreign words, difficult languages,
into our mother tongue; then how simple they are and how
beautiful, and that which was a difficulty before becomes a gate
opening upon a wide liberty. We need a man who can interpret
to us the meaning of confused and confusing and bewildering
events; some man with a key from heaven, some man with divine
insight, the vision that sees the poetry and the reality of things,
and a man with a clear, simple, strong, penetrating voice who
will tell us that all this confusion will one day be shaped into
order, and all this uproar will fall into the cadences of a celestial
and endless music. We shall know that man when we meet him;
there is no mistaking the prophet; he does not speak as other
men speak, he is not in difficulty or in trouble as other men are;
on his girdle hangs the key, the golden key, that can open the
most difficult gates in providence and in history, and in the daily
events that make up our rough life from week to week. How
distressing is the possibility that a prophet may have been amongst
us, and we may have mistaken him for a common man! How
much more we might have elicited from him if we had listened
more intently to his wonderful voice! What miracles of music he
might have wrought in our nature; but we take the prophet
sometimes as a mere matter of course: he is a man in a crowd,

his specialty we overlook, and we know not that he is talking to us from the mountain of the heavens, from the altar of the temple unseen. . . .

"It is the prophet's business to interpret things to us, to tell us that everything has been from the beginning, to assure us that there are no surprises in providence, to calm our hearts with the deep conviction that God has seen the end from the beginning, and that nothing has occurred on all this theatre of time which God did not foresee and which God cannot control. The devil is but a black servant in the kitchen of God; the devil has limited chains; he counts the links, he would like to make seven eight, he strives to strain the links into greater length, he cannot do it, he was chained at the first, he has been chained ever since, he will be chained for ever—hallelujah! the Lord reigneth! There is but one throne, and all hell is subject to the governance and the authority of that throne . . .

" 'Which being interpreted.' We need the interpreter every day. We say, Affliction, and he says, I will interpret that word to you; it needs interpretation, it is a very bitter word, but affliction being interpreted is chastening, refining, sanctifying, making meet for the Master's use. The Cross being interpreted is law, righteousness, pardon, redemption, atonement, salvation. Being misinterpreted, it is to one class a sneer, to another an offence, to another foolishness; but to believe its interpretation at its best, it is the power of God and the salvation of God. Man being interpreted is child of God, son of the Eternal, a creature made in the image and likeness of God, and meant to live with God and to glorify Him for ever. The Church being interpreted is the most vital centre of the most blessed influence, an association of souls that love the Cross, that live in Christ, that are saved by Christ, and that have no joy that is not consonant with the purposes of God. God being interpreted is Love."

Probably in no department of Biblical and theological study has there been such a lack of worthwhile literature in the twentieth century as in the field of Biblical hermeneutics. The nineteenth century witnessed the appearance of the best hermeneutical works the Church has ever known: the twentieth century has seen practically none that are important—trivial, wretchedly written, fragmentary works, without exact scholarship and incapable of making real contributions to this study. The older works are now all out of print, and some of them would prove too bulky, too exhaustive for present needs. Moreover, so much has occurred in the last sixty years bearing directly upon Biblical interpretation that a new volume on hermeneutics has long been overdue. Vast discoveries in the ancient lands of the Bible, great strides in linguistics, in the understanding of ancient Hebrew, and Ugaritic, and the earlier Semitic languages, new emphases on certain portions of the Word of God, and the sudden appearance in history of a resurrected Israel, along with the crazy interpretations of certain parts of the Word of God by cults that are now winning converts by the thousands—all these call for a new work in the field of Biblical interpretation. I have taught hermeneutics from time to time, and unless I have missed something more important than anything I have been able to discover for use in classroom work, it is my opinion that this volume by Dr. Ramm is the only work covering the entire field of hermeneutics that has been published in the last forty years suitable and satisfactory for seminary work.

The author of this volume, from whom I believe many notable works will yet be forthcoming, if the Lord wills, Dr. Bernard Ramm, received his B.A. degree from the University of Washington in 1938, followed by a B.D. degree from Eastern Baptist Seminary in Philadelphia. In 1947 Mr. Ramm received his M.A. degree from the University of Southern California, and in the spring of 1950 had conferred upon him by the same institution the degree of Doctor of Philosophy, in the preparation for which he specialized in the field of the philosophy of science. While at Eastern Baptist Theological Seminary, he earned the Middler's Scholarship Award, and the Church History prize. After a

short period as pastor of the Lake Street Baptist Church of
Glendale, California, Mr. Ramm for one year, 1943–1944,
was Professor of Biblical Languages in the Los Angeles
Baptist Theological Seminary; from 1944 to the spring of
1950, he was the head of the Department of Philosophy and
Apologetics at the Bible Institute of Los Angeles. During
this time he was a Mid-Term Lecturer at Western Baptist
Theological Seminary, the lectures later appearing in his
first work, *Problems in Christian Apologetics*. As this book
comes from the press, Dr. Ramm begins his new work as
Associate Professor of Philosophy in Bethel College and
Seminary in St. Paul, Minnesota.

Personally, it amazes me that one as young as Dr. Ramm
has been able to produce such a mature work as this volume
will immediately appear to be to those who know something
of the problems and the literature of hermeneutics. Teachers in Bible institutes and professors in theological seminaries will unite in gratitude to this young man for making
available for them a greatly needed textbook. I predict that
in the next two years it will be the accepted text for hermeneutical studies in the majority of conservative schools in
this country, where men are being trained in that holiest of
all work, the interpretation of the Word of God, the group
which Dr. Alexander Whyte called "that elect and honorable
and enviable class of men that we call students of New
Testament exegesis . . . the happiest and the most enviable
of all men who have been set apart to nothing else but to
the understanding and the opening up of the hid treasures
of God's Word and God's Son."

                                              Wilbur M. Smith

Pasadena, California

Note: Dr. Parker's sermon, '"The Interpreter," appears in his *City
       Temple Pulpit*, London, 1899, pp. 40–47.
       The words quoted from Dr. Whyte are to be found in his
       inimitable work, *The Walk, Conversation, and Character of
       Jesus Christ Our Lord*, p. 53.

TABLE OF CONTENTS

Chapter I

INTRODUCTION

A. The Need for Hermeneutics

HERMENEUTICS is the science and art of Biblical interpretation. It is a science because it is guided by rules within a system; and it is an art because the application of the rules is by skill, and not by mechanical imitation. As such it forms one of the most important members of the theological sciences. This is especially true for conservative Protestantism which looks on the Bible as *sola fidei regula* and not as just *prima fidei regula*. *Sola fidei regula* is the Reformation position that the Bible is the only authoritative voice of God to man. The Roman Catholic Church and the Eastern Oriental Church accept the Bible as the first or primary authority among other authorities, *e.g.*, the moral unanimity of the Fathers, the ancient Creeds, the decisions of the ecumenical councils, and oral tradition.

These additional authorities function to help interpret the Scriptures. In that conservative Protestantism takes *only* the Bible as authoritative, there is no secondary means of making clear the meaning of the Bible. Therefore we know what God has said by the faithful and accurate interpretation of the Scriptures. The authorities of the Roman Catholic and Eastern Oriental Churches will not be ignored by a careful exegete, but he will consider them as helps and assistants, human and fallible, not as divine authorities.

1. *The Primary Need*

That God has spoken in Holy Scripture is the very heart of our faith and without this certainty we should be left to the relativity and dubiousness of *human* knowledge. God has spoken! But what has He said?

This is the primary and basic need of hermeneutics: *to ascertain what God has said in Sacred Scripture; to determine the meaning of the Word of God.* There is no profit to us if God has spoken and we do not know what He has said. Therefore it is our responsibility to determine the meaning of what God has given to us in Sacred Scripture.

To determine what God has said is a high and holy task. With fear and trembling each should be ever so careful of that which he has adopted as his method of Biblical interpretation. Upon the correct interpretation of the Bible rests our doctrine of salvation, of sanctification, of eschatology, and of Christian living. It is our solemn responsibility to know what God has said with reference to each of these. This can be done only if we have carefully, thoroughly, and systematically formulated that system of Biblical interpretation which will yield most readily the native meaning of the Bible.

Further, we need to know the correct method of Biblical interpretation so that we do not confuse the voice of God with the voice of man. In every one of those places where our interpretation is at fault, we have made substitution of the voice of man for the voice of God. We need to know hermeneutics thoroughly if for no other reason than to preserve us from the folly and errors of faulty principles of understanding God's Word.

Because Scripture has not been properly interpreted the following has been urged as the *voice of God:* in that the patriarchs practiced polygamy we may practice it; in that the Old Testament sanctioned the divine right of the king of Israel, we may sanction the divine right of kings everywhere; because the Old Testament sanctioned the death of witches, we too may put them to death; because the Old Testament declared that some plagues were from God, we may not use methods of sanitation, for that would be thwarting the purposes of God; because the Old Testament forbade usury in the agrarian commonwealth of Israel we may not employ it in our economic system; because the Scripture makes certain remarks about the suffering of women in childbirth we may not approve any method of easing the pain; because tithing was a law (*de jure*) in Israel, it is a law to the Church—and, incidentally, when it was so considered the people were tithed to such a point of penury that the Church had to check it before complete economic exhaustion prevailed.

A sound hermeneutics would have prevented all of this. It would prevent an uncritical and unrealistic application of the Old Testament to Christian morality. It would prevent an expositor from using some mere phrase as an eternal principle of morality. It would prevent the effort of trying to force some binding principle upon contemporary life from an obscure Old Testament incident. It would prevent the justification of ritualism and priestcraft from an improper extension of the Tabernacle worship and sacrificial system.

The result of an erratic hermeneutics is that the Bible has been made the source of confusion rather than light. "There is no folly, no God-dishonouring theology, no iniquity, no sacerdotal puerility," writes Edward White, "for which chapter and verse may not be cited by an enslaved intelligence. And under these circumstances it is impossible to express in adequate terms the importance of a correct estimate and exposition of 'The Bible' " (*Inspiration*, p. 153). In Bassanio's mouth Shakespeare puts these words: "In religion, what damned error but some sober brow will bless it, and approve it with a text, hiding the grossness with fair ornament" (*The Merchant of Venice*, Act III, scene 2).

Certainly many of the doctrinal variations in Christendom are due to differences in interpretation. As our subsequent historical study will reveal there are major differences in approach to the interpretation of the Bible among the Roman Catholics, Eastern Oriental Church, and Protestantism. The hermeneutical systems of orthodoxy, neo-orthodoxy, and religious liberalism have very important divergences. Even a cursory reading of the literature of Christian Science will bring to light the fact that a different system of Biblical interpretation is being employed than that which is characteristic of historic Protestantism. Cults and sects employ one or more specialized principle of Biblical interpretation which makes their basic hermeneutics a different species from that of the Reformers and historic Protestantism. Differences in eschatology arise from the adoption of different principles of prophetic interpretation.

The only way to clear the atmosphere and to determine what is right and wrong, proper and improper, orthodox and heretical, is to give one's self to a careful study of the science of Biblical hermeneutics. Otherwise we deal with symptoms, not with causes; we debate about superstructure when we should be debating about foundations.

It is important, therefore, to determine how God's Word is to be understood that we may know what God has said. This is the chief and foremost need for hermeneutics.

2. *The Secondary Need*

The second great need for a science of hermeneutics is *to bridge the gap between our minds and the minds of the Biblical writers.* People of the same culture, same age, and same geographical location understand each other with facility. Patterns of meaning and interpretation commence with childhood and early speech behaviour, and by the time adulthood is reached the principles of interpretation are so axiomatic that we are not aware of them.

But when the interpreter is separated culturally, historically, and geographically from the writer he seeks to interpret, the task of interpretation is no longer facile. The greater the cultural, historical, and geographical divergences are, the more difficult is the task of interpretation. In reading the Bible we find ourselves with a volume that has great divergences from us.

The most obvious divergence is that of *language*. The

Bible was written in Hebrew, Aramaic, and Greek. To formulate rules to bridge this gap is one of the most important tasks of Biblical hermeneutics. The basic problem at this point is that languages are structurally different. The English language is analytic in structure. The *sense* of a sentence depends largely on word order. "The rat ate the cheese" does not have the same meaning as "the cheese ate the rat" although the same words are used in both sentences. Greek is an agglutinative language, and so declines nouns and adjectives, and conjugates verbs. Hence one can alter the order of a Greek sentence two or three different ways and still get the same meaning, for meaning is not basically dependent on *word order*, but on *word endings*.

To translate from Greek to English is not the simple task of finding an English word for each Greek word. The translator has to tack back and forth between languages that are structurally different. He has the tricky job of trying to find equivalents in the English verb system of forms in the Greek verb system.

Nor is it easy to find words in English that closely match the word in the Hebrew or Greek text. Each word is a little pool of meanings. Here again it taxes the learning and judgment of the wisest scholars to decide out of the pool of meanings which is the meaning intended in a given sentence, and then to try to match it with some word in the English language which is itself a pool of meanings.

There is also the *culture-gap* between our times and Biblical times which the translator and interpreter must bridge. Culture, in the anthropological sense, is all the ways and means, material and social, whereby a given people carry on their existence. Until we can recreate and understand the cultural patterns of the various Biblical periods we will be handicapped in our understanding of the fuller meaning of Scripture. For example, the web of relationships among husband, wife, concubines and children that existed in Abraham's time, has now been recovered from clay tablets. Abraham's treatment of Hagar is now seen as protocol in terms of these relationships. Joseph's shaving before he saw Pharaoh, his receiving Pharaoh's ring, and his wearing the gold chain about his neck, are now understood as Egyptian practices. Many of the features in the parables of our Lord are drawn from the manners and customs of the people of his day, and the better understanding of the parables is dependent upon a knowledge of the Jewish culture of that century.

A knowledge of marriage customs, economic practices, military systems, legal systems, agricultural methods, etc., is all very helpful in the interpretation of Scripture.

The *geography* of the various Bible lands is very instrumental for understanding the Sacred Text. The geography of Egypt is apparent in many of the features of the Ten Plagues as recorded in Exodus. Some light is shed on the life of Christ and the travels of Paul by a knowledge of Palestinian and near-East geography. References to towns, places, rivers, mountains, plains, lakes, and seas all lend a flicker of light to the meaning of the Bible if we will study them with the help of geographical science.

The understanding of most passages of Scripture is dependent on some understanding of *history*. If geography is the scenery of Scripture, history is the plot of Scripture. Each incident is dependent on a larger historical context for its better understanding. To understand the life of Christ it is necessary to know what occurred during the inter-Biblical period. We must know something of the Roman rule of the entire ancient world; Roman practices with reference to local governments; and the history of Roman rule in Palestine.

To understand Paul's travels, it is necessary to know the history of the various provinces of Asia Minor. Sir William Ramsay has demonstrated how much such historical knowledge helps to interpret the book of Acts. And what may be said of the life of Paul and of the life of our Lord, pertains to the entire Bible.

In summary, the two great needs for the science of hermeneutics are: (i) that we may know what God has said, and (ii) that we may span the linguistical, cultural, geographical, and historical gaps which separate our minds from those of the Biblical writers. Speaking of the fact that in modern times a host of data have come to light with reference to the geography, culture, and history of the Bible, Barrows correctly says:

> The extended investigations of modern times in these departments of knowledge have shed a great light over the pages of inspiration, *which no expositor who is worthy of the name will venture to neglect.*[1]

B. GENERAL INTRODUCTION

1. *Assumptions*

The conservative Protestant interpreter comes to his text believing in its divine inspiration. This is not an assumption but the demonstration of the theologian and the apologist. Exegesis itself is involved in demonstrating the divine inspiration of Scripture, to be sure. But exegetical work is carried on within a circle of theological conviction, and the conservative Protestant works within a circle which affirms the divine inspiration of the Holy Bible. This also involves the demonstration of the true canon of Scripture. Theological considerations and historical criticism unite to settle the problem of the canon. The Jewish faith accepts its Hebrew Old Testament as the only inspired Scripture. The Roman Catholic faith adds to these books the Apocryphal books and the New Testament. The Protestants accept the Jewish canon for the Old Testament rejecting the Apocryphal books, and have the same canon in the New Testament as the Catholics.

When an interpreter sets out to interpret *Scripture*, the

[1] *Companion to the Bible*, p. 525. Italics are ours.

boundary of Scripture must be determined. It is the study of the Sacred Canon which determines the boundary of Scripture. The interpreter presumes that the Protestant canon has been demonstrated to be the true content of Sacred Scripture.

After the Sacred Canon has been settled, the next task is to determine its truest text. There is no single manuscript of the Old or New Testament which is *the official manuscript*. There are *manuscripts*. A study of these manuscripts reveals many differences. The first task is to collect all the manuscripts and other materials which will help to determine the true text. The second task is to work out *basic theory* concerning how the true text is to be determined. The third task is to determine how the basic theory determines the text of any given verse.

The publication of the Revised Standard Version and the discussion it provoked revealed how improperly many ministers understood the problems of textual criticism. The deletion of a phrase or verse was judged as tampering with the Bible. But if some previous copyist added to the Scripture, the only sane thing to do is to delete his addition. The textual critic is not trying to add to nor take away from the Word of God, *but to determine what was the original wording of the Word of God.*

Textual criticism is complicated and difficult. Enormous labors have been spent on collecting, collating, and interpreting the readings. This material is presented in critical editions of the Hebrew and Greek Testaments. Textual criticism is absolutely necessary. The careful and faithful interpreter will avail himself of the findings of textual criticism and will endeavor to determine his text before he commences his actual exegesis.

After the most careful scrutiny by scholars of the Old and New Testament texts, it is now evident that the Old and New Testaments are the best preserved texts from antiquity. The number of really important textual variations of the New

Testament that cannot be settled with our present information is very small, and the new manuscripts available from
the various caves around the Dead Sea show the remarkable
purity of our present Old Testament text.

After the canon and text have been settled, the matters of
historical criticism must be discussed. Lower criticism is the
Biblical science which determines the text of Scripture. Historical criticism deals with the literary and documentary
character of the books of the Bible. Historical criticism deals
with such matters as authorship of the book, date of its
composition, historical circumstances, the authenticity of its
contents, and its literary unity. Historical criticism is a
necessary Biblical science if we wish a faith that is neither
gullible nor obscurantistic.

Because men with little regard for traditional views of
historical criticism and some with no respect for the divine
inspiration of Scripture have written much in this field, historical criticism is sometimes known as *radical* criticism or
German rationalism. It was called *radical* because of the nov-
elty and extremeness of many of the positions defended in
contrast to traditional views. It was called *German rationalism* because many of the leaders in the radical movement
were Germans. Sometimes it is called *higher criticism.*
"Higher" in contrast to "lower" meant no more than historical or literary criticism in contrast to lower or textual
criticism. But unfortunately the term *higher criticism* became
synonymous with *radical* criticism, and so the expression is
now ambiguous. Because these radical critics engaged in
many innovations they were also called *neologists* and their
views, *neologism.*

Unfortunately, due to the heated controversy of radical
criticism with conservative and traditional [2] scholarship, the

---

[2] By traditional in this sentence we mean referring to those opinions
about dates and authorships of Biblical books as held from great antiquity by the Jews and by the early Christian Church, which though
not infallible, are held as reliable until proven otherwise. The *conserva-*

entire task of historical criticism has not been given the attention by conservative scholarship that it deserves. Literary and historical criticism of the Bible is not an evil but a necessity, and no man can do full justice to a book of the Bible till he has done the best he can to determine who wrote the book, when it was written, if its contents are authentic, and if the book is a literary unit or not.[3]

These three things hermeneutics assumes as having been accomplished. It is at this point that exegesis begins. The study of the canon determines the inspired books; the study of the text determines the wording of the books; the study of historical criticism gives us the framework of the books; hermeneutics gives us the rules for the interpretation of the books; exegesis is the application of these rules to the books; and Biblical theology is the result.

2. *Definitions*

The word *interpretation* occurs in both Testaments. The Hebrew word *pathar* means "to interpret," and *pithron* means an interpretation. Most of the usages in the Old Testament refer to the interpretation of dreams for they were usually symbolic in form and their meaning therefore was not obvious.

The word occurs many times in many forms in the New Testament (*hermēneia*, interpretation; *hermēneuō*, to interpret; *diermēneuō*, to interpret, to explain; *methermēneuomai*, to interpret, to translate; *dysermēneutos*, difficult to interpret; *diermēneutes*, interpreter; *epilusis*, interpretation).

---

tive position is frequently the *traditional* position, but not uniformly so. The belief in the authenticity and genuineness of Scripture involves *ex hypothesi* that many of the traditional views are the correct ones.

[3] "Exegesis proper presupposes textual and literary criticism of the document. The exegete of the New Testament has to know, for instance, whether the text upon which he works represents the original text of the autographs, or the textual form of the fourth century. His work also presupposes knowledge of the historical background of the author, the document, and its subject matter." Otto A. Piper, "Principles of New Testament Interpretation," *Theology Today*, 3:192, July, 1946.

Most of the references are to translations from Hebrew or Aramaic into Greek.

The word *hermeneutics* is ultimately derived from Hermes the Greek god who brought the messages of the gods to the mortals, and was the god of science, invention, eloquence, speech, writing, and art.

As a theological discipline hermeneutics is the science of the correct interpretation of the Bible. It is a special application of the general science of linguistics and meaning. It seeks to formulate those particular rules which pertain to the special factors connected with the Bible. It stands in the same relationship to exegesis that a rule-book stands to a game. The rule-book is written in terms of reflection, analysis, and experience. The game is played by concrete actualization of the rules. The rules are not the game, and the game is meaningless without the rules. Hermeneutics proper is not exegesis, but exegesis is applied hermeneutics.

Hermeneutics is a *science* in that it can determine certain principles for discovering the meaning of a document, and in that these principles are not a mere list of rules but bear *organic* connection to each other. It is also an *art* as we previously indicated because principles or rules can never be applied mechanically but involve the skill (*technē*) of the interpreter.

3. *Divisions*

There is no set number of divisions to the study of hermeneutics. Some writers make *psychological hermeneutics* (the requisite spiritual qualifications of the interpreter) a basic division. Others do not. Most books follow at least the two-fold division of *general* and *special* hermeneutics. General hermeneutics refers to those rules which pertain to the interpretation of the entire Bible. Special hermeneutics refers to those rules which are developed with reference to special parts of Scripture, e.g., parables, prophecy, apocalypse, and poetry.

4. *Limitations of a Mere Knowledge of Hermeneutics*

Learning the rules of hermeneutics does not make a student a good interpreter. A person with a good memory may memorize the rules of chess and yet be a mediocre player. A person may be limited in his native mental endowment, and although able to memorize the rules of hermeneutics unable to apply them with skill. A person with a good mind may go astray due to the pressure of very strong biases. Equally great scholars are to be found among Jewish, Catholic, and Protestant interpreters. It can hardly be denied that bias in this regard will prevent one scholar from seeing an opposing position sympathetically, and will in turn see his own position glow with invulnerability. Millennial and eschatological biases are the source of many over-statements, under-statements, and unguarded statements found in the literature of this subject.

A good knowledge of hermeneutics may aid a poor education but it cannot supply what is lacking from an inadequate education. To know that a man should resort to the original languages for the best interpretation does not give the interpreter the knowledge of the languages. An interpreter unfamiliar with the history of interpretation may fall into some error of long standing.

5. *Qualifications of an Interpreter*

That spiritual qualifications have an important place in the list of qualifications cannot be debated. If spiritual things are spiritually discerned only the spiritual man can discern them. If the natural or carnal mind is at enmity with God, only a regenerate mind will be at home in Scripture. That an interpreter must have the same Spirit who inspired the Bible as the *sine qua non* for interpreting the Bible has been well stated by Marcus Dods:

In order to appreciate and use the Bible, the reader of it must himself have the same spirit which enabled its writers to understand their revelation of God and to record it. The Bible is a record, but it is not a dead record of dead persons and events, but a record inspired by the living Spirit who uses it to speak to men now. . . . It is the medium through which the living God now makes himself known. But to find in it the Spirit of God the reader must himself have that Spirit.[4]

The first spiritual qualification of the interpreter is *that he be born again.* Angus and Green write: "This first principle of Bible interpretation is taken from the Bible itself. It occupies the same place, too, in the teaching of our Lord, who, in His first recorded discourse, assured Nicodemus that 'except a man be born again, he cannot see'—can neither understand the nature nor share the blessedness—of the kingdom of God." [5]

The second spiritual qualification is that a man have *a passion to know God's word.* He must have the zeal that consumes; and the enthusiasm that breeds both reverence and industry.

The third spiritual qualification is this: *let the interpreter have always a deep reverence for God.* Meekness, humility, and patience are prime virtues for understanding Holy Scripture, and these virtues are a reflection of our reverence for God. The devout and scholarly Dean Alford has said: "Approach the Holy Gospels from the side of trust and love, and not from that of distrust and unchristian doubt. . . . Depend upon it, FAITH is the great primary requisite for the right use of the Gospels." [6]

The final spiritual qualification is that of *utter dependence on the Holy Spirit to guide and direct.* A good proverb for a student of Scriptures is: *Bene orasse est bene studuisse.*[7] "To pray well is to study well." Aquinas used to pray and fast

---

[4] *The Nature and Origin of the Bible,* p. 102. Cf. Cellérier, *Biblical Hermeneutics,* "Psychological Hermeneutics." Pp. 56–72.

[5] Angus and Green, *Cyclopedic Handbook to the Bible,* p. 179.

[6] H. Alford, *How to Study the New Testament,* p. 13. Caps are his.

[7] Angus and Green, *op. cit.,* p. 179.

when he came to a difficult passage of Scripture. Most of the scholars whose Biblical studies have blessed the church have mixed prayers generously with their studies. The heart must be kept sensitive to the indwelling Spirit who in turn has inspired the Word.

This leading of the Holy Spirit will never be as crystal clear as the original inspiration of the Scriptures. This would be a confusion of inspiration and illumination. Inspiration is infallible, but not illumination. No man can say he has had *infallible* illumination from the Holy Spirit. The illumination of the Spirit is not the conveyance of truth for that is the function of inspiration. The Holy Spirit influences our attitudes and spiritual perception. Devout expositors who do not understand the distinction between illumination and inspiration should weigh well the words of Angus and Green:

It is necessary to complete this truth by adding that the Spirit of God does not communicate to the mind of even a teachable, obedient, and devout Christian, any doctrine or meaning of Scripture which is not *contained already in Scripture itself*. He makes men wise *up to* what is written, not beyond it.[8]

Matters of fact cannot be settled solely by spiritual means. One cannot pray to God for information about the authorship of Hebrews and expect a distinct reply. Nor is it proper to pray for information with reference to other matters of Biblical introduction expecting *a revelation* about *the revelation*.

An interpreter should have the proper educational requirements. No man in the history of the Christian church has possessed *all* such requirements. The person with an average measure of intelligence can with industry and adequate guidance from teachers and books discover the central meaning of the majority of the passages of the Bible. The requirements for understanding the principal truths of the Bible are not so strict as to shut the Bible up to the *literati*.

[8] *Loc. cit.* Italics are theirs.

Rowley has very adequately stated this truth when he wrote:

Not every interpreter can have the ideal equipment. Indeed, nor can attain to the ideal, and all that any can hope to do is to attain a reasonable balance of the qualities and varieties of equipment his task demands. To ask that every interpreter of the Bible should possess a wide linguistic equipment would be to deny the task of its interpretation to all but a handful of specialists, who might lack other equally essential qualities even though they possessed the linguistic knowledge. It does not seem unreasonable to ask, however, that all who would interpret the Bible to others should have some acquaintance with Hebrew and Greek. We should be astonished at one who claimed to be a specialist in the interpretation of Greek tragedy but who could not read Greek, or who offered to expound the Confucian classics without any knowledge of Chinese. But too often the biblical interpreter has little or no access to the original texts that he so confidently handles.[9]

In the Middle Ages theology was the queen of the sciences and therefore a student was not prepared for theology until he had been through the arts. The wisdom of a liberal arts education prior to a theological training has been justified by centuries of theological education. A short-cutting to theological education without a study of the liberal arts almost uniformly results in a cutting-short of the true dimensions of Christian theology. A good liberal arts education is the basis for good interpretation, especially a course that has been rich with studies in literature, history, and philosophy.

This should be followed by a standard theological education which should include studies in Hebrew, Greek, and theology. To be a competent Biblical interpreter a knowledge of the original languages is indispensable. It is true that not all ministers have ability in languages. However, it is also true that all our language experts should not be theological professors but as Barrows observes: "It is a principle of

[9] H. H. Rowley, "The Relevance of Biblical Interpretation," *Interpretation*, 1:10–11, January, 1947.

Protestantism, the soundness of which has been confirmed by the experience of centuries, that there should always be in the churches a body of men able to go behind the current versions of the Scripture to the original tongues from which these versions were executed." [10] These men complement the men in the seminaries for they are in turn able to judge the worth of the commentaries written by the professional scholar.

The specialists must know various cognate languages. Old Testament scholars must now delve into Aramaic, Arabic, Ugaritic, Akkadian, and Latin. New Testament scholars can profit from a knowledge of Aramaic and Latin. Ancient tablets and inscriptions are important in the study of the alphabet, ancient culture, and in the understanding of Hebrew words and grammar. A knowledge of the Aramaic and Latin enables the scholar to study ancient, valuable versions of the Hebrew and Greek Testaments.

Finally, there are intellectual requirements for good interpretation. Hermeneutics is not only a science but an *art*. The rules must be applied with skill and this requires intellectual ability. There must be an *openmindedness* to all sources of knowledge. The standards of the finest scholarship must be employed with insight. A judicious use of intellectual abilities reflects itself in a high quality of exegesis. Such men as Lightfoot, Ellicott, Calvin, Maclaren, and G. Campbell Morgan exhibited remarkable skill and taste in their expositions of Scripture.

C. The Equipment of the Interpreter

An interpreter must work with tools. Certainly he ought to work with the latest critical editions of the Hebrew, Greek, and Septuagint texts. He must have those works which deal with the inspiration, canon, and criticism of Scripture. He should have standard grammars, lexicons, and concordances of the Hebrew and Greek languages. He should consult the

[10] Barrows, *op. cit.*, p. 525.

learned commentaries of the past and present. For those students who need some guide through the labyrinth of books we suggest: Wilbur Smith, *Profitable Bible Study* (revised edition); John R. Sampey, *Syllabus for Old Testament Study;* A. T. Robertson, *Syllabus for New Testament Study; A Bibliography of Bible Study*, and, *A Bibliography of Systematic Theology* (published by The Theological Seminary Library, Princeton, New Jersey); and the list we shall submit in the next section.

Supplementary material of importance is to be had from Bible dictionaries, Bible encyclopedias, Bible atlases, and specialized books on such subjects as Bible history, archaeology, manners and customs, and Bible backgrounds.

Exegetical and expository material of worth will be found in such journals as: *Interpretation, The Expository Times, The Evangelical Quarterly, Bibliotheca Sacra, The Journal of the Society of Biblical Literature, New Testament Studies*, and *Theological Studies.*

It is often asserted by devout people that they can know the Bible competently without helps. They preface their interpretations with a remark like this: "Dear friends, I have read no man's book. I have consulted no man-made commentaries. I have gone right to the Bible to see what it had to say for itself." This sounds very spiritual, and usually is seconded with *amens* from the audience.

But is this the pathway of wisdom? Does any man have either the right or the learning to by-pass all the godly learning of the Church? We think not.

First, although the claim to by-pass mere human books and go right to the Bible itself sounds devout and spiritual *it is a veiled egotism*. It is a subtle affirmation that a man can adequately know the Bible apart from the untiring, godly, consecrated scholarship of men like Calvin, Bengel, Alford, Lange, Ellicott, or Moule. In contrast to the claim that a man had best by-pass the learned works of godly expositors, is a man like Henderson, author of *The Minor*

Prophets. He spared no mental or intellectual pains to equip himself with the necessary linguistic ability to understand the Bible, and then he read patiently and thoroughly in all the literature that might help him in his interpretation of the Scriptures. He consecrated his *entire mind* and all that that involved to the understanding of Sacred Scripture. This is truly the higher consecration.

Secondly, such a claim is the old confusion of the inspiration of the Spirit with the illumination of the Spirit. The function of the Spirit is not to communicate *new* truth or to instruct in *matters unknown*, but to illuminate what is revealed in Scripture. Suppose we select a list of words from Isaiah and ask a man who claims he can by-pass the godly learning of Christian scholarship if he can out of his own soul or prayers give their meaning or significance: Tyre, Zidon, Chittim, Sihor, Moab, Mahershalahashbas, Calno, Carchemish, Hamath, Aiath, Migron, Michmash, Geba, Anathoth, Laish, Nob, and Gallim. He will find the only light he can get on these words is from a commentary or a Bible dictionary.

It is true that commentaries can come between a man and his Bible. It is true that too much reliance on commentaries may make a man bookish, and dry up the sources of his own creativity. But the abuse of commentaries is by no means adequate grounds to forsake the great, godly, and conservative commentaries which have been to our blessing and profit.

Thomas Horne has given us some excellent advice on the use of commentaries.[11] The advantages of good commentaries are: (i) they present us with good models for our interpretation; (ii) they give us help with difficult passages. But he also warns us that: (i) they are not to take the place of Bible study itself; (ii) we are not to slavishly bind ourselves to them as to authorities; (iii) we are to use only the best ones; (iv) where their interpretations are conjectures

[11] Thomas Horne, *An Introduction to the Critical Study and Knowledge of the Holy Scriptures* (eighth edition), I:353–354.

they are to be used with utmost care; and (v) we should use original commentaries rather than those that are mere compilations of previous works.[12]

D. A Suggested Minimum Bibliography
for Exegetical Work

(1). *Biblical Texts.* Hebrew: R. Kittel, *Biblia Hebraica* (fourth edition). Greek: Nestles, *Greek New Testament* (nineteenth edition). Septuagint: Editions of Rahlfs or Sweet.

(2). *Biblical Grammars.* Hebrew: Any of the standard introductory grammars, e.g., Yates, A. B. Davidson, or Gesenius-Kautzsch. Greek: Any of the standard introductory grammars as Machen, *New Testament Greek for Beginners,* and one or two of the intermediate and advanced grammars such as: H. Dana and J. Mantey, *A Manual Grammar of the Greek New Testament.* A. T. Robertson and W. Davis, *A New Short Grammar of the Greek New Testament.* W. D. Chamberlain, *An Exegetical Grammar of the Greek New Testament.* A. T. Robertson, *A Grammar of the Greek New Testament in the Light of Historical Research.*

(3). *Lexicons.* Hebrew: Translations and revisions of Gesenius, *Hebrew and Chaldee Lexicon to the Old Testament Scriptures* by Tregelles; or Robinson; or Brown, Driver and Briggs. L. Koehler and W. Baumgartner, *Lexicon in Veteris Testamenti Libros* (in German and English). Greek: J. H. Thayer, *A Greek Lexicon of the New Testament.* J. H. Moulton and G. Milligan, *The Vocabulary of the Greek New Testament.* H. Cremer, *Biblical Theological Lexicon of New Testament Greek.* Bauer's *Deutsches Wörterbuch zu den Schriften des Neuen Testaments* (fourth edition) will appear in English translation as a cooperative effort of the Concordia Theological Seminary and the University of Chicago Press. De-

[12] Further bibliographical data on commentaries will be found in: Wilbur Smith, *Profitable Bible Study* (revised edition), pp. 94–202; James Orr, "Commentaries," *The International Standard Bible Encyclopedia,* II, 680–85; C. H. Spurgeon, *Commenting and Commentaries*; R. M. Grant, "Commentaries," *Interpretation,* 2:454–64, October, 1948.

tails of this venture will be found in *Concordia Theological Monthly*, 26:33–37, January, 1955. Since 1927 under the direction of G. Kitte, German scholars have been working on a lexicon like Cremer's only on a much larger scale. It is called the *Theologisches Wörterbuch zum Neuen Testament*. Four of these masterful studies of words of the New Testament have appeared in English translation in a work edited by J. R. Coates (*Bible Key Words:* "Love," "The Church," "Sin," "Righteousness"). Some monographs on individual words have been published in English, and more translations like Coates' are sure to appear.

(4). *Concordances.* Hebrew: *Englishman's Hebrew and Chaldee Concordance.* A. B. Davidson, *Concordance of the Hebrew and Chaldee Scriptures.* Wigram, *A Handy Hebrew Concordance.* Septuagint: Hatch and Redpath, *A Concordance to the Septuagint.* Greek: W. Greenfield, *A Concordance to the Greek New Testament* (abridgment of Schmidt). *Englishman's Greek Concordance.* Hudson, *A Critical Greek and English Concordance.* Moulton and Geden, *A Concordance of the Greek New Testament.*

(5). *Dictionaries. The International Standard Bible Encyclopedia.* W. Smith, *Dictionary of the Bible.* Hastings, *Dictionary of the Bible. Dictionary of Christ and the Gospels. Dictionary of the Apostolic Church.*

(6). *Atlases.* G. A. Smith, *Historical Geography of the Holy Land.* G. A. Smith, *Historical Atlas of the Holy Land.* G. Wright and F. Filson, *The Westminster Historical Atlas of the Bible.* G. Dalman, *Sacred Sites and Ways.* J. M. Adams, *Biblical Backgrounds.* B. Maisler, *The Graphic Historical Atlas of Palestine.* Various articles in the journal, *The Biblical Archeologist.*

(7). *Archeology, History, and Culture.* W. Thomson, *The Land and the Book.* H. Dana, *The New Testament World.* S. Angus, *The Environment of Early Christianity.* C. Cobern, *The New Archeological Discoveries and their Bearing on the New Testament.* A. Deissmann, *Light from the Ancient East.*

S. Caiger, *Bible and Spade*. J. Muir, *How Firm a Foundation*. M. Burrows, *What Mean These Stones*. M. Unger, *Archaeology and the Old Testament*. W. Albright, *From the Stone Age to Christianity*. W. Albright, *Archaeology and the Religion of Israel*. W. Albright, *The Archaeology of Palestine*. J. Finegan, *Light from the Ancient Past*. G. Barton, *Archeology and the Bible* (seventh edition). M. Muir, *His Truth Endureth*. J. Adams, *Ancient Records and the Bible*. A. Olmstead, *The History of Palestine and Syria to the Mohammedan Conquest* (somewhat outdated by archeology). W. Blaikie, *A Manual of Bible History* (with C. Mathews, revised, 1940). S. Caiger, *Archaeology of the New Testament*. *The Biblical Archeologist*.

(8). *Biblical Introduction*. H. Miller, *General Biblical Introduction*. Willoughby (editor), *Study of the Bible Today and Tomorrow*. C. Manley (editor), *The New Bible Handbook*. Woolley and Stonehouse (editors), *The Infallible Word*. J. Young, *Introduction to the Old Testament*. J. Raven, *Old Testament Introduction*. M. Unger, *Introductory Guide to the Old Testament*. J. Bewer, *Literature of the Old Testament*. R. Pfeiffer, *Introduction to the Old Testament*. R. Pfeiffer, *History of New Testament Times with an Introduction to the Apocrypha*. H. Thiessen, *Introduction to the New Testament*. E. Scott, *Literature of the New Testament*. J. Moffatt, *An Introduction to the Literature of the New Testament*. F. Kenyon, *Our Bible and the Ancient Manuscripts*. W. Green, *Introduction to the Old Testament: Text*. A. T. Robertson, *Introduction to the Textual Criticism of the New Testament*.

(9). *Commentaries*. *The International Critical Commentary*. J. Lange, *Commentary on the Holy Scriptures*. *Cambridge Bible for Schools and Colleges*. *The Westminster Commentaries*. J. Ellicott (editor), *The Bible Commentary for English Readers*. Jamieson, Faussett, and Brown, *Critical and Experimental Commentary*. *The Interpreter's Bible*. C. Cooke (editor), *The Bible Commentary*. J. Calvin, *Commentaries*. Keil and Delitzsch, *Commentaries on the Old Testament*. W. Nicoll (editor), *The Expositor's Greek Testament*.

C. Wordsworth, *Greek Testament with Notes. Cambridge Greek Testament for Schools and Colleges.* H. Alford, *The Greek Testament.* M. Vincent, *Word Studies in the New Testament.* A. T. Robertson, *Word Pictures in the New Testament.* H. Meyer, *Critical and Exegetical Commentary on the New Testament* (kept up to date in German but not English). *The Moffatt New Testament Commentary.* R. Lenski, *The Interpretation of the New Testament.*

There are several single volume commentaries on the entire Bible, e.g., *The New Bible Commentary.* They are better than no help at all, but satisfactory exegesis requires more space than a one volume commentary can afford. The famous Strack-Billerbeck, *Kommentar zum Neuen Testament aus Talmud und Midrasch*, with its wide learning in rabbinical materials yet awaits translation.

For further elaboration and evaluation of such materials see Wilbur Smith, *Profitable Bible Study* (revised edition), p. 94 ff. Also see the following articles in *Interpretation.* John Bright, "Biblical Geographies and Atlases," 2:324–36, July, 1948. James L. Kelso, "Archaeology," 2:66–73, January, 1948. Bruce M. Metzger, "Grammars of the Greek New Testament," 1:471–85, October, 1947. Balmer H. Kelley, "Hebrew Grammars and Lexicons," 2:186–98, April, 1948. Howard Tillman Kuist, "New Testament Lexicons," 1:226–37, April, 1947. Charles T. Fritsch, "Bible Dictionaries and Encyclopedias," 1:363–71, July, 1947. Robert M. Grant, "Commentaries," 2:454–64, October, 1948. Donald G. Miller, "Concordances," 1:52–62, January, 1947. John Wick Bowman, "The Rabbinic Writings," 3:437–449, October, 1949.

CHAPTER II

HISTORICAL SCHOOLS

FEW studies are so rewarding in granting insight and perspective into problems as historical studies. This is true of the history of hermeneutics.

Terry has well said:

A knowledge of the history of biblical interpretation is of inestimable value to the student of the Holy Scriptures. It serves to guard against errors and exhibits the activity and efforts of the human mind in its search after truth and in relation to noblest themes. It shows what influences have led to the misunderstanding of God's word, and how acute minds, carried away by a misconception of the nature of the Bible, have sought mystic and manifold meanings in its content.[1]

One of the cardinal mistakes in interpretation is provincialism, i.e., believing that the system in which one has been trained is the *only* system. Another mistake is to assume that certain traditional or familiar interpretations are the only adequate interpretations. Certainly hermeneutics ought to be purged of subjectivism and provincialism, and fewer studies are more capable of doing this than historical studies in interpretation.

Rather than trace the long history of interpretation from Ezra until today, the typical schools of interpretation will be presented, and this will preserve much of the historical element.

[1] M. S. Terry, *Biblical Hermeneutics* (revised edition), p. 31.

A. Allegorical Schools

1. *Greek Allegorism*

Allegorical interpretation believes that beneath the letter (*rhētē*) or the obvious (*phanera*) is the real meaning (*hyponoia*) of the passage.[2] Allegory is defined by some as an extended metaphor. There is the literary allegory which is intentionally constructed by the author to tell a message under historical form. Bunyan's *Pilgrim's Progress* is such a one and such allegories occur in Scripture too.[3] If the writer states that he is writing an allegory and gives us the cue, or if the cue is very obvious (as in an allegorical political satire), the problem of interpretation is not too difficult. But if we presume that the document has a secret meaning (*hyponoia*) and there are no cues concerning the hidden meaning interpretation is difficult. In fact, the basic problem is to determine if the passage has such a meaning at all. The further problem arises whether the secret meaning was in the mind of the original writer or something found there by the interpreter. If there are no cues, hints, connections, or other associations which indicate that the record is an allegory, and what the allegory intends to teach, we are on very uncertain grounds.

It may seem strange to list as our first school of interpretation the Greek school, but this is necessary to understand the historical origins of allegorical interpretation. The Greeks were not concerned with Sacred Scripture but with their own writings, and in this sense it is improper to classify them within the context of Biblical interpretation. But in that their allegorical method was adopted by both Jew and Christian they deserve this special attention.

---

[2] H. A. Wolfson, *Philo*, I, 115. For Greek allegorical interpretation see: *Wolfson*, ibid., I, 131–133. J. Geffcken, "Allegory," *Hastings Encyclopedia of Religion and Ethics*, I, 327–331. F. W. Farrar, *History of Interpretation*, pp. 131–136. H. P. Smith, *Essays in Biblical Interpretation*, Chapter III, "The Triumph of Allegory." K. Fullerton, *Prophecy and Authority*, p. 59 ff.

[3] Terry, *op. cit.*, Part Second, Chapter VII.

The Greeks had two noble traditions. (i) They had a religious heritage in Homer and Hesiod. Homer's influence seemed to increase with the extension of time rather than diminish. The "Bible" of the Greek was the writings of Homer and Hesiod. To question or to doubt them was an irreligious or atheistic act. (ii) They had an astute philosophical (Thales, *et al.*) and historical tradition (Thucydides and Herodotus), which developed principles of logic, criticism, ethics, religion, and science.

The *religious tradition* had many elements which were fanciful, grotesque, absurd, or immoral. The philosophical and historical tradition could not accept much of the religious tradition as it lay in the written documents. Yet, the hold of Homer and Hesiod was so great, popularly and with the thinkers, that Homer and Hesiod could not be declared worthless and forsaken. How was the tension of the two traditions to be resolved? The problem is at once *apologetic* and *hermeneutical*. It is interesting that the religious apology and the allegorical method of hermeneutics have the same historical root. The tension was relieved by *allegorizing* the religious heritage. The stories of the gods, and the writings of the poets, were not to be taken *literally*. Rather underneath is the secret or real meaning (*hyponoia*). Wolfson, Farrar, Geffcken and Smith have demonstrated how widespread this allegorical method became in Greek thought.

The important item to notice here is that this Greek tradition of allegorizing spread to Alexandria where there was a great Jewish population and eventually a large Christian population.

2. *Jewish Allegorism*

The Alexandrian Jew faced a problem similar to his fellow Greek. He was a child of Moses instructed in the law and the rest of a divine revelation. But as he mingled with the cosmopolitan population of Alexandria he soon learned of the Greek literature with its philosophical heritage. Some of these Jews were so impressed that they accepted the teachings of Greek philosophy.

The Greek faced the tension of a religious-poetic-myth tradition and a historical-philosophical tradition. The Jew faced the tension of his own national Sacred Scriptures and the Greek philosophical tradition (especially Plato). How could a Jew cling to both? The solution was identical to the Greek's solution to his problem. In fact, the Jew even got it from the Greek for Farrar writes, "The Alexandrian Jews were not, however, driven to invent this allegorical method for themselves. They found it ready to their hands." [4]

Here is one of the strange fates of history. The allegorical method arose to save the reputation of ancient Greek religious poets. This method of interpretation was adopted by the Alexandrian Greeks for the reasons stated above. Then it was bequeathed to the Christian Church. "By a singular concurrence of circumstances," continues Farrar, "the Homeric studies of pagan philosophers suggested first to the Jews and then, through them, to Christians, a method of Scriptural interpretation before unheard of which remained unshaken for more than fifteen hundred years." [5]

The first writer who seems to have written in this Jewish tradition of allegorism was Aristobulus (160 B.C.). His works exist only through fragments and quotations by other writers. Wolfson,[6] a leading Philonian scholar, believes that Philo actually cites from Aristobulus, thus aligning himself with those who believe that the writings (or oral teachings) of Aristobulus antedate Philo. Aristobulus asserted (i) that

---

[4] Farrar, *op. cit.*, p. 134.

[5] *Ibid.*, p. 135. Wolfson (*op. cit.*) qualifies this by noting that the rabbis themselves had commenced to do some allegorizing to make ancient laws relevant to contemporary situations. Feldman (*The Parables and Similes of the Rabbis*) has some important material about the use of allegorical interpretation among the rabbis. P. 3 ff. Philo was not influenced at this point only by the Greeks but by his own rabbinic traditions.

[6] *Op. cit.*, I, 95.

Greek philosophy borrowed from the Old Testament, especially from the Law of Moses; and (ii) that by employing the allegorical method the teachings of Greek philosophy could be found in Moses and the prophets.

The outstanding Jewish allegorist was Philo (born about 20 B.C.; died about A.D. 54). He was a thoroughly convinced Jew. To him the Scriptures (primarily in the Septuagint version) were superior to Plato and Greek philosophy. He teaches practically a dictation-theory of inspiration he so emphasizes the passivity of the prophet. Yet, he had a great fondness for Greek philosophy, especially Plato and Pythagoras. By a most elaborate system of allegorizing he was able to reconcile for himself his loyalty to his Hebrew faith and his love for Greek philosophy.

One scholar notes that Philo actually had about twenty rules which indicated that a given Scripture was to be treated allegorically. Most of his rules however, can be classed under general headings.[7] Philo did not think that the literal meaning was useless, but it represented the immature level of understanding. The literal sense was the body of Scripture, and the allegorical sense its soul. Accordingly the literal was for the immature, and the allegorical for the mature. Nor did Philo believe that the allegorical method denied the reality of the historical events.

There were three canons which dictated to the interpreter that a passage of Scripture was to be allegorically interpreted: (i) If a statement says anything unworthy of God; (ii) if a statement is contradictory with some other statement or in any other way presents us with a difficulty; and (iii) if the record itself is allegorical in nature.

However, these three canons spill over into many sub-

---

[7] Special attention to Philo's allegorical system is given by Gilbert, *Interpretation of the Bible*, Chapter II. Farrar, *op. cit.*, pp. 136–157. Briggs, *Biblical Study*, p. 305 ff. Wolfson, *op. cit.*, p. 115 ff. Jean Daniélou (*Origen*) sets forth the data showing how much Origen was influenced by Philo. Pp. 178–191.

canons. (i) *Grammatical* peculiarities are hints that underneath the record is a deeper spiritual truth. (ii) *Stylistic* elements of the passage (synonyms, repetition, etc.) indicate that deeper truth is present. (iii) *Manipulation* of punctuation, words, meaning of words, and new combinations of words can be so done as to extract new and deeper truth from the passage. (iv) Whenever *symbols* are present, we are to understand them figuratively not literally. (v) Spiritual truth may be obtained from *etymologies* of names. (vi) Finally, we have the law of *double-application*. Many natural objects signify spiritual things (heaven means the mind; earth means sensation; a field, revolt, etc.).

Actual examples of this method may be found in the literature. Some of this is sound (major canon iii, and sub-canon iv) for there are allegorical and figurative elements in Scripture. But most of it led to the fantastic and the absurd. For example, Abraham's trek to Palestine is *really* the story of a Stoic philosopher who leaves Chaldea (sensual understanding) and stops at Haran, which means "holes," and signifies the emptiness of knowing things by the holes, that is the senses. When he becomes Abraham he becomes a truly enlightened philosopher. To marry Sarah is to marry abstract wisdom.[8]

3. *Christian and Patristic Allegorism*

The allegorical system that arose among the pagan Greeks, copied by the Alexandrian Jews, was next adopted by the Christian church and largely dominated exegesis until the Reformation, with such notable exceptions as the Syrian school of Antioch and the Victorines of the Middle Ages.

The early Christian Fathers had as their Bible the Old Testament in Greek translation. This had been the Bible of Christ and the Apostles judging from their citations of the Old Testament in the New. One of the most basic convictions

[8] The validity of allegorical and typological interpretation will be discussed in the chapter on prophecy.

of the early church was that the Old Testament was a Christian document. C. H. Dodd's work, *According to the Scripture*, is an effort to isolate out these *testimonia* of the New Testament wherein Old Testament Scriptures are used to show the Messianic witness of the Old Testament to Christianity. The New Testament itself is replete with Old Testament citations, allusions, and references. The apologetic of Matthew and Hebrews is directly a proof of the fulfilment of the Old in the New. The allegorical method of interpretation sprang from a proper motive, in spite of the fact that it was usually improper in practice.

The proper motive was the firm belief that the Old Testament was a Christian document. This ground the Church can never surrender without retreating to Marcionism in some revived form. The allegorical method was its primary means of making the Old Testament a Christian document.

It must also be kept in mind that although these writers used the allegorical method to excess, they did unconsciously use the literal method. If we underscore everything they interpret literally (even though they might not spend too much time defending the literal sense of Scripture), we discover how much the literal approach was used in actual practice. In some cases the historical (approximating the literal) is actually made part of their hermeneutical system.

Two things may be said for the allegorizing of the Fathers: (i) They were seeking to make the Old Testament a Christian document. With this judgment the Christian Church has universally agreed. (ii) They did emphasize the truths of the Gospel in their fancies. If they had not done this, they would have become sectarian.

The difficulties with the method are many. (i) There was a lack of a genuine historical sense in exegesis. The historical connections of a passage of Scripture were usually completely ignored. (ii) Their method of citing the Old Testament revealed that they had a very infantile understanding of the progress of revelation. They had the basic understanding that a great shift had taken place from the Old to the New Testament. But citing verses in the Old Testament, in themselves frequently very obscure, as if superior to verses in the New, revealed no understanding of the significance of historical and progressive revelation for hermeneutics. (iii) They considered the Old (especially) and the New Testaments filled with parables, enigmas, and riddles. The allegorical method alone sufficed to bring out the meaning of these parables, enigmas, and riddles. (iv) They confused the allegorical with the typical, and thus blurred the distinction between the legitimate and the improper interpretation of the Old Testament. The "allegorical," the "mystical," the "pneumatic," and the "spiritual," are practically synonymous. (v) They believed that Greek philosophy was in the Old Testament and it was the allegorical method which discovered it. (vi) In that the method is highly arbitrary, it eventually fostered dogmatic interpretation of the Scripture. Fullerton's judgment against the allegorical method at this point is very sharp:

Instead of adopting a scientific principle of exegesis they introduce Church authority under the guise of Tradition as the norm of interpretation. The movement of thought which we have been following now becomes associated with the great dogmatic consolidations of the second and third centuries that led directly to ecclesiastical absolutism.[9]

The curse of the allegorical method is that it obscures the true meaning of the Word of God and had it not kept the Gospel truth central it would have become cultic and heretical. In fact, this is exactly what happened when the gnostics allegorized the New Testament. The Bible treated allegorically becomes putty in the hand of the exegete. Different doctrinal systems could emerge within the framework of allegorical hermeneutics and no way would exist to determine

[9] K. Fullerton, *Prophecy and Authority*, p. 81. Italics have been omitted.

which were the true. This was precisely one of the problems in refuting the gnostics. The orthodox wished to allegorize the Old Testament, but not the New. The gnostics accused them of inconsistency. The only method of breaking an exegetical stalemate created by the use of the allegorical method is to return to the sober, proper and literal interpretation of the Scriptures. The allegorical method puts a premium on the subjective and the doleful result is the obscuration of the Word of God. To cite Fullerton again:

> *When the historical sense of a passage is once abandoned there is wanting any sound regulative principle to govern exegesis.* . . . The mystical [allegorical] method of exegesis, is an unscientific and arbitrary method, reduces the Bible to obscure enigmas, undermines the authority of all interpretation, and therefore, when taken by itself, failed to meet the apologetic necessities of the time.[10]

To present a clearer picture of some of the patristic hermeneutical theory we shall briefly study Clement, Origen, Jerome, and Augustine.

(1). *Clement.* Clement of Alexandria found five possible meanings to a passage of Scripture.[11] (i) The *historical* sense of Scripture, i.e., taking a story in the Old Testament as an actual event in history; (ii) the *doctrinal* sense of Scripture, i.e., the obvious moral, religious, and theological teachings of the Bible; (iii) the *prophetic* sense of Scripture including predictive prophecy and typology; (iv) the *philosophical* sense which follows the Stoics with their cosmic and psychological meaning (which sees meanings in natural objects and historical persons); and (v) a *mystical* sense (deeper moral, spiritual and religious truth symbolized by events or persons).

(2). *Origen.* Patristic scholarship is indebted to Jean Daniélou for a thorough study of Origen in his book entitled *Origen.* Part II of this work is devoted to "Origen and the Bible."

---

[10] *Ibid.*, p. 75. Italics are his.
[11] R. M. Grant, *The Bible in the Church*, p. 64, in which he summarizes the findings of C. Mondésert, *Clément d'Alexandrie.*

Origen is in the Aristobulus-Philo-Pantaenus-Clement tradition. Daniélou shows how deeply Origen's system was marked by Philo. Origen had an apologetic motivation to be sure. He wanted to escape the crudities of lay people who were literalists to the point of taking everything symbolic or metaphorical or poetic literally. He was motivated to show that the New Testament does have its roots in the Old and so reply to the Jews. He wished to eliminate what were absurdities or contradictions in Scripture and make Scripture acceptable to the philosophically minded. His approach can be summed up as follows: [12]

(i). The *literal meaning* of the Scripture is the preliminary level of Scripture. It is the "body," not the "soul" (moral sense) nor the "spirit" (allegorical sense) of the Bible. The literal sense is the meaning of Scripture for the layman. Actually we perhaps should say "letterism" rather than literalism for reasons we pointed out in the previous paragraph.

Further, the literal sense would leave us in Judaism. If we were to take the Old Testament in a strict literal sense we would believe and practice exactly as the Jews. We escape Judaism by spiritualizing the Old Testament.

Again, the literal in Scripture is the sign of the mysteries and images of things divine. It is to provoke us to a deeper and more spiritual study of the Bible. History, for example, is to be taken symbolically. Origen has a Platonic view of history which he reinterprets by means of Christian theology. The symbolization of history does not deny the actual historicity of the story.

(ii). To understand the Bible *we must have grace given to us by Christ.* Christ is the inner principle of Scripture and only those with the Spirit of Christ can understand Scripture.

(iii). The true exegesis is *the spiritual exegesis of the Bible.* "The Bible is one vast allegory, a tremendous sacrament in which every detail is symbolic," writes Daniélou of Origen's

---

[12] Origen's hermeneutics is treated in *De Principiis*, Book IV.

fundamental thesis.[13] The Bible is a spiritual book, and its meaning is found only by spiritualizing it. Even the New Testament has elements in it which cannot be taken literally, and so must be spiritualized. In many cases this means nothing more than that a figure of speech has no literal meaning.

Origen's *spiritual* exegesis is a mixture of the typological and the allegorical. Daniélou knows that the allegorical method was greatly abused, and is not in high regard among scholars. He seeks to rescue Origen from the charge of being an allegorist by insisting that he has basically a typological exegesis. That Origen allegorized Daniélou does not deny. That his theory was much better than his practice he strongly affirms. But he does object to classifying Origen as an allegorist, pure and simple, and then condemning him because he is an allegorist. Daniélou believes that Origen has the correct Christian principle of interpretation, but that Origen poorly practiced it, and that subsequent scholarship misrepresents him.

(iv). Origen believed that *the Old is the preparation for the New*. This implies two further assertions: (a) If the Old is the preparation of the New, the New is in the Old in a concealed manner, and it is the function of the Christian exegete to bring it to the surface. This is *typological exegesis* and is based on the fundamental harmony of the Old and New Testaments. (b) If the New fulfils the Old, the Old is now superseded. There is continuity and divergence in the relationship between the New and the Old. Continuity means that the New is like the Old and therefore the Old is capable of typological interpretation. There is divergence between the New and the Old, and this means the Old is now out of date.

(3). *Jerome.* Jerome was a great Bible scholar in terms of the scholarship of antiquity. He translated the Bible into

---

[13] *Origen*, p. 184. Cf. Grant (*op. cit.*, p. 65 ff.) for a less sympathetic treatment of Origen.

Latin (*Latin Vulgate*) which required him to become proficient in Greek and Hebrew. He noticed that the Hebrew Bible did not contain the Apocrypha and suggested its secondary nature and that it ought to be put between the Testaments. This suggestion was not carried out until Luther. Jerome placed great emphasis on the historical and the literal.

Jerome is similar to Augustine. In theory he developed some sound principles, especially because he was influenced by the literal school of Antioch. In practice he was an allegorist. He started out as an extreme allegorist, but influenced by the school of Antioch, he retreated from the allegorical tradition in theory or principle and emphasized the historical and literal.

He insisted that the literal is not contradictory to the allegorical as the extremists in the Alexandrian school asserted. On the other hand he evaded the *letterism* of the Jews. But in practice he was a typical allegorist even to allegorizing the New Testament.

(4). *Augustine.* Augustine developed a handbook of hermeneutics and homiletics called *De Doctrina Christiana.*[14] One very interesting aspect of this treatment is that *Augustine endeavors to develop a theory of signs.* This is missed by practically all the hermeneutical studies, yet in the light of contemporary philosophy it is most important. Here is a Father of the church that in so many words indicates that a theory of signs is basic to any theory of hermeneutics. Or, Biblical hermeneutics is but a special case of semantics (or semiotic). Augustine speaks of natural objects which are percepts but not signs, e.g., a piece of wood or metal. Next he speaks of things which signify other things. A tree may signify forestry service, a shoe a shoemaker, and an anvil

---

[14] A new translation of this is: *The Fathers of the Church.* Vol. IV: *The Writings of Saint Augustine.* "Christian Instruction" translated by John J. Gavigan. Besides treatments of Augustine in standard histories of hermeneutics cf. David S. Schaff, "St. Augustine as an Exegete." *Nicene and Post-Nicene Fathers* (first series), VI, vii–xii.

the blacksmith guild. Then there are things whose sole function is to signify other things, i.e., words.

He defines a sign as: "A thing which apart from the impression that it presents to the senses, causes of itself some other thing to enter our thoughts." [15] These signs are conventional or natural. Smoke is a natural sign of fire. Conventional signs "are those which living creatures give to one another." [16] From this he proceeds to discuss sounds and speech; God's method of communication to man through speech; and speech incarnate in the written Scripture. This is typical of the genius of Augustine to have put his finger on a critical point in a discussion which sometimes took a millennium or more to realize. It is regrettable that: (i) he did not follow through with complete consistency from his theory of signs to hermeneutics; (ii) that others did not catch any glimmer of light in his remarks about signs; and (iii) that historians of hermeneutics for the most part ignore Augustine's treatment of signs.

Augustine was driven to the allegorical interpretation of Scripture by his own spiritual plight. It was the allegorical interpretation of Scripture by Anselm which illuminated much of the Old Testament to him when he was struggling with the crass literalism of the Manicheans. He justified allegorical interpretation by a gross misinterpretation of 2 Cor. 3:6. He made it mean that the *spiritual* or *allegorical* interpretation was the real meaning of the Bible; the *literal* interpretation kills.[17] For this experimental reason Augustine could hardly part with the allegorical method.

[15] *Christian Instruction*, Bk. II, Ch. 1, paragraph 1.

[16] *Ibid.*, II, 2, 3.

[17] This abuse of this Scripture has continued throughout history and to this hour. Orthodoxy uses it to put criticism in its place ("A spiritual understanding of the Bible gives life but an academic, critical and scholarly study of the Bible kills"). Neo-orthodoxy uses it to rout the orthodox ("Existential interpretation gives life; literal interpretation is the wooden, lifeless letter"). Religious modernism also so used it against orthodoxy. Cults use it to justify their fanciful impositions on Scripture. Cf. *Confessions*, VI, 4, 6 for Augustine's statement.

Summing up Augustine's hermeneutics we would say his controlling principles were:

(i) A genuine Christian faith was necessary for the understanding of the Scriptures. The inner spirit of the exegete was as important as his technical equipment. (ii) Although the literal and historical are not the end of Scripture we must hold them in high regard. Not all of the Bible is allegorical by any means, and much of it is both literal and allegorical. Augustine's great theological works indicate that the literal method was employed far more than he admitted on paper. (iii) Scripture has more than one meaning and therefore the allegorical method is proper. The supreme test to see whether a passage was allegorical was that of love. If the literal made for dissension, then the passage was to be allegorized. Besides this he had seven other somewhat farfetched rules for allegorizing the Scriptures. He did work on the principle that the Bible had a hidden meaning, and so in his allegorical interpretations he was frequently as fanciful as the rest of the Fathers. However, whatever was allegorized was in theory to be built upon the literal and historical meaning of the text. (iv) There is significance in Biblical numbers. Augustine regarded the entire world of logic and numbers as eternal truths, and therefore numbers played a special role in human knowledge. If this is so then we can get much truth by an allegorical or symbolic interpretation of numbers in Scripture. (v) The Old Testament is a Christian document because it is a Christological document. In finding Christ in too many places however he obscured the genuine Christology of the Old Testament. (vi) The task of the expositor is to get the meaning out of the Bible, not to bring a meaning to it. The expositor is to express accurately the thoughts of the writer. (vii) We must consult the *analogy of faith*, the true orthodox creed, when we interpret. If orthodoxy represents Scripture, then no expositor can make Scripture go contrary to orthodoxy. To this must be added *love*. No man understands Scripture if he is not built up in love to God and man. Love and analogy of faith are apparently the two major controlling principles in his hermeneutics. In truth, love may be a form of spiritual intuition necessary for the deeper apprehension of Scripture. (viii) No verse is to be studied as a unit in itself. The Bible is not a string of verses like a string of beads, but a web of meaning. Therefore we must note *the context* of the verse; what the Bible says on the same subject somewhere else; and what the orthodox creed states. (ix) If an interpretation is insecure, nothing in the passage can be made a matter of orthodox faith. (x) We cannot make the Holy Spirit our substitute for the necessary learning to understand Scripture. The able interpreter must know Hebrew; Greek; geography; natural history; music; chronology; numbers; history; dialectics; natural science; and the ancient philosophers. (xi) The obscure passage must yield to the clear passage. That is, on a given doctrine we should take our primary guidance from those passages which are clear rather from those which are obscure. (xii) No Scripture is to be interpreted so as to conflict with any other —the harmony of revelation. But to do this we must *distinguish the times*. Augustine's statement ("Distinguish the times [*tempora* not *saeculae*] and you harmonize the Scriptures") means that we must take into account *progressive revelation*. Polygamy conflicts with monogamy only if we fail to note that revelation progresses. If we are aware of the progressive character of revelation we shall not make Scripture conflict. This is very different from the dispensational interpretation put on these words, which is only possible by taking *tempora* as if it meant *saeculae*.

As magnificent an effort as this appears, it is disheartening to realize how far short in so many instances Augustine came. There is hardly a rule he made which he did not frequently violate. What compensated for this was: (i) the actual usage of the literal understanding of Scripture even though such a principle was not fully developed in his hermeneutical theory; and (ii) his great theological genius which could not help but see the theological grandeur of the Scriptures.

4. *Catholic Allegorism*

It would be over-simplification to assert that the only method of exegesis during the Middle Ages was the allegorical. It would not, however, be an exaggeration to assert that the preponderance of exegetical work was allegorical.[18] To clarify terminology we should note that the scholastics divided the meaning of the Bible into the literal and the spiritual (i.e., the *spirit* is more central to human personality than the body, so the spiritual meaning of the Bible is the more important one) or the mystical (i.e., it is more refined, subtle, less obvious). Under the spiritual or mystical are the three divisions of (i) allegorical or what passes as a combination of typology and allegorism, (ii) tropological or moral interpretation, and (iii) anagogical or how the church *now* anticipates the church glorified, the eschatological sense.

The Catholic Church in imitation of the Fathers has maintained the validity of the allegorical method or the spiritual method of interpretation. We shall not try to survey the history of interpretation during the Middle Ages but will present the Catholic theory which eventually emerged from it.

In studying Catholic pronouncements on hermeneutics it is very clear that the advancement of Biblical studies by Protestants has had its telling influence on the very spirit of the Catholic approach. (i) Catholic scholars admit the extremes that allegorism was carried to by some of the Fathers and some of the Scholastics. There is no stout defense of these exaggerations in Catholic hermeneutical literature except from real patristic sentimentalists. (ii) The importance and primacy of the literal meaning of Scripture is extolled.

---

[18] Besides the general histories of hermeneutics listed at the end of this chapter, material for exegesis in the Middle Ages may be found in Beryl Smalley, *The Study of Bible in the Middle Ages* (second edition, 1952). We shall note later the literalistic Victorines.

No longer is the literal declared to be for spiritual infants or to be the mere surface of the Scripture. The position of the Alexandrians at this point especially is repudiated.

(1). Catholic scholars accept the Latin Vulgate as the authentic version for *public lectures, disputations, sermons,* and *expositions.*[19] This includes the apocryphal books as listed by the Council of Trent (Fourth Session). This puts the Catholic Church in odd position because the Hebrews wrote their Bible in Hebrew and Aramaic and the Apostles in Greek. This is common information to all Biblical scholars. It thus appears rather unusual for a translation to be given authentic status when the document may be had in the original languages. If the entire dogmatic structure of Catholic theology is based on the Latin it could be disconcerting to find it at variance with Greek and Hebrew.

One Catholic scholar states very directly the implied essence of the Catholic position: "The Greek and Hebrew texts are of the greatest value, as means in order to arrive at the genuine sense and full force of many passages in the Latin Vulgate." [20] Another scholar, however, has tried to use the Greek and Hebrew as his more basic sources in translating the Bible, and has been charged with duplicity.[21] This is a surface admission of the authenticity of the Latin but a tacit admission of the priority of the Hebrew and Greek.

(2). The Catholic interpreter obediently accepts whatever the Catholic Church has *specifically* said about matters of Biblical Introduction, and authorship of the books of the Bible.

[19] So decreed by the *Council of Trent,* Session IV. Also repeated in the *Dogmatic Decrees of the Vatican Council.*

[20] Humphry (a Jesuit) quoted by Salmon, *Apocrypha,* I, xxix (*Holy Bible Commentary*). Note that this is exactly the opposite of the Protestant position. The Protestant uses the Latin to help him understand the inspired Hebrew and Greek. Humphry says the Greek and Hebrew help in understanding the authentic Latin.

[21] Cf. the scholarly review of Knox's (Roman Catholic) translation of the Bible in the *London Times* (Literary Supplement, December 23, 1949, p. 834).

(3). The Catholic interpreter accepts all verses which the Church has officially interpreted in the sense in which they have been interpreted. All told not more than twenty such verses have been officially interpreted. Further, in some instances the Church has indicated what meaning a verse cannot have. However, the number is actually much more than this because many of the official documents of the Church involve certain definite interpretations of certain verses. The official definition of the meaning of a verse is not usually made unless the verse has become controversial and the interpretation of it must be made.

(4). The literal and historical interpretation of Scripture is the foundation of the study of the Bible.[22] Maas and Fuller both make a strong point that Catholic exegesis considers itself built on the substantial ground of the literal interpretation and historical interpretation of Scripture. This is not exactly new in their tradition. Aquinas emphasized the importance of the literal and even stated that no doctrine could be erected on spiritual exegesis. But making literal and historical interpretation such virtues is certainly due to the impact of Protestant Biblical scholarship.

(5). The Scriptures do possess a spiritual or mystical meaning which is beyond the literal. Thomas Aquinas taught very clearly that Scripture may have more than one sense because the author of Scripture is God.[23] God was able to inspire men in such a way that they wrote not only literal and his-

---

[22] Cf. A. J. Maas, "Exegesis," *The Catholic Encyclopedia*; V, 692–706, and "Hermeneutics," *Ibid.*, VII, 271–276. R. C. Fuller, "The Interpretation of Scripture," *A Catholic Commentary on Holy Scripture*, pp. 53–60. Maas calls the First Law of hermeneutics to be the grammatical, philological, contextual and historical study of a passage of Scripture.

[23] *Summa Theologica*, I, 1, 10, "Whether in Holy Scripture a Word may have Several Senses." Cf. "The author of Holy Scripture is God, in Whose power it is to signify His meaning, not by words only (as man also can do) but also by things themselves. . . . That signification whereby things signified by words have themselves also a signification is called the spiritual sense, which is based on the literal and presupposes it."

torical truth but spiritual and figurative truth. Therefore, Thomas concludes, it is not proper to limit the meaning of Scripture to the literal sense.

This spiritual or mystical interpretation which is an outgrowth of the allegorizing of the early church became codified during the Middle Ages under three rules. (i) A passage may have an *allegorical* meaning. This refers to its future or prophetic meaning and includes allegorical and typological interpretation. In view of the abuses of the allegorical method many contemporary Catholics prefer the word *typological* to *allegorical*. (ii) A passage may have an *anagogical* (eschatological) meaning. It may "lead up" to the Church Triumphant. Thus the Church militant has features about it which anticipate the Church in glory. (iii) A passage may have a *tropological* meaning, i.e., teach a *tropos*, a way of life. This is the moral significance of the passage.

This spiritual meaning must be built upon the literal and historical meaning. Modern Catholic scholarship is making a serious effort to take the arbitrariness out of spiritual and allegorical exegesis. It is fully aware of the sordid history of fanciful allegorical interpretation. The Protestant scholar too must face the typical and predictive in the Old Testament, and so he likewise has a problem. It is the actual *practice* which reveals a very fundamental cleavage. When the manna in the wilderness, the passover of the exodus, the bread and wine of Melchisedec, and the diet of meal and oil by Elijah are made types of the Eucharist the Protestant objects. When Newman argues that the change of the Old Testament worship system as demanded by the New does not make a profound alteration from the material to the spiritual, again the Protestant objects.[24] Reading back into the Old Testament the sacramental and clerical system of Catholicism appears as simple *eisegesis* (reading into) and not *exegesis* (reading out of). It was this necessity of making all the Bible

[24] Jaak Seynaeve, *Cardinal Newman's Doctrine of Holy Scripture*, Part II, Newman's Hermeneutics. Pp. 197–396. Cf. pp. 260–261.

sacramental and *sacerdotal* which was one of the reasons Newman wrote that "it may be almost laid down as a historical
fact, that the mystical [allegorical] interpretation and orthodoxy will stand or fall together." [25]

(6). The Catholic Church is the official interpreter of Scripture. There are several important considerations here. First,
the Church is the *custodian* of Scripture. The Bible was not
given to the world but deposited in the Church. Hence one
of the rights of the Church is to interpret the Scriptures.
Another consideration is that the Catholics believe that
Christianity is *The Deposit of Faith* deposited in the Catholic
Church in an oral and written form. The usual Protestant
notion that the Catholics have the Bible to which they add
tradition is not quite accurate. There is the Original Tradition, or Revelation, or Deposit of Faith which is transmitted
through the centuries in an oral form (tradition), and a written form (Bible). The final consideration is that the written
form is obscure and needs an official interpreter. The average
man is not competent to interpret the Scripture because it is
a task beyond his abilities. For example a Catholic writes
that "Every biblical scholar knows perfectly well that there
is no book in the world more difficult than the Bible. It is
a sheer absurdity to say that ordinary people, with no knowledge of Hebrew or Greek or archaeology or of the writings
of the Fathers of the Church, are competent to interpret it." [26]

(i). The Church which bears the true Tradition (oral and
written) is thereby the official interpreter of the Scriptures.
Only that Church which bears the mark of apostolicity can
know the real meaning of the written tradition.

(ii). No passage of Scripture can be interpreted to conflict
with the Roman Catholic doctrinal system. "Any meaning
[of a passage of Scripture] . . . not in harmony with the fact
of inspiration and the spirit of the Church's interpretation

[25] J. H. Newman, *An Essay on Development of Christian Doctrine.*
P. 344.
[26] M. Sheehan, *Apologetics and Catholic Doctrine*, I, 149, fn. 13.

cannot be the true sense of Scripture," writes a Catholic author.[27] This was also maintained by the Council of Trent (Fourth Session) in which not only the Church's right as interpreter was set forth, but individual interpretation condemned. Sometimes this is called interpretation by *the analogy of faith.*

Councils, commissions, and congregations do not have the virtue of infallibility, but their interpretations of Scripture enjoy a high authority.

(7). The Fathers are to be a guide in interpretation according to three principles:

(i). The interpretation must be solely about *faith and morals.* Statements about natural or scientific matters, or historical matters are not binding.

(ii). The Father must be bearing witness to the Catholic Tradition (the *Quod ubique, quod semper, quod omnibus creditum est* [what has been believed everywhere, always, by everyone] of Vincent, the classical definition of orthodoxy), and not to personal opinion.

(iii). The Fathers must have a unanimous witness to the given interpretation.

However, even when not all three canons may be applied to a given interpretation, nevertheless the opinions of the Fathers are to be held in veneration. This veneration of the Fathers resulted in much medieval exegesis being really studies in patristics and not exegesis in the proper sense.

(8). Obscure and partial teaching of the Scripture is to be explained by the fuller teaching in the unwritten tradition of the Church. The Roman Catholic believes that he has two sources of revelation which mutually interpret each other. Scripture makes clear matters of the unwritten tradition, and unwritten tradition makes clear obscure matters

[27] A. J. Maas, "Hermeneutics," *Catholic Encyclopedia,* VII, 272. He also wrote: "Since the Church is the official custodian and interpreter of the Bible, her teaching concerning the Sacred Scriptures and their genuine sense must be *the supreme guide* of the commentator." *Ibid.,* V, 698. Italics are ours in both quotes.

in Scripture.[28] Hence the Catholic scholar does not feel it necessary to find full teaching of all his doctrines in the Bible but allusions are sufficient (e.g., prayers for the dead, veneration for Mary, confession, the supremacy of Peter). The Catholic Church does not intend to limit itself entirely to the word of Scripture. Its source of revelation is the Deposit of Faith in an unwritten and written form. The unwritten tradition may then be used to fill out what is deficient in the written form (Scripture).

(9). The Bible is to be understood in terms of *the principle of development.* No one will deny that there is considerable difference between a modern cathedral and its worship services and the fellowship gatherings of the Christians as recorded in the book of Acts. The Catholic theologian believes that the doctrines of the New Testament are *seeds* which grow and develop so that what is seen in a modern Catholic cathedral was contained in seed form in the apostolic Church of the book of Acts.

(i). First, this is justified by the principle of implication. We are bound to believe all that is in the Scriptures and that which may be *properly deduced.* The Trinity is not taught in so many words in the New Testament but the Christian Church has believed it to be a *proper deduction.*

(ii). Secondly, this is justified by the principle of *epigenesis.* Seeds do not merely enlarge. New doctrines are not determined solely by construing the necessary implications of Scripture. Seeds grow, develop and change. Yet in a real sense the "truth" of the tree is identical with the "truth" of the seed. This notion of the *epigenetic growth* of seed doc-

[28] Cf. "Thus the knowledge of apostolic Tradition can make up for the silence of the ambiguity of the letter of the New Testament and restore the exact sense it wanted to transmit to us." A. Bubarle, "Introduction to Holy Scripture," in A. M. Henry, *Introduction to Theology*, I, 67. "What is contained by way of outline in the written Gospel has light thrown upon it by traditions which are in their own way also bearers of the mystery of Christ." A. Liégé, "The Sources of the Christian Faith," *Ibid.*, I, 12.

trines into the elaborate doctrines of the Roman Catholic Church was classically elaborate by J. H. Newman in his famous work, *The Development of Christian Doctrine.* The essay is a tacit admission that the present Catholic Church is far removed from the apostolic Church of the New Testament.[29]

(10). The attitude of the Catholic Church toward the Protestants is contained in the Encyclical, *Providentissimus Deus* of Leo XIII.

Though the studies of non-Catholics, used with prudence, may sometimes be of use to the Catholic student, he should, nevertheless, bear well in mind . . . that the sense of Holy Scripture cannot be expected to be found in writers, who being without the true faith, *only gnaw the bark of Sacred Scripture, and never attain its pith* [italics are ours].

B. Literal Schools

1. *Jewish Literalism*

The literal method of interpreting the Bible is to accept as basic the literal rendering of the sentences unless by virtue of the nature of the sentence or phrase or clause within the sentence this is not possible. For example, figures of speech or fables or allegories do not admit of literal interpretation. The spirit of literal interpretation is that we should be satisfied with the literal meaning of a text unless very substantial reasons can be given for advancing beyond the literal meaning, and when *canons of control* are supplied.

Ezra is considered the first of the Jewish interpreters and the ultimate founder of the Jewish, Palestinian, hyperliteralist school. The Jews in the Babylonian captivity ceased

[29] Modern Catholic scholarship has approved rather than disavowed Newman's principle claiming although not in scholastic form it still reflects what has been Catholic teaching. Cf. A. M. Dubarle, *op. cit.,* I, 65. G. H. Joyce, "Revelation," *The Catholic Encyclopedia,* XIII, 4. Walter P. Burke, "The Beauty Ever Ancient," *American Essays for the Newman Centennial,* pp. 206–207.

speaking Hebrew and spoke Aramaic. This created the language gap between themselves and their Scriptures. It was the task of Ezra to give the meaning of the Scriptures by paraphrasing the Hebrew into the Aramaic or in other ways expounding the sense of the Scriptures. This is generally admitted to be the first instance of Biblical hermeneutics.[30]

Far removed from the land of Palestine, the Jews in captivity could no longer practice their accustomed religion (Mosaism) which included the land, their capitol city, and their temple. There could be no Mosaism with no temple, no land about which there were many regulations, and no harvest. Robbed of the national character of their religion the Jews were led to emphasize that which they would take with them, their Scriptures. Out of the captivities came Judaism with its synagogues, rabbis, scribes, lawyers, and traditions.

There is no simple manner by which Jewish exegesis can be *adequately* summed up. It is a complex system contained in a voluminous corpus of literature. Through the course of the centuries many talented rabbis expressed themselves on hermeneutics and various schools emerged (e.g., Karaites and Cabbalists). The Karaites were the literalists and the Cabbalists were the allegorists.

The Palestinian Jews did develop some sound principles of exegesis which reflected a token approach to the literal understanding of the Scriptures. Hillel formulated seven rules, Isamel thirteen, and Eliezer thirty-two. Some of these principles are still part of a valid hermeneutics.

(i). They insisted that a word must be understood in terms of its sentence, and a sentence in terms of its context.

(ii). They taught that Scriptures dealing with similar topics should be compared, and that in some instances a third Scripture would relieve the apparent contradiction between two Scriptures.

[30] See Farrar's fine tribute to Ezra. *Op. cit.*, p. 54. However Davidson (*Old Testament Prophecy*, p. 80) lists the prophets as the first interpreters. He appeals to Isaiah 43:27. However others translate the word as "ambassador." The RSV has "mediators."

(iii). A clear passage is to be given preference over an obscure one if they deal with the same subject matter.

(iv). Very close attention is to be paid to spelling, grammar, and figures of speech.

(v). By the use of logic we can determine the application of Scripture to those problems in life Scripture has not specifically treated. In this connection some of the valid forms of the logic of deduction or implication were used by the rabbis. This is still standard procedure in theological hermeneutics.

(vi). Their insistence that the God of Israel spoke in the tongues of men was their way of asserting that the God of Israel had adapted His revelation to the recipients of it. This implies a measure of accommodation and cultural conditioning of the divine revelation.

It would not be unfair to rabbinic exegesis to assert that it did not develop a profound self-conscious and critical theory of hermeneutics. Nor would it be unfair to state that they wandered far off from the good rules they did construct.

The major weakness of their system was the development of a hyperliteralism or a *letterism*. In the intense devotion to the details of the text, they missed the essential and made mountains out of the accidental. This was based on the belief that *nothing* in Scripture was superfluous and therefore all the grammatical phenomena of the text (pleonasm, ellipsis, etc.) had an import to the interpreter. Further, because the Bible was given of God the interpreter could expect numerous meanings in the text. The combination of these two principles led to the fantastic interpretations of the rabbis. The errors were then compounded by the enormous authority given to tradition.

Eventually this system developed into the system of the Cabbalists wherein *letterism* and *allegorism* form a grotesque alliance. By the use of *notarikon* all sorts of exegetical gymnastics were performed. Each letter of a word was made to stand for another word. By use of *gemetria* they endowed words with numerical values which became grounds for arbitrary and odd associations of verses. Let the modern student who wishes to play with the numbers of the Bible first read what the Jews did with *gemetria* and so learn moderation and restraint. By the use of *termura* they permutated the letters of a word and so extracted new meanings from old words.

Fortunately the Karaites and the Spanish Jews started a more intelligent procedure for the understanding of the Old Testament, and from this new inspiration has come much valuable exegetical literature.[31]

There is one major lesson to be learned from rabbinical exegesis: the evils of *letterism*. In the exaltation of the very letters of the Scripture the true meaning of the Scripture was lost. The incidental is so exaggerated as to obscure the essential.[32] Any exegesis will go astray which bogs itself down in trivialities and *letterism*.

2. *Syrian School of Antioch*

It has been said that the first Protestant school of hermeneutics flourished in the city of Antioch of Syria, and had it not been crushed by the hand of orthodoxy for its supposed heretical connections with the Nestorians, the entire course of Church history might have been different. The Christian community was influenced by the Jewish community and the result was a hermeneutical theory which avoided the *letterism* of the Jews and the *allegorism* of the Alexandrians.

---

[31] Farrar, (*op. cit.*, Lecture II, "Rabbinic Exegesis," and, "Notes to Lecture II," and, "Notes to Lecture V"), should be read for first-hand examples of Jewish exegetical fantasies. But one must bear in mind the judgment of Abrahams that Farrar is not always fair, and that buried amidst this exegesis are some very substantial contributions to exegetical science. Cf. Israel Abrahams, "Rabbinic Aids to Exegesis," *Cambridge Biblical Essays*, pp. 159–192.

[32] Gilbert (*op. cit.*, Chapter I) lists five major criticisms of Jewish exegesis but they all boil down to one, *viz.*, the failure to develop an adequate theory of hermeneutics. In process of publication is a commentary which hopes to summarize the Jewish exegetical wisdom of the ages, *viz.*, Kasher, *Encyclopedia of Biblical Interpretation* (vol. I, 1953).

It boasted of such names as Lucian, Dorotheus, Diodorus, Theodore of Mopsuestia and Chrysostom. As a school it influenced Jerome and modulated the allegorism of Alexandria in the West. It also had an influence on medieval exegesis, and found itself again in the hermeneutics of the Reformers.

The Syrian school fought Origen in particular as the inventor of the allegorical method, and maintained the primacy of the literal and historical interpretation of the Scripture. It is true that in practice some of the Antiochenes were found dipping into allegorizing, nevertheless in hermeneutical theory they took a stout stand for literal and historical exegesis. They asserted that the literal was plain-literal and figurative-literal. A plain-literal sentence is a straightforward prose sentence with no figures of speech in it. "The eye of the Lord is upon thee," would be a figurative-literal sentence. According to the Alexandrians the literal meaning of this sentence would attribute an actual eye to God. But the Syrian school denied this to be the literal meaning of the sentence. The literal meaning is about God's omniscience. In other words literalism is not the same as *letterism*.

Further, they avoided dogmatic exegesis. Dogmatic exegesis, which kept growing in the West due perhaps to so many controversies with the heretics, eventually developed into Roman Catholic authoritarian exegesis. But the Syrians insisted that the meaning of the Bible was its historical and grammatical meaning, and interpretations must so be justified.

The Syrians insisted on the reality of the Old Testament events. They accused the allegorists of doing away with the historicity of much of the Old Testament and leaving a shadowy world of symbols. The literal and historical approach guarantees to the Old Testament history its important reality.

In place of an allegorical interpretation of the Old Testament the Syrians presented a more sane typological approach. According to the allegorists, floating above the obvious historical meaning of the Old Testament events was another more spiritual or theological meaning. But according to the Syrians the historical and the Messianic were blended together like woof and warp. The Messianic did not float above the historical, but was implicit in it. This not only weeded out much of the fanciful Old Testament Christological interpretation of the allegorists, but it rested the subject on a far more satisfactory basis. The relationship of the Old and New Testaments was made typological and not allegorical.

This also enabled the Syrians to defend the unity of the Bible from a better vantage point. They admitted the development of revelation. An allegorist might find something far richer about Jesus Christ and salvation in Genesis than in Luke. But if progressive revelation is correctly understood such a maneuver by an exegete is impossible. Secondly, they admitted that the unity of the Bible was Christological. The bond between the Two Testaments is prophecy (predictive and typological) understood in terms of (i) progressive revelation and (ii) the literal and historical exegesis of Messianic passages.

The result of these principles was some of the finest exegetical literature of ancient times. As Gilbert says, "The commentary of Theodore [of Mopsuestia] on the minor epistles of Paul is the first and almost the last exegetical work produced in the ancient Church which will bear any comparison with modern commentaries." [33] Grant observes that this school had a remarkable influence in the Middle Ages and became the pillar of the Reformation, and finally became the "principal exegetical method of the Christian Church." [34]

---

[33] *Op. cit.*, p. 135. Commenting on the good hermeneutical taste yet oratorical ability of Chrysostom (the "golden-mouthed," or in our idiom "the silver tongued") M. B. Riddle wrote: "Great pulpit orators do not need to indulge in mystical fancies nor does their power arise from dogmatic warping of the sense of Scripture." "St. Chrysostom as an Exegete," *Nicene and Post-Nicene Fathers* (first series), X, p. xix.

[34] Grant, *op. cit.*, p. 84.

3. *The Victorines*

Scholars of the medieval period have established the fact that a strong historical and literal school existed in the Abbey of St. Victor in Paris.[35] Its outstanding men were Hugo of St. Victor, Richard of St. Victor, and Andrew of St. Victor. Just as the Jewish scholarship in Antioch of Syria influenced the Christian scholars there for literalism, so the Jewish scholars of the medieval period influenced the Victorines for literalism. Miss Smalley at several points in her exposition notes the friendly relations and interactions of this school with the Jewish scholars.

The Victorines insisted that liberal arts, history, and geography were basic to exegesis. History and geography especially form the natural background for literal exegesis. Literal exegesis gave rise to doctrine, and doctrine was the natural background for allegorization. A close check is hereby put on allegorization for none is permitted that does not root in doctrine established by the literal sense.

The literal, rather than a preliminary or superficial study, was the basic study of the Bible. The Victorines insisted that the mystical or spiritual sense could not be truly known until the Bible had been literally interpreted. By literalism they did not mean *letterism* but the true and proper meaning of a sentence. This emphasis on the literal carried over into an emphasis on syntax, grammar, and meaning. True interpretation of the Bible was *exegesis*, not *eisegesis*.

4. *The Reformers*

The tradition of the Syrian school was reflected among the Victorines and became the essential hermeneutical theory of the Reformers. Although historians admit that the West was ripe for the Reformation due to several forces at work

[35] Cf. Beryl Smalley, *The Study of the Bible in the Middle Ages* (revised edition), Chapters III and IV. The older historians of interpretation apparently were ignorant of the existence of this school.

in European culture, nevertheless there was a *hermeneutical Reformation* which preceded the ecclesiastical Reformation.

There were two main factors that prepared the way for the Reformation in terms of hermeneutics. The first of these was the philosophical system of Occam. Occam was a nominalist, and much of the training which Luther had was in the philosophy of Occam. In Occam we find a separation of revelation and human reason. Human reason had as its territory nature, philosophy, and science. Revelation which was received through faith had for its territory salvation and theology. This was a radical separation of two elements that existed on friendlier terms in the philosophy of Aquinas. In Thomism reason not only dealt with philosophy but with natural religion, and natural religion became the mediating link between philosophy and revelation.

The two realms of grace and nature were separated by Occam. Therefore, whatever we know of God we know by divine revelation, not by human reason. The authority for theological dogma rested solely on divine revelation, and therefore upon the Bible. Thus Luther was so trained as to magnify the authority of the Bible as over against philosophy. When called upon to prove his position he appealed to Scripture and reason (logical deductions from Scripture). A traditional Catholic theologian would appeal to Scripture and reason but also to Thomistic philosophy, councils, creeds, and the Fathers. (The traditional interpretation of Luther and Occamism has been challenged by B. Haegglund: "Was Luther a Nominalist?" *Theology*, 59:226–234, June, 1956.)

The second factor was the renewed study of Hebrew and Greek. Beryl Smalley (*The Study of the Bible in the Middle Ages*) had demonstrated that Hebrew studies were not as completely lacking among the scholastics as scholars formerly thought. It was Reuchlin, a humanist and a lawyer, who translated Kimchi's Hebrew grammar into Latin so that if a man had the time he could decipher some main elements of the Hebrew language.[36] With the Renaissance came a renewed interest in Greek, and Erasmus published the first Greek New Testament in modern times in 1516. The entire Bible in its original languages was now available for study, for a Hebrew Testament had been printed by 1494. Luther learned his Latin for the priesthood and could so handle the Latin Vulgate, and he also learned his Greek and Hebrew. He had a photographic memory and this did him good service in public debate for he could recall the reading of the Greek or Hebrew on a given passage. When he thought he might be shut up in prison, he selected as his two books of consolation a Hebrew and a Greek Testament.

Luther's hermeneutical principles were: [37]

(1). *The psychological principle.* Faith and illumination were the personal and spiritual requisites for an interpreter. The believer should seek the leading of the Spirit and depend on that leading. In his *Table Talk* he writes: "We ought not to criticise, or judge the Scriptures by our mere reason, but diligently, with prayer, meditate thereon, and seek their meaning" (*On God's Word*, IV). In that Scripture was inspired it demanded a spiritual approach by the interpreter for he also wrote: "The Bible should be regarded with wholly different eyes from those with which we view other productions" (*On God's Word*, IX).

(2). *The authority principle.* The Bible is the supreme and final authority in theological matters, and is therefore above all ecclesiastical authority. Its teaching cannot be countermanded nor qualified nor subordinated to ecclesiastical authorities whether of persons or documents.

[36] For the details of Hebrew learning at the time of the Reformation and for Luther's own knowledge of the language see W. H. Koenig, "Luther as a Student of Hebrew," *Concordia Theological Monthly*, 24:845–853, Nov., 1953.

[37] Besides the standard works on history of interpretation see R. F. Surburg, "The Significance of Luther's Hermeneutics for the Protestant Reformation," *Concordia Theological Monthly*, 24:241–261, April, 1953. Farrar (*op. cit.* 326 ff.) gives two different lists of Luther's hermeneutical principles.

(3). *The literal principle.* In place of the four-fold system of the scholastics, we are to put the literal principle. The scholastics had developed their hermeneutics into two divisions, the literal and the spiritual. The spiritual had been divided into three divisions (allegorical, anagogical, and tropological). Luther maintained strongly the primacy of the literal interpretation of Scripture. In the *Table Talk* he affirms that "I have grounded my preaching upon the literal word" (*On God's Word*, XI). Farrar cites him as writing: "The literal sense of Scripture alone is the whole essence of faith and of Christian theology." [38] Briggs cites him as saying: "Every word should be allowed to stand in its natural meaning, and that should not be abandoned unless faith forces us to it." [39]

The literal principle implies three sub-principles:

(i). Luther rejected allegory. He calls allegorical interpretation "dirt," "scum," "obsolete loose rags," and likens allegorizing to a harlot and to a monkey game. Yet this is not the entire story. This was his opinion of allegory as used by the Catholics. He was not adverse to allegory if the content were Christ and not something of the papacy. In fact students of Luther have indicated his inconsistency at this point for Luther himself engages in some typical medieval allegorization. But in principle he broke with it, and in much practice he repudiated it even though he was not entirely free from it.

(ii). Luther accepted the primacy of the original languages. He felt that the original revelation of God could not be truly recovered until it was recovered from the Hebrew and Greek Testaments. His advice to preachers was: "While a preacher may preach Christ with edification though he may be unable to read the Scriptures in the originals, he cannot expound or maintain their teaching against the heretics without this in-

[38] *Op. cit.*, p. 327.
[39] C. A. Briggs, *History of the Study of Theology*, II, 107.

dispensable knowledge." Luther did a great deal to sponsor the revival of Hebrew and Greek studies.

(iii). The historical and grammatical principle. This is inseparable from the literal principle. The interpreter must give attention to *grammar;* to the *times, circumstances, and conditions* of the writer of the Biblical book; and to the *context* of the passage.

(4). *The sufficiency principle.* The devout and competent Christian can understand the true meaning of the Bible and thereby does not need the official guides to interpretation offered by the Roman Catholic Church. The Bible is a *clear* book (the *perspicuity* of Scripture). Catholicism had maintained that the Scriptures were so obscure that only the teaching ministry of the Church could uncover their true meaning. To Luther the *perspicuity* of the Bible was coupled with the *priesthood of believers,* so that the Bible became the property of all Christians.

The competent Christian was *sufficient* to interpret the Bible, and the Bible is *sufficiently* clear in content to yield its meaning to the believer. Further, the Bible was a world of its own and so *Scripture interprets Scripture.* At points where the Bible was obscure the Catholic referred to the unwritten tradition of the Church. But Luther shut the interpreter up within the Bible and made the obscure passage yield to a clear passage. Much of Catholic exegesis was nothing more than studies in patristics. This Luther rejected:

I ask for Scriptures and Eck offers me the Fathers. I ask for the sun, and he shows me his lanterns. I ask: "Where is your Scripture proof?" and he adduces Ambrose and Cyril . . . With all due respect to the Fathers I prefer the authority of the Scripture.[40]

A corollary at this point is: *the analogy of faith.* The scholastics interpreted by glosses and catena of citations from the Fathers. This was arbitrary and disconnected.

[40] Cited by Farrar, *op. cit.,* p. 327.

Luther insisted on *the organic, theological unity of the Bible*. All of the relevant material on a given subject was to be collected together so that the pattern of divine revelation concerning that subject would be apparent.

(5). *The Christological principle.* The literal interpretation of the Bible was not the end of interpretation. The function of all interpretation is to find Christ. Luther's rule at this point was: "Auch ist das der rechte Prüfstein alle Bücher zu tadeln, wenn man siehet ob sie Christum trieben oder nicht." [41] Smith cites Luther as saying: "If you will interpret well and securely, take Christ with you, for he is the man whom everything concerns." [42]

This is Luther's method of making the entire Bible a Christian book. The Fathers did it with their allegorical method. Luther does it with his Christological principle.

This has been one of Luther's most controversial utterances. (i) One group (especially the neo-orthodox) claims that Luther did not hold to a narrow verbal inspiration view of Scripture. Luther felt free to challenge anything in Scripture not Christological. (ii) The strict orthodox Lutheran theologians claim that this is purely a hermeneutical principle, and not a principle of Biblical criticism. They adduce numerous statements of Luther to prove that he held to an infallible, inerrant Bible. Fortunately, the study of hermeneutics does not have to await the outcome of this debate for it is crystal clear that this principle is first of all a hermeneutical maxim of Luther's.

(6). *The Law-Gospel principle.* Luther saw the root heresy of the Galatian churches transposed into a different key in the Catholic Church. The Galatians had been taught to (i) be circumcized—the seal of the Old Testament Covenant and (ii) to believe in Christ—the center of the New Covenant, and they would be saved. The Catholic Church taught that

---

[41] Farrar, *op. cit.*, p. 333. "This is the correct touchstone to censure (or test) all [biblical] books, if one sees if they urge Christ or not."
[42] H. P. Smith, *Essays in Biblical Interpretation*, p. 78.

(i) to do religious works, and (ii) believe in Christ would save them. Justification by faith alone not only repudiated the Judaizers of the Gospel, but the Roman Catholic system of salvation.

Luther taught that we must carefully distinguish Law and Gospel in the Bible, and this was one of Luther's principal hermeneutical rules. Any fusion of the Law and Gospel was wrong (Catholics and Reformed who make the Gospel a new law), and any repudiation of the Law was wrong (antinomianism). The Law was God's word about human sin, human imperfection, and whose purpose was to drive us to our knees under a burden of guilt. The Gospel is God's grace and power to save. Hence we must never in interpreting the Scriptures confuse these two different activities of God or teachings of Holy Scripture.

*　　　*　　　*

With reference to Calvin, Fullerton observes that "Calvin may not unfittingly be called the first scientific interpreter in the history of the Christian Church." [43] Is there any other man in the history of the Christian Church who has turned out such a scientific, able, and valuable commentary on almost the entire Scriptures and also made one of the greatest contributions to theology in his *Institutes*? It is true that to Luther we owe the honor of having broken through to a new Protestant hermeneutics, but it was Calvin who exemplified it with his touch of genius. Speaking of Calvin's commentaries Wright says: "The more one studies these commentaries, the more astonished he becomes at their scholarship, lucid profundity, and freshness of insight. Although biblical studies have moved a long way since the sixteenth century,

[43] *Prophecy and Authority*, p. 133. Cf. also P. T. Fuhrman, "Calvin, the Expositor of Scripture," *Interpretation*, 6:188–209, April, 1952. For a description of the sheer genius of Calvin see A. M. Hunter, "The Erudition of John Calvin," *The Evangelical Quarterly*, 18:199–208, July, 1946.

there is still little which can be held to be their equal." [44]

(i). Calvin insisted that the *illumination of the Spirit* was the necessary spiritual preparation for the interpreter of God's Word.

(ii). Calvin, with Luther, rejected allegorical interpretation. Calvin called it Satanic because it led men away from the truth of Scripture. He further stated that the inexhaustibility of Scripture *was not in its so-called fertility of meanings.*

(iii). "Scripture interprets Scripture" was a basic conviction of Calvin. This meant many things. It meant *literalism* (as defined in this book) in exegesis with a rejection of the medieval system of the four-fold meaning of Scripture. It meant listening to the Scripture, not reading Scripture to justify a host of dogmatic presuppositions—although scholars are not sure that Calvin escaped doing this himself. Calvin wrote: "It is the first business of an interpreter to let his author say what he does, instead of attributing to him what we think he ought to say," [45] and in the dedicatory letter to one of his commentaries he added:

We were both of this mind that the principal point of an interpreter did consist in a lucid brevity. And truly, seeing that this is in a manner his whole charge, namely, to show both the mind of the writer whom he hath taken upon himself to expound, look, by how much he leadeth the readers away from the same, by so much he is wide of the mark . . . Verily the word of God ought to be so revered by us that through a diversity of interpretation it might not be drawn asunder by us, no not so much as a hair's breadth . . . It is an audacity akin to sacrilege to use the Scriptures at our own pleasure and to play with them as with a tennis ball, which many before us have done.[46]

The "Scripture interprets Scripture" principle led Calvin to make a strong emphasis on grammatical exegesis, philol-

[44] G. E. Wright, "The Christian Interpreter as Biblical Critic," *Interpretation*, 1:133 ff., April, 1947.

[45] Quoted by Farrar, *op. cit.*, p. 347.

[46] Quoted by Fullerton, *op. cit.*, p. 134.

ogy, the necessity of examining the context, and the necessity of comparing Scriptures which treated common subjects.

(iv). Calvin showed a marked independence in exegesis. He not only broke with Catholic exegetical principles, but with any sort of exegesis which was shoddy, superficial, or worthless. He rejected arguments for very orthodox doctrines if the exegesis involved was unworthy.

(v). Finally, Calvin anticipated much of the modern spirit with reference to the interpretation of Messianic prophecy. He showed caution and reserve in these matters, and stated that the exegete ought to investigate the historical settings of all prophetic and Messianic Scriptures.

5. *Post-Reformation*

In general the spirit and the rules of the Reformers became the guiding principles of Protestant orthodox interpretation. To name the scholars who followed in the footsteps of Luther and Calvin would be to name most of the great exegetes from Reformation times until now. Briggs claims that the Puritans worked out the Protestant hermeneutics to a fine point.[47]

Not all post-Reformation exegesis was of the same high standard as that of Calvin, and that there were extremists no one can doubt although Farrar's judgment on these men is extreme. However, a very significant advance was made by Ernesti, who was a classical scholar. He published his *Institutio Interpretis* in 1761 and in it maintained the thesis that the skills and tools of classical studies were basic to New Testament exegesis. Ernesti stated that grammatical exegesis has priority over dogmatic exegesis, and that literal interpretation was preferred over allegorical exegesis. His principal emphasis was on the necessity of sound philology in exegesis. Of Ernesti Briggs writes: "It is the merit of Ernesti in modern times that he so insisted upon grammatical

[47] Cf. his discussion of the rules of the Puritans in *Biblical Study*, p. 335 ff.

exegesis that he induced exegetes of all classes to begin their work here at the foundation" [grammatical interpretation].[48]

D. Devotional Schools

The devotional interpretation of Scripture is that method of interpreting Scripture which places emphasis on the edifying aspects of Scripture, and interpreting with the intention of developing the spiritual life.

1. *Medieval Mystics*

The medieval period produced both scholasticism and mysticism. The mystics read the Scriptures as means of promoting the mystical experience. Such representative men were the Victorines (Hugo but more especially, Richard) and Bernard of Clairvaux. The principal book of the mystics was the *Song of Songs* which they readily interpreted as the love relationship between God and the mystic resulting in spiritual delights told in terms of physical delights.

2. *Spener and Francke—Pietism*

The post-Reformation period was a period of theological dogmatism. It was a period of heresy hunting and rigid, creedal Protestantism. Farrar's account of it although perhaps extreme is nevertheless depressing.[49] He says it was characterized by a three-fold curse: "The curse of tyrannous confessionalism; the curse of exorbitant systems; the curse of contentious bitterness." [50] Speaking of bitterness among theologians, he writes: *"They read the Bible by the unnatural glare of theological hatred."* [51]

It was in reaction to this situation that *pietism* developed.

[48] *Op. cit.*, p. 352. However, there are some items in Ernesti's system which are not acceptable to historic Christianity. These principles are stated and challenged in Carson, *Examination of the Principles of Biblical Interpretation.*

[49] *Op. cit.*, p. 357 ff.

[50] *Ibid.*, p. 359.

[51] *Ibid.*, p. 363. Italics are ours.

Pietism was the effort to recover the Bible as spiritual food and nourishment to be read for personal edification. It was a distinct reaction against dogmatic and fanciful exegesis. Spener, who was influenced by Richard Baxter, published his *Pia Desidera* in 1675 and maintained that the Bible was the instrument in God's hands for effecting true spirituality. Spener organized his *Collegia pietatis* wherein believers met together for Bible study, devotions, and prayer.

The second great pietist was A. H. Francke who was much more the scholar, linguist and exegete. Francke organized with Anton and Schade a *Collegium Philobiblicum* for the study of the Scriptures with an emphasis on philology and the practical bearing of Scripture on life. Later he went to the University at Halle which became the center of pietism. Francke insisted that the entire Bible be read through frequently; that commentaries were to be used but with discretion so as not to take the place of the study of Scripture itself; and that only the regenerate could understand the Bible.

Farrar says that Bengel was the "heir and continuator of all that was best in Pietism." [52] Bengel studied under the pietists and was impressed by their spirituality, their wonderful Christian fellowship, their emphasis on grammatical and historical interpretation, and their emphasis on the application of Scripture to spiritual life. Bengel eventually wrote his famous *Gnomon* which is concise, grammatical, penetrating, and which emphasizes the unity of the Scriptural revelation. His work in textual criticism represents one of the great landmarks in the development of New Testament textual criticism.

The influence of pietism was great. It influenced the Moravians and Zinzendorf. Others in the pietistic tradition

[52] *Op. cit.*, p. 392. Cf. J. Pelikan, "In Memoriam: Joh. Albrecht Bengel," *Concordia Theological Monthly*, 23:785–796, November, 1952. Charles T. Fritsch, "Bengel, Student of Scripture," *Interpretation*, 5:203–215, April, 1951.

(or at least emphasizing the devotional, practical, and edifying study of the Bible) are the Puritans, Wesley, Edwards, Matthew Henry, and the Quakers.[53]

3. *Modern Emphasis*

The insights of the pietists have not been lost. It would not be amiss to say that the average Christian reads his Bible in the devotional tradition, i.e., for his own blessing and spiritual food. The devotional material on our book shelves is imposing and the preacher is expected to have a devotional emphasis in every sermon above and beyond whatever doctrinal or exegetical remarks he may have to make.

The devotional and practical emphasis in Bible teaching is *absolutely* necessary. The purpose of preaching is more than doctrinal communication or exposition of the meaning of Scripture. It must reach over into life and experience, and this is the function of the devotional teaching of Scripture. The vital, personal, and spiritual *must be present in all the ministries of the Word*.

There are two weaknesses of devotional interpretation:

(i). It falls prey to allegorization especially in the use of the Old Testament. In the effort to find a spiritual truth or application of a passage of Scripture the literal and therefore primary meaning of the passage is obscured. If it is not a case of bald allegorizing it may be excessive typology. Given enough allegorical and typological rope one may prove a variety of contradictory propositions from the Old Testament. One may prove Calvinistic security (the central board in the wall of the Tabernacle) or Arminian probationalism (the failure of faith at Kadesh-Barnea). A Reformed expositor may prove that the soul feeds on Christ while discuss-

---

[53] Cf. Dana's discussion. *Searching the Scriptures*, p. 81 ff. Immer claims that the chief error of the pietists was that "the Scriptures were not so much explained as overwhelmed with pious reflections." Cited by Terry, *op. cit.*, p. 62 fn.

ing the sacrificial system, and a Catholic prove his doctrine of the mass.

All sorts of distortions have been made of the historical records of the Old Testament (and occasionally the New) in order to derive a spiritual blessing or to make a devotional point.

(ii). Devotional interpretation may be a substitute for the requisite exegetical and doctrinal studies of the Bible. Strong doctrinal sinews and solid exegetical bones are necessary for spiritual health. If the emphasis is completely devotional the requisite doctrinal and expository truth of Scripture are denied God's people.

D. LIBERAL INTERPRETATION

As early as Hobbes and Spinoza rationalistic views were held about the Bible. The debate over the Bible in modern times is a debate of rationalism versus authoritarianism. Rationalism in Biblical studies boils down to the fundamental assertion that whatever is not in harmony with *educated* mentality is to be rejected. The critic defines *educated* in a very special way. The authoritarian position asserts that if God has spoken, the human mind must be obedient to the voice of God. That there is a blind or credulous authoritarianism cannot be denied, but it is not true that authoritarianism is anti-intellectual.[54] The rationalistic premise has led to radical criticism of the Scriptures.

This radical treatment of Scriptures reached its full tide in the nineteenth century. Suffice it to say that by the middle of the twentieth century most theological seminaries have accepted the basic theses of radical criticism, and many of its conclusions. The Barthian reaction will be discussed later. In broad perspective the following rules have governed the

[54] Protestants accept authority when underwritten by the criteria of truthfulness. Cf. E. Carnell, *An Introduction to Christian Apologetics.* P. 71.

religious liberals as they approached the study of the Bible: [55]

(i). *Religious liberals believe that "modern mentality" is to govern our approach to Scripture.* This "modern mentality" is made up of a complex of presuppositions, e.g., standards of scholarship as practiced in higher education, the validity of the scientific *outlook* as well as *method*, and the ethical standards of educated people. Whatever in the Scriptural account does not measure up to these criteria is rejected. Scholarship claims that all books are to be treated as human documents and by the same methods and the Bible is no exception.[56] Science presumes the regularity of nature so miracles are not accepted. The doctrines of sin, depravity, and hell offend the liberals' moral sensitivities so these doctrines are rejected. This also means a rather free use of the text of the Bible. If a book of the Bible seems "patched" the text may be re-arranged, e.g., as Moffatt does with the Gospel of John in his translation. If the text is obscure the text may be remade, e.g., as is done too frequently in the Old Testament part of the *Revised Standard Version.*[57]

(ii). *Religious liberals redefine inspiration.* All forms of genuine inspiration (verbal, plenary, dynamic) are rejected. If liberalism rejects all transcendental and miraculous activity of God, then it must reject a supernaturalistic doctrine of inspiration and revelation which it does.[58] In its place it puts Coleridge's principle that the inspiration of the Bible is its power to inspire religious experience. Revelation is redefined as human insight into religious truth, or human dis-

[55] Generally speaking radical views of the Bible have accompanied liberal views of theology. However, an atheist may hold to radical criticism and reject liberal theology. There are scholars who have accepted radical criticism and maintained orthodox theology, as is evident from W. B. Glover's *Evangelical Nonconformists and Higher Criticism in the Nineteenth Century* [in Great Britain].

[56] Cf. E. C. Colwell, *The Study of the Bible,* Chapters III, IV, and V. Also, H. E. Fosdick, *The Modern Use of the Bible.*

[57] Cf. Piper's sharp criticism of rationalism in the hermeneutics of religious liberalism. Otto A. Piper, "Principles of New Testament Interpretation," *Theology Today,* 3:202, July, 1946.

[58] Fosdick, *op. cit.,* pp. 30–31.

covery of religious truths. Or as Fosdick puts it: "The under side of the process is man's discovery; the upper side is God's revelation." [59]

The canon of criticism is "the spirit of Jesus." Whatever in the Bible is in accord with the "spirit of Jesus" is normative, and whatever is below the ethical and moral level of the "spirit of Jesus" is not binding. Bewer writes quite clearly at this point: "To the Christian the only norm and standard is the spirit of God as revealed in Jesus . . . . all those parts of the Old Testament which are contrary to the spirit of Jesus, or which have no direct spiritual meaning to us, are for us without authority." [60]

This means that the doctrinal or theological content of Scripture is not binding. It was Sabatier who argued that religious experience was fundamental and theology was the afterthought of this experience. But the religious experience could not be completely expressed in thought-form so theological expression was but symbolical of the religious experience. With this essential thesis Fosdick agrees, for to him religious experience is the heart of religion and theological forms are temporary. One of the chapters of his book has the title, "Abiding Experiences and Changing Categories." His thesis is expressed in these words: "What is permanent in Christianity is not mental frameworks but abiding experiences that phrase and rephrase themselves in successive generations' ways of thinking and that grow in assured certainty and richness of content." [61]

(iii). *The supernatural is redefined.* The supernatural may mean: that which is extraordinary, miraculous, oracular, not

[59] *Ibid.*, p. 30. This thesis is found widely in the literature of religious liberalism and no clearer expression of it has been given than in A. Sabatier's *Outlines of a Philosophy of Religion based on Psychology and History.* See p. 34 ff.

[60] Bewer, *Authority of the Old Testament* in T. Kepler's *Contemporary Religious Thought,* p. 127.

[61] Fosdick, *op. cit.,* p. 103. Cf. also his remarks in Kepler, *op. cit.,* pp. 13–20. But is not this thesis itself *a theological proposition?* Therefore, *this* theological proposition is prior to religious experience. Result: his basic position is contradictory.

attainable in knowledge or power by ordinary human nature. Or it may mean: above the material order, or beyond mere natural processes, e.g., prayer, ethics, pure thought, immortality. Historic orthodoxy has accepted supernaturalism in both these meanings. Religious liberalism accepts only the latter.

Everything in the Bible which is supernatural in the first sense is rejected. Colwell argues that the *same* methodology must be used in interpreting the Bible as is used in interpreting the classics; no special principle may be appealed to by Christians. If, therefore, we reject all reports of miracles in the classics as violating our scientific good sense, then we must reject miracles in the Scriptures.[62] When the miracle or supernatural is found in Scripture it is treated as folklore or mythology or poetic elaboration.

(iv). *The concept of evolution is applied to the religion of Israel and thereby to its documents.* Fosdick's book, *The Modern Use of the Bible*, is considered a most lucid presentation of the Wellhausenian interpretation of the Old Testament. The primitive and crude, ethically and religiously, is the earlier; and the advanced and elevated, is the later. We can thereby recreate the evolution of the religion of Israel and rearrange our documents accordingly. "We know now that every idea in the Bible started from primitive and childlike origins and, with however many setbacks and delays, grew in scope and height toward the culmination of Christ's Gospel," is Fosdick's point of view.[63]

[62] Colwell, *op. cit.*, p. 122 f. Piper's comment is: "Critics who had no experience of the supernatural concluded, for instance, that everything in the Bible which referred to the supernatural was wrong. Sound criticism would have contented itself with saying: 'My judgment as to the truthfulness of these documents has to be suspended because I know nothing of these things.' " *Op. cit.*, p. 201.

[63] *Op. cit.*, p. 11. H. P. Smith (*Essays in Biblical Interpretation*) speaking of the application of evolutionary principles to Biblical criticism says that such application is widely accepted because men see evolution in *history* as well as nature. However, a great reversal has taken place in anthropological theory and the evolutionary principle of social cultural no longer dominates anthropological theory. P. 141.

In the study of the canon this put the prophets *before* the law. The basic Wellhausen position calls for considerable rearrangement of books and materials.[64]

The same procedure has been applied to the New Testament. Harnack's *What is Christianity?* is considered the finest and clearest expression of religious liberalism. Its thesis is that Jesus, a good man in the highest prophetic order, is transmuted by theological speculation and Greek metaphysics into the strange God-man of the creeds. The critic of the New Testament must be an expert archeologist and geologist to uncover the strata of accretions imposed on the true Jesus of history.

However, archeological work, further work in criticism, and the uncovering of much papyri demonstrated that all such stratigraphy was due to fail. In *Formgeschichte* (form or historical criticism) an effort is made to develop a preliterary theory for accounting for the New Testament. The New Testament was the creation of the Christian community out of its spiritual needs, and so the Gospels are not the life of Christ as much as they are the life of the early church.

(v). *The notion of accommodation has been applied to the Bible.* Much of the theological content of the Bible is weakened or destroyed by asserting that the theological statements are in the transitory and perishable mold of ancient terminology. For example, the only terms in which Paul could describe the death of Christ were from bloody Jewish sacrifices or the blood-baths of Mythraism. Thus Paul's doctrine of the atonement is accommodated to the expressions of his time and these are not binding on us. It is claimed that our Lord in dealing with the Jews had to accommodate his teaching to their condition, especially in matters of Bibli-

[64] However, this entire concept is now under severe criticism. Cf. Albright, *From the Stone Age to Christianity,* and, *Archeology and the Religion of Israel.* John Bright, "The Prophets Were Protestants," *Interpretation,* I:153–82, April, 1947.

cal Introduction, e.g., the historicity of Adam and Eve, of Jonah, of the Davidic authorship of the Psalms.[65]

The religious liberal feels it is his assignment to recast the essence of the New Testament doctrine in the language of his contemporaries, and in so doing must strip off the concepts and images of the Old and New Testament cultures.

(vi). *The Bible was interpreted historically—with a vengeance.*[66] The historical interpretation is used in a special leveling and reductionist sense by the religious liberal. He means more than painting the historical backdrop of the various passages of the Bible. It is a method which endeavors to break the uniqueness of the Scriptures. It makes religion a changing, shifting phenomenon so that it is impossible to "canonize" any period of its development or its literature. It believes that there are social conditions which create theological beliefs and the task of the interpreter is not to defend these theological beliefs (as in orthodoxy) but to understand the social conditions which produced them. It stresses the continuity of Biblical religion with surrounding religion, and emphasizes "borrowing," "syncretism," and "purifying."

Further, in so stressing the necessity of finding the meaning of a passage for the original hearers of it, it repudiates the prophetic or predictive element of prophecy. It rejects typology and predictive prophecy as Christian abuses (although in good faith) of the Old Testament.

(vii). *Philosophy has had an influence on religious liberalism.* Immanuel Kant made ethics or moral will the essence

[65] That our Lord did not accommodate himself in this sense is thoroughly argued by C. J. Ellicott, *Christus Comprobatur.* Horne (*An Introduction to the Critical Study and Knowledge of the Holy Scriptures,* eighth edition) has an able refutation of this type of accommodation, too, that although written more than a hundred years ago is still relevant. Gore's essay in *Lux Mundi* argued that the incarnation involved ignorance and so Christ knew only what a typical Jew would know about matters of Biblical Introduction.

[66] Cf. Colwell, (*op. cit.,* Chapter VI), for the results of a religious liberal's use of the historical principle in criticism. Also, H. P. Smith (*op. cit.*), Chapter XIII, "Historical Interpretation."

of religion. Kant shut himself up almost completely to the *moral* interpretation of Scripture. Whatever was not of this he rejected. This emphasis on the moral element of Scripture with its tacit rejection of theological interpretation has played a major role in the liberals' use of the Scripture.

Deism made ethics the essence of religion too. In a typically deistic fashion Jefferson went through the Gospels picking out the ethical and moral, and rejecting the theological and so published his *Jefferson Bible*.

Hegelianism has had its influence on Biblical interpretation. According to Hegel progress in the clarification of an idea involves three terms: the thesis, the antithesis, and the synthesis. This Hegelian waltz was applied to the totality of human culture including religion. Hegelian students were not slow in applying it to the Biblical records. Wellhausen applied it to the Old Testament, and Strauss and the Tuebingen school to the New. Thus in the Tuebingen school the strife between Pauline factions and Petrine factions is harmonized by the Lucan approach.

Ethical idealism and idealism with strong ethical and religious elements has had its influence on American religious liberalism. At the headwaters of much of our American religious philosophy were Josiah Royce and Borden Parker Bowne. Bowne's personalism through his students and their students has had a real influence on much of Methodist and liberal theology in America.

E. NEO-ORTHODOXY

Karl Barth ushered in a new era in Biblical interpretation when he published his *Römerbrief* at the end of World War I. This was a new approach to the theological interpretation of the book of Romans. This new movement has been called "crisis theology" because it so emphasized God's judgment of man; "Barthianism," because it stems from the original thought of Karl Barth; "neo-orthodoxy" because it dissevers itself from liberalism and seeks to recover the insights of the

Reformers; "neo-supernaturalism" because in contradiction to modernism it reënstates the category of the transcendental; "logotheism" because it is a theology of the Word of God; "neo-evangelicalism" because it seeks to recover the Christian gospel in contrast to the social gospel of liberalism; "neo-liberalism" because it is claimed that although differing in many ways from liberalism it has not really broken with it; and "Biblical realism" because it makes a new effort to rediscover the theological interpretation of the Bible.[67]

The movement has been fractured into a series of submovements rendering simple description difficult. We shall try to set forth those hermeneutical principles which would more or less characterize the center of this movement.

(i). *The revelation principle.* This movement makes it very clear that the historic, orthodox position with reference to inspiration, revelation, and Biblical criticism can no longer be maintained.[68] The *infallibility* of the Bible is denied. The Bible is not one harmonious whole but a series of conflicting theological systems and ethical maxims. Some parts of the Bible are definitely sub-Christian and perhaps it would not be too strong to say even anti-Christian.[69] The *inerrancy* of the Bible is denied. In matters of science, anthropology, history, and geology, the Bible is flatly contradicted by modern science. The Hebrews had the typical Semitic cosmology and outlook on nature. The traditional notion of *revelation* is denied. Revelation as a communication of that truth not

---

[67] The literature of neo-orthodoxy has become voluminous. For discussions of hermeneutics which come right to the point see Edwin Lewis, *The Biblical Faith and Christian Freedom* (especially chapter II); B. W. Anderson, *Rediscovering the Bible* (especially chapter I); Brunner, *Dogmatic*, I & II; and Niebuhr, *Nature and Destiny of Man.* Barth discusses hermeneutics in *Die Kirchliche Dogmatik*, I, 2, pages 513 ff., 546 ff., 810 ff., 515 ff., 546 ff., and 812 ff.

[68] This entire story from the neo-orthodox viewpoint is told directly and energetically by Lewis, *op. cit.*, chapter III, "The Emancipation of the Word of God."

[69] Cf. Lewis, *op. cit.*, p. 121.

ascertainable by human powers is strongly repudiated. It is dubbed "propositional revelation" and an attack on "propositional revelation" is one of the typical themes of neo-orthodoxy. All historical and orthodox forms of *inspiration* are denied (verbal, conceptual, plenary),[70] and in more than one neo-orthodox treatise the word inspiration never even makes the index. Those who believe in verbal inspiration are guilty of a *mechanical* or *dictational* theory of inspiration and the additional charge of *bibliolatry* is made against them.

Although neo-orthodoxy has challenged some of the theses of radical criticism it has accepted in main the results of the same. Lewis puts it bluntly but he expresses the opinion of the movement when he writes: "The one certain thing about the new Biblicism is that it is not a revamped fundamentalism." [71]

However, no matter how strongly neo-orthodoxy has reacted to the orthodox view of the Bible, it has not capitulated to modernism. It finds its normative use of the Bible in terms of its doctrine of revelation. Very briefly the essence of the doctrine is this: *Only God can speak for God.* Revelation *is* when, and only when, God speaks. But God's speech is not words (orthodox view) but is *His personal presence.* "The Word of God" is God Himself present to my consciousness. The "objective" form of this speech is Jesus Christ which is God present in mercy, grace, and reconciliation. When God addresses me by Jesus Christ and I respond, then revelation

[70] Brunner's attack on verbal inspiration will be found throughout his work, *Revelation and Reason,* and also in his *Dogmatics,* I., and, *The Philosophy of Religion.* Barth rejects it in his *The Doctrine of the Word of God* (cf. pp. 126, 156, 309 f.). Niebuhr's attack on "theological literalism" will be found in *The Nature and Destiny of Man* (*in passim*) and in, *Faith and History,* pp. 33–34. Monsma accuses Barth of breaking with the literal sense of Scripture (Cf. his *Karl Barth's Idea of Revelation*). Hamer accuses Barth of being a spiritualizer (in *The Hibbert Journal,* 48:84, October, 1949). For a sharp criticism of Barth's hermeneutics cf. Behm, *Pneumatische Exegese?*

[71] Lewis, *op. cit.,* p. 46.

occurs. Revelation is thus *both* God speaking to me of grace and forgiveness in Jesus Christ *and* my response of faith to this personal address.

The Bible is thus not revelation or the word of God directly, but a *record* and a *witness* to revelation. It is not the word of God directly. It is the word of God in the indirect sense that the Bible contains the normative *witness* of revelation of the past, and the *promise* of revelation in the future. The Bible is a trustworthy yet fallible witness to revelation. Although a man may unmistakably experience revelation, he never gets a *pure* communication. The revelation is always *broken* or *diffracted* through the prism of its medium. Therefore the Bible, a record of revelation, can never be directly the revelation of God nor a pure communication of it.

The neo-orthodox interpreter then looks for the Word behind the words. The religious liberal saw no Word behind the words of Scripture, but only a record of remarkable religious experiences. The orthodox identified the human words of the Bible with the Word behind the words.[72] The neo-orthodox thinker proposes to dig through the human, fallible words of the Bible to discover *the original witness to the Word of God.*

(ii). *The Christological principle.* God's Word to man is Jesus Christ. Only that part of the Bible which is witness to the Word of God is binding. This introduces the second fundamental hermeneutical principle of neo-orthodoxy, the Christological principle. Only that which witnesses to Christ is binding, and doctrines are understood only as they are related to Jesus Christ, the Word of God.

As we read the Old Testament we encounter a variety of incidents. Whatever is not in harmony with Jesus Christ the

---

[72] "Criticism has made impossible all those conceptions of the Bible which depend upon the identity of the words of the Bible with God's own 'word.'" Lewis, *op. cit.*, p. 11. "The critical movement has issued in our time in the emancipation of the Word of God from identification with the words of men and there will be no return to this bondage." *Ibid.*, p. 44.

Word of God is not valid witness. Lewis declares that there is nothing in the Old Testament about God that is binding upon Christian men which "cannot be reconciled with what God has disclosed himself to be in the Incarnate Word, and with the requirement of human life and thought and action that is the proper issue and concomitant of this disclosure." [73]

Further, it is argued by Brunner that no doctrine is a Christian doctrine unless it receives a Christological orientation. Such doctrines as creation and sin are not to be directly approached in the Old Testament for only in Christ do we truly know what it means to be a creature (and thereby have the proper grounds for understanding creation in Genesis) and only in Christ do we know what sin is (and thereby understand Genesis 3). The rule for understanding *"all* Christian articles of faith is the Incarnate Word, Jesus Christ." [74]

(iii). *The totality principle.* Barth, Brunner, Lewis, and Niebuhr argue that one cannot prove a doctrine by the citation of a text of Scripture or a few texts of Scripture. The teaching of the Bible is determined by a consideration of the totality of its teaching. Lewis insists that crass literalism does not yield the true meaning of Scripture. The Scriptures are properly interpreted only when we apply the totality principle and Brunner argues that "we are not bound by any Biblical passages taken in isolation, and certainly not by isolated sections of the Old Testament." [75] No doubt the Bible interpreted *in particular* leads to orthodox doctrines. To take the Bible seriously (as neo-orthodoxy intends to do) without taking it with a crass literalism, is to interpret each

[73] *Ibid.,* p. 117. These sentiments can be heavily documented from neo-orthodox literature.

[74] Emil Brunner, *Dogmatics,* II, 6. Italics are his. Cf. also pp. 8, 52, 53, 90.

[75] *Ibid.,* p. 52. This is not really a totality principle, but an ignoration principle, for under the guise of taking all the Scripture says on a subject, they take only that which concurs with their presuppositions and *ignore* the rest.

doctrine from the totality of the Biblical perspective guided by the Christological principle.

(iv). *The mythological principle.* The Bible contains discussions about such topics as the creation of the universe, the creation of man, the innocency of man, the fall of man, and the second coming of Christ. The liberal either rejected these teachings forthright, or altered them so as to change their Biblical character. Neo-orthodoxy seeks to interpret these doctrines *seriously* (as liberals failed to do), but not *literally* (as the orthodox do). The *via media* is to interpret them *mythologically.* [76]

The myth is a form of theological communication. It presents a truth about man's religious existence in historical dress. *Creation* is such a myth for it is a truth about religious existence in historical form. Genesis 1 is not meant to tell us actually how God created the universe. Rather it tells us on the one hand of our creaturehood, and on the other of the limits of scientific investigation. Creation really means that eventually science comes to the end of the line in its explanation of the universe and must there surrender to truth of another dimension. The *Second Coming* of Christ is a religious truth in historical form to the intent that man can never find his happiness nor his meaning in purely historical existence. The *Fall* is the myth which informs us that man inevitably corrupts his moral nature. The *Incarnation* and the *cross* are myths telling us that the solution to man's problems of guilt and sin is not to be found in a human dimension but must come from beyond as an act of God's grace.

Neo-orthodox writers make it clear that Biblical myths are radically different from pagan and classical myths. The latter are the productions of human imagination and the elaboration of tradition. The Biblical myths are a serious and meaningful (although imperfect) method of setting forth that

[76] See Anderson, *op. cit.,* Chapter X; Niebuhr, *Faith and History,* pp. 33–34; Alan Richardson, "Adam," *A Theological Word Book of the Bible*; Kierkegaard, *The Concept of Dread.*

which is transcendental about man's religious existence and can best be represented in historical form. Because myths do not actually teach literal history but the conditions of all religious existents, mythological interpretation may sometimes be called *psychological* interpretation as suggested in Kierkegaard's subtitle to *The Concept of Dread* ("A simple psychological deliberation oriented in the direction of the dogmatic problem of original sin").

(v). *The existential principle.* The existential principle of interpretation has its roots in Pascal's method of Bible study and received its initial formulation in Kierkegaard's meditation on "How to Derive True Benediction from Beholding Oneself in the Mirror of the Word." [77] According to Kierkegaard the grammatical, lexical, and historical study of the Bible was necessary but preliminary to the true reading of the Bible. To read the Bible *as God's word* one must read it with his heart in his mouth, on tip-toe, with eager expectancy, in conversation with God. To read the Bible thoughtlessly or carelessly or academically or professionally is not to read the Bible as God's word. As one reads it as a love letter is read, then one reads it as the word of God. The Bible is not God's word to the soul until one reads it as one *ought* to read the word of God. "He who is not alone with God's Word is not reading God's Word," pens Kierkegaard.[78]

Kierkegaard gives the illustration of a boy who stuffs the seat of his pants with napkins to soften the blows of the licking he is expecting. So the scholar stuffs his academic britches with his grammars, lexicons, and commentaries and thus *the Bible as God's word* never reaches his soul.

This existential approach to the reading of Scripture has

[77] *For Self-Examination and Judge for Yourselves*, p. 39 ff.   Cf. Minear and Morimoto, *Kierkegaard and the Bible* for a brief sketch of Kierkegaard's hermeneutics.   No doubt pietistic interpretation had existential elements in it.

[78] *Ibid.*, p. 55.   Regardless of the incipient neo-orthodoxy in this essay it is one of the finest in theological literature in the field of psychological hermeneutics.

been taken up by neo-orthodoxy. The Bible contains a special history (*Heilsgeschichte*), the history of salvation. Some of it is mythological in form, and some is actual history. This history within the Bible is the record that revelation has occurred, and so constitutes a promise that as men read the Scriptures revelation may occur again. This *Heilsgeschichte* is normative for all men and the instrument of occasioning revelation. From the human standpoint revelation may be invited by reading the Bible *existentially*, i.e., as Kierkegaard suggested with eagerness, anticipation, with a spirit of obedience, with a passionate heart.

The existential situation is a profound situation of life. It is an experience involving decisions about the most fundamental issues of life. Brock defines it as follows:

Existenz is an attitude of the individual to himself, which is called forth by such concrete situations as the necessity for choice of profession or a conflict in love, a catastrophic change in social conditions, or the imminence of one's own death. It leads immediately to sublime moments in which a man gathers his whole strength to make a decision which is taken afterwards as binding upon his future life. Furthermore, Existenz never becomes completed, as does life through death. In its different manifestations it is only a beginning which is faithfully followed or faithlessly forgotten. Moreover, Existenz is not real in being known, it is real only in being effectuated, in remembrance of it, and in resolutions for the future which are taken to be absolutely binding.[79]

The Bible is not primarily history, although it contains history. It is not primarily a theological textbook although it contains theology. It is a book about existence, about life at its most comprehensive expression, about God. To understand it at this level one must read it existentially. By this existential reading the Bible may become the word of God to the reader. Speaking of this Grant says:

[79] Quoted by H. R. Mackintosh, *Types of Modern Theology*, p. 219, from Brock's *Contemporary German Philosophy*, pp. 83–84.

The deepest interpretation of Scripture is that concerned with 'existential' situations: life and death, love and hate, sin and grace, good and evil, God and the world. These are not matters of ordinary knowledge like the multiplication table or the date of the council of Nicea. There is . . . no special method for the attainment of these deeper insights; the historical method is not replaced but deepened.[80]

It is precisely at this point that the famous continental scholar, Eichrodt, levels one of his major criticisms at Fosdick. Fosdick has read *into* the Old Testament his evolutionary theory of the progress of religious ideas. Had he read the Bible with *existential* insight he would have noted more carefully the mighty redemptive and revelatory acts of God in making Himself known to the people, and the corresponding insight into the meaning of these acts which the prophets and real believers in Israel shared.[81]

Grant mentions also the German scholar Oepke,[82] who attacks the liberal's historical-critical method in that it is dead and fruitless, and suggests in its place the super-historical method—the existential method. The scholar reads his Bible with the full apparatus of his learning, yet personally he might be very nominal in his spiritual life. The scholar has an intellectual knowledge of the Bible. In contrast to this is the devout believer who has little of the scholar's critical apparatus yet who derives a rich blessing for his soul from his Bible reading. The latter reads his Bible *existentially* whereas the former reads it historically and critically.

---

[80] Grant, *op. cit.*, p. 162.

[81] W. Eichrodt, "Fosdick, A Guide to Understanding the Bible," *Journal of Biblical Literature*, 65:205 ff., June, 1946. Eichrodt calls Fosdick's book, "The obituary of a whole scholarly approach and investigation." P. 205. Further references on the existential approach are, Brunner, *Dogmatics*, I and II, and, Bernard Ramm, "The Existential Interpretation of Doctrine," *Bibliotheca Sacra*, 112:154–163, April, 1955, and July, 256–264.

[82] *Op. cit.*, p. 163.

(vi). *The paradoxical principle*.[83] It was Kierkegaard who not only developed the existential principle but also the paradoxical. This full story is too long to tell. The heart of it is this: Hegel, a German philosopher, made much of *divine immanence* and *logical rationality*. He was a pantheist and because of his belief in the pervasiveness of his logic his system has been called *pan-logism*. Kierkegaard challenged these categories with the counter-categories of *divine transcendence* and *logical paradox*.

If man is a limited and sinful creature, and if God is Wholly Other (that is, very different from man), then man cannot have unambiguous knowledge of God. The truth of God must appear to man as dialectical or paradoxical. Any given doctrine must be defined in terms of assertion and counter-assertion. Assertion and counter assertion appear to man as paradoxical. Exposition of doctrine by means of assertion and counter-assertion is what is meant by the expression *dialectical* theology.

This dialectical procedure and the resultant paradoxes is not wilful indulgence in irrationalism. It is not the contention of the neo-orthodox to assert flat contradictions. Rather, it is the inevitable nature of theological truth, and an uncritical application of the law of contradiction leads to a premature and inaccurate formulation of Christian doctrine.

Examples of these paradoxes are: man is a creature of nature, yet possessing spirit he transcends nature; man must use reason to understand God, yet God is beyond human reason; man is responsible for his sin, yet he inevitably sins; man's historical existence is at the same time destructive and constructive; man must lose his life to save it; God is One

---

[83] Cf. Roger Hazelton, "The Nature of Christian Paradox," *Theology Today*, 6:324–335. R. Niebuhr, "Coherence, Incoherence and Christian Faith," *Christian Realism and Political Problems*, pp. 175–203. H. De-Wolf, *The Religious Revolt Against Reason*. Tillich, however, makes a distinction between the paradoxical and dialectical (cf. "Reinhold Niebuhr's Doctrine of Knowledge," *Reinhold Niebuhr: His Religious, Social, and Political Thought*, p. 39).

yet Three; the cross is foolishness yet wisdom; God is absolute holiness yet unmeasured love.

The truths of man's religious existence can never be precisely or rationally defined, but are tensions between contrarities not capable of complete rational explication yet sufficiently adequate for our religious understanding. Religious reality is too rich in meaning and content to be stated in strict, non-contradictory form.

F. THE HEILSGESCHICHTLICHE SCHOOL

Amidst the orthodoxy and liberalism of the nineteenth century, von Hofmann of Erlangen endeavored to break through to a fresh Biblical-theological synthesis. He tried to combine the insights of Schleiermacher concerning religious experience as the point of departure for theological thought, the critical study of the Bible, and orthodox Lutheran theology. He attempted to ground religious authority on the tripod of: (i) the experience of regeneration; (ii) the history and fact of the church; and (iii) Scripture.[84]

His principal contribution to hermeneutics is his notion of holy history or salvation-history. For his basic insight he is indebted to Schelling (as Tillich is in our century), for Schelling saw history as the manifestation of the eternal and absolute and not as so many events to be chronicled. Revelation is a higher form of history reaching backward into the past and forward into the future. The supreme content of this superhistorical history, this metaphysics of history, is Jesus Christ.

With this clue from Schelling, von Hofmann said that a historical event had roots in the past, meaning in the present, and portent for the future. In the study of prophecy we must know: (i) the history of Israel, (ii) the immediate historical

[84] Cf. Christian Preus, "The Contemporary Relevance of von Hofmann's Hermeneutical Principles," *Interpretation*, 4:311–321, July, 1950; and, J. L. Neve and O. W. Heick, *A History of Christian Thought*, II. 132 ff.

context of the individual prophecy; and (iii) the fulfilment intended. This is what von Hofmann considered to be the *organic* view of Scripture. All Scripture was bound together in this holy history for every event looked backwards, to the present, and to the future. Preuss says that "it was the first time in the history of Biblical interpretation that an organic view of history was applied to the problems of exegesis in a systematic way." [85]

Christ is the central point of history. God is the active agent; Christ, the focal point. Yet this does not exhaust the content of history, for the present age portends another age, the millennium. Von Hofmann thus takes his place with the Lutheran millenarians of the nineteenth century.

Further, von Hofmann taught that the Holy Spirit not only inspired the Scriptures, but He guides the church. We are never to formalize, dogmatize, or canonize our interpretations of Scripture but ever be sensitive to more teaching from the Holy Spirit. Interpretation is not to be static, but dynamic moving along under the leadership of the Spirit.

Revelation was first historical. It is God's acts in history. But with these events was given a divine interpretation of them. Communication of ideas was necessary to make the event meaningful. Scripture is thus the product of historical event plus inspired interpretation.

Further, the older method of proving a doctrine by piecing together a catena of Scripture from all over the Bible is seriously challenged by Hofmann. He insists that *every* verse or passage be given its historical setting which should in turn give it its true meaning and its weight in proving any doctrine.

The outstanding American representative of this school is Otto Piper.[86] Piper admits indebtedness to von Hofmann and

[85] Preus, *op. cit.*, p. 314.

[86] Cf. Otto Piper, "Principles of New Testament Interpretation," *Theology Today*, 3:192–204, July, 1946. "The Authority of the Bible," *Theology Today*, 6:159–173. "The Theme of the Bible," *Christian*

to his Salvation history principle. He claims to be neither neo-orthodox nor liberal nor fundamentalist. One of the major theses of von Hofmann was that inspiration and criticism were not disjunctively related, and this major thesis Piper also accepted. Accordingly he is not appreciated by the liberals who deny any real inspiration nor by the fundamentalists who believe that concessions to criticism are fatal.

The authority of the Bible, according to Piper, is not its claim to verbal inspiration (for this claim is really the claim of the post-Reformation dogmatists) nor is it some higher type of knowledge which it seeks to communicate (for this is the error of gnosticism), but rather "that the Bible confronts us with facts that are more comprehensive and more important than anything else we know." [87] The Bible speaks to us of Jesus Christ and God's offer of forgiveness and salvation through faith. We find that out of our experience with life, this is precisely what our souls need, and upon faith we find ourselves blessed with the blessedness of the gospel. Hence Scriptures are not rationally vindicated, but they are vindicated out of life. The Bible is thus the Word of God (not the words of God as in verbal inspiration) because I *sense* that it is true. God speaks to me out of the Bible. He speaks of sin and forgiveness. The general address of the Bible becomes God's Word to me when I receive it by faith. Piper admits this is subjectivity (i.e., the Bible is the Word of God only to those who respond to it), but this need not alarm us. First, as long as we are willing to relate our experience to other knowledge it is not a solipsistic principle, and secondly, all *important* knowledge is subjective.

In the interpretation of the Bible Piper accepts in principle the critical treatment of the Bible for he pens, "All the attempts to exempt the Bible from the kind of criticism that

Century, 63:334 f., March 13, 1946. "The Bible as Holy History," Christian Century, 63:362 f., March 20, 1946. "Discovering the Bible," Christian Century, 63:266 f., Feb. 27, 1946. "How I Study my Bible," Christian Century, 63:299 f., March 6, 1946.

[87] "The Authority of the Bible," op. cit., p. 163.

we apply to other historical documents are just as futile as
were the theological protests against the discoveries of pale-
ontology." [88] But to be sure he does not follow this to drastic
measures for at times he stoutly resists the efforts of the
critics to do away with the supernatural. But he does insist
that the interpreter must engage in the preliminary and critical studies of Biblical introduction, canon, and text.

Assuming that the critical study of the Bible has been
made, the interpreter is then guided by three major hermeneutical principles (the quest for the life-movement of the
given book; the comprehension of its message; and the appropriation of its message).[89]

In the study of the life-movement of a document we perform the following: we attempt to discover the unity of the
book; we ascertain the persons to whom the book is communicated and its bearing on the interpretation of the book;
we try to follow the succession of ideas or arguments in the
book; we note the literary mold or form or structure of the
book; and we must note the basic unity of the entire New
Testament in its kerygmatic preaching and witness.

Comprehension of the document, Piper's second step, is
(i) locating each idea in the author's total view of life and
reality, and (ii) determining "the relationship which exists
between the ideas of the documents and the ideas of our own
mind." [90] This involves, among other things, the determination of the world view of the New Testament writers. The
cogency or believability of this world view lies in "the fact
that it is most comprehensive and most consistent taking all
kinds of facts and experiences into consideration and that it
reaches into depths of meaning not fathomed by any world
view." [91] If an interpreter fails to discover this world view
and insists on interpreting the New Testament from the so-

[88] "How I Study my Bible," *op. cit.*, p. 299.
[89] Set forth in "Principles of New Testament Interpretation," *op. cit.*
[90] *Ibid.*, 197.
[91] *Ibid.*, 198.

called modern scientific world view he can only *misinterpret* the New Testament.

The fallacy of allegorical interpretation is that it is reading into Scripture the views already held by exegetes, rather than the discovery of the world view and system of values held by the writers of Scripture. Equally at fault is a narrow literalism, for communication is too complex to be limited to simple, literal interpretation. The *real* literal interpretation is the meaning found "in the original text when its component words are understood in the world view and according to the scale of values of the author." [92]

The final stage is appropriation which is our reply to the challenge of the Bible. Appropriation means that we critically study the Scriptures for we should not take seriously a spurious or unauthentic document. After criticism establishes the genuineness and the authenticity of a document we may proceed to its appropriation. The rationalist and liberal are so out of harmony with the supernatural character of the Scriptures that they are not able to truly appreciate them. The post-Reformation orthodox and their modern orthodox and fundamentalist counterparts equally fail to properly appreciate the Bible. The Reformers have showed us the way through the Protestant Circle. Coming to Scriptures out of faith we believe them to be the Word of God, and by properly reading them we in turn discover them to be the Word of God. Only *by* response and *in* response to Scripture do we appreciate it and truly know it as the Word of God.

Summary: The various efforts to understand the Bible have now been surveyed. It has not been our purpose to refute each of these methods here suggested, as that in principle is involved in the next chapter. In this following chapter we define and defend what we believe to be the conservative Protestant method of Biblical interpretation for we deem it the only adequate one to unlock the meaning of Sacred Writ.

[92] *Ibid.*, 200.

We believe it was the essential method of our Lord, of His Apostles, and all others who have been successful in understanding the pages of God's Holy Word.

BIBLIOGRAPHY

F. W. Farrar, *History of Interpretation*.

———, *Interpretation of the Bible: A Short History*.

R. M. Grant, *The Bible in the Church: A Short History of Interpretation*.

K. Fullerton, *Prophecy and Authority: A Study in the History of the Doctrine of the Interpretation of Scripture*.

B. Smalley, *The Study of the Bible in the Middle Ages* (revised edition).

C. Briggs, *Biblical Study*, Chapter X, "The Interpretation of the Bible."

H. P. Smith, *Essays in Biblical Interpretation*.

The Interpreter's Bible, I, p. 106 ff., "History of the Interpretation of the Bible."

C. W. Dugmore (editor), *The Interpretation of the Bible*.

M. S. Terry, *Biblical Hermeneutics*, Introduction, Chapter III, "Historical Sketch."

G. H. Gilbert, *The Interpretation of the Bible: A Short History*.

Wolfgang Schweitzer, "Annotated Bibliography on Biblical Interpretation," *Interpretation*, 4:342–357, July, 1950.

Fr. Torm, *Hermeneutik des Neuen Testaments*, Section 10, "Kurze Übersicht über die Geschichte der Exegese."

(W. Schweitzer's *Schrift und Dogma*, a survey of contemporary hermeneutics, came into our hands too late to include it in this chapter.)

Chapter III

THE PROTESTANT SYSTEM OF HERMENEUTICS

A. Inspiration: The Foundation

The divine inspiration of the Bible is the foundation of historic Protestant hermeneutics and exegesis. With the Jews Protestants accept the inspiration of the Old Testament, and with the Roman Catholic and Eastern Oriental Churches they accept the inspiration of the New Testament. Protestants differ from Orthodox groups in rejecting the Apocrypha.

Historic Protestant interpretation shares much in common with the classicists in that it has documents coming from antiquity in ancient languages, and in terms of the cultures of those times. Both the Biblical interpreter and the classicist have the problem of determining the text, of translating, and of stating ancient concepts in their modern counterparts. For example, the classicist must explain that Aristotle's word for matter (*hyle*) is not the equivalent of our word *matter*. Likewise the Biblical interpreter must take a word like soul (*psyche*) and relate it by comparison and contrast with our present usage of the word in English.

The classicist has no documents he considers inspired although he may greatly value and admire them. One life-time scholar of the classics said in the hearing of the author that his idea of heaven was a group of Greek students sitting around a seminar table reading through the Greek literature again and again. The Protestant, however, is professedly dealing with inspired documents. At the point of inspiration a new dimension for interpretation is added. This new dimension has the following features:

(i). It has a *moral* or *spiritual* aspect. There is no moral or spiritual qualification necessary to understand the classics unless a man defends the brief that only a moral man can understand great art. The spiritual requisite is, however, central in Protestantism. The Bible: being a spiritual book demands of its interpreter a minimum of spiritual qualifications which are not necessary for the classicist.

(ii). It has a *supernatural* aspect so that what is suspect in classical studies is sober history in the Biblical records. The myths and marvels of Greek mythology are taken by the classicists as inventions of the human imagination. The Protestant accepts the existence of an Almighty God who in the progress of redemption performed mighty miracles. Therefore, in interpreting his text the Protestant takes soberly the miraculous whereas the classicist rejects it in his documents —and rightly so.

(iii). It has a *revelational* aspect adding new content to old words. Granted that the bulk of New Testament vocabulary is derived from classical and *Koinē* Greek, and that many of the meanings remain unchanged in the New Testament, there is yet no question that added depth is given to words in the New Testament. We are not here defending the notion— exploded by Deissmann—that there is a special or ecclesiastical Greek. But the New Testament does add new depth, new connotations, to such words as *faith, love, mercy, redemption, salvation, heaven,* and *judgment.*

The evangelical Protestant interpreter in accepting the plenary inspiration of Scripture severs company with all forms of rationalism, e.g., neo-orthodoxy, religious liberalism, or Reformed Judaism. Many of the critical judgments of the nineteenth century are today either discarded or modified. The imposition of an evolutionary theory of religion on the Scriptures has undergone some modification and even rejection by some scholars. The archeological researches have shown that much more is sober history in the Old Testament than was previously believed. Archeology has also shown the radical contrasts of Israelitish religion with surrounding religions. The conservative trend in Old Testament studies is one of the unexpected phenomenon of the mid-twentieth century.[1]

The position of the evangelical is that only a *full-fledged, intelligent Biblicism is adequate to the present day situation in science, philosophy, psychology,* and *religion.*

Because historic Protestantism accepts the plenary inspiration of Scripture certain over-all attitudes characterize it. (i) It approaches the Bible from the spiritual dimension of faith, trust, prayer, and piety. (ii) It engages in Biblical criticism to save it from being deceived or deluded or naïve. It is not foundationally anti-critical. Unfortunately some representatives of the conservative viewpoint have unenlightened opinions as to the nature and purpose of criticism, but anti-criticism is not part of the necessary structure of evangelicalism. Evangelicalism, however, is patient and watchful when confronted with critical problems, trusting that further research and investigation will weigh the evidence in its favor. The rewards of such an approach have been many, particularly from archeological research. (iii) It exercises the utmost care and scruples to discover the true text of both Testaments, to discover the true rules of interpretation, and to apply them with the greatest of pains and care that the word of man may not be intruded into the Word of God. It therefore does not indulge in the wholesale reconstruction of texts, histories, and documents which characterizes liberalism.

[1] Liberals may well note that there is a considerable number of erudite scholars of the Jewish and Catholic faiths that have not capitulated to rationalism in criticism. Cf. Felix A. Levy, "Contemporary Trends in Jewish Bible Study," *The Study of the Bible Today and Tomorrow* (Willoughby, editor), pp. 98–115; and, James Harrel Cobb, "Current Trends in Catholic Biblical Research," *ibid.*, pp. 116–128. Other essays showing how liberalism has failed to really understand the Bible are: G. E. Wright, "The Christian Interpreter as Biblical Critic," *Interpretation*, 1:131–152, April, 1947; and, H. H. Rowley, "The Relevance of Biblical Interpretation," *Interpretation*, 1:3–20, January, 1947.

B. Edification: The Goal

Not only is Protestant interpretation grounded in the plenary inspiration of the Scriptures, but it takes also as the counterpart of that truth the great purpose of the Bible, namely, to produce a spiritual effect in the life of the man that reads it. Augustine was not wrong when he said the guide of interpretation was *LOVE*—love to God and love to man. All the historical, doctrinal, and practical truth of the Bible is for one purpose: *to promote the spiritual prosperity of man. The Bible is not an end; it is a means.* Its purpose is first of all to make us wise unto salvation, and secondly to benefit us in our Christian life through doctrine, reproof, correction, and instruction in righteousness (2 Tim. 3:15–17). The end result is that we might be *men of God* completely equipped in good works. The prostitution of the Bible from *means* to *end* is an ever present danger for little groups who study the Bible for no other reason than to study the Bible. Such groups frequently fall prey to such spiritual maladies as Pharisaism, spiritual pride, and popishness in interpretation.

This is to say the goal of all interpretation is *spiritual results* in the listeners. Hobart correctly says that "no man does good interpretation who does not look for results in men as the final aim of his interpretation." [2] Nor can we gainsay Rowley when he wrote:

There is yet another principle of interpretation which remains to be mentioned, without which no interpretation can be adequately relevant. . . . This means that the theological interpretation of the Bible which is often called for, and which indeed is to be desired, is not sufficient. For the Bible is more than a theological book. It is a religious book; and religion is more than theology. Its study should do more than develop right views about God, man, and duty; it should nurture right relations to God. [3]

[2] Hobart, *A Key to the New Testament*, p. 11.
[3] Rowley, *op. cit.*, p. 16.

The practical significance of this is that the crowning method of preaching is the expository method. This method puts the Holy Bible at the center of the public ministry of the preacher. It is a professed acknowledgment that the only dependable source for preaching is the Scriptures. It enables the full power and pungency of the Word of God to be released among the people of God. When resigning a church a pastor gave to his people this advice for the selection of his successor which shows directly the necessity for an expository ministry: *"Do not choose a man who always preaches on isolated texts, I care not how powerful and eloquent he may be. The effect of his eloquence will be to banish a taste for the Word of God and substitute a taste for the preacher in its place."* [4]

C. The Historic Protestant Method: Literal, Cultural, and Critical

1. *Literal*

The word *literal* is certainly ambiguous. To some scholars it means *letterism*—the exaggerated importance of the insignificant elements of grammar and spelling. To other scholars it means a metaphysical (or philosophical) belief that words signify things directly, and to express a given thought one and only one set of words may be used. It is this sort of "literalism" to which neo-orthodoxy takes so much exception. The term may also stand for a drab, unimaginative, "flat" approach to the meaning of the Bible.

Because the word "literal" has been used so odiously in polemics—both liberals and neo-orthodox accusing the conservative of being a wooden literalist—other terms have been suggested such as "normal," or "literary," or "proper." However we shall use the word *literal* and explain precisely what we mean by it, and so expect to be understood throughout the rest of the book.

[4] *The Moody Monthly* (editorial), 45:261, January, 1945. Italics are ours. Cf. also Chafer's discussion of "Animation" (the power of the Bible to influence life and conscience), *Systematic Theology*, I:120–123.

In the science of semantics the process of associating words (oral or written) with objects is called *designation*. How our first parents commenced speaking is not known save that speech was a divine gift as the necessary correlate of the rationality of the *imago Dei*. However, the process of designation is observable in the development of speech in children, and in the adoption of new words into a language. For communication designation must be a mutual or social process. We may create our own individual designations but we cannot communicate with others if we do. *The customary, socially-acknowledged designation of a word is the literal meaning of that word*.

To be sure this is a complex process for we not only designate objects (cows, barns, feet, sticks, etc.), but actions (running, walking, eating), attitudes (fear, hate, love), adverbs (rapidly, slowly, falteringly), adjectives (gray, beautiful, small, large), and abstractions (history, justice, morality, force). One word may have two or three basic designations (e.g., bar, lug, tear), and one object (or action, etc.) may have more than one designation as is the case with synonyms (e.g., barrister, lawyer, attorney, counsel). But there is enough usage of terms in speech and writing to create *a common language mentality*, if we may so speak, and the literal meaning of terms is their native meaning in this common language mentality.

Not only does customary social usage help determine the native or literal meaning of a word, but the context of speech does also. The meaning of the word "ball" would be determined by the context of the conversation. If it were about dancing it would mean one thing, and if about sports, another.

The literal meaning of a word is the *basic, customary, social designation of that word*. But speech is a very complicated and flexible activity. It is actually the most complicated activity man engages in, and the toil necessary to learn another language is testimony to this. On top of the basic, native, primitive meanings of words are heaped many shades, nuances, and figures of speech, i.e., the entire retinue of rhetorical use of language. These secondary, tertiary, and even quaternary meanings depend upon and are derived from the literal meanings in the sense literal is here defined.

Therefore, in so-called *spiritual or mystical or pneumatic* interpretation, the literal is primary and basic, and the spiritual, pneumatic, or mystical derives from the literal.

To interpret literally (in this sense) is nothing more or less than interpreting words and sentences in their *normal, usual, customary, proper designation.* Let us set before us two definitions of literal interpretation which bear out what we have here been advocating. Horne's definition is:

"Further, in common life, no prudent and *conscientious* person, who either commits his sentiments to writing or utters anything, intends that a diversity of meanings should be attached to what he writes or says; and, consequently, neither his readers, nor those who hear him, affix to it any other than the true and obvious sense. . . . *The Literal Sense* of any place of Scripture is that which the words signify, or require, in their natural and proper acceptation, without any trope, metaphor, or figure, and abstracted from any mystic meaning.[5]

Craven's excellent comments are as follows:

Normal is used instead of literal . . . as more expressive of the correct idea. No terms could have been chosen so unfit to designate the two great schools of prophetic exegetes than *literal* and *spiritual.* These terms are not antithetical, nor are they in any proper sense significant of the peculiarities of the respective systems they are employed to characterize. They are positively misleading and confusing. *Literal* is not opposed to *spiritual* but to *figurative; spiritual* is an antithesis on the one hand to *material,* and on the other to *carnal* (in a bad sense). The *Literalist* . . . is not one who denies that *figurative* language, that *symbols* are used in prophecy, nor does he deny that great *spiritual* truths are set forth therein; his position

[5] T. Horne, *An Introduction to the Critical Study and Knowledge of the Holy Scriptures* (eighth edition), I, 322. Italics are his.

is simply, that the prophecies are to be *normally* interpreted (i.e., according to the received laws of language) as any other utterances are interpreted—that which is manifestly literal being regarded as literal, and that which is manifestly figurative being so regarded. The position of the *Spiritualist* . . . is not that which is properly indicated by the term. He is one who holds that certain portions are to be *normally* interpreted, other portions are to be regarded as having a *mystical* . . . sense. Thus for instance, Spiritualists . . . do not deny that when the Messiah is spoken of as 'a man of sorrow and acquainted with grief,' the prophecy is to be normally *interpreted;* they affirm, however, that when He is spoken of as coming 'in the clouds of heaven' the language is to be 'spiritually' (mystically) interpreted . . . The terms properly expressive of the schools are *normal* and *mystical.*[6]

The reader will note in these citations the emphasis on "natural," "proper," "obvious," and "normal." These are but other ways of expressing the social designation of the primitive meanings of words. This is not *letterism*—the exaggerated importance attached to incidentals, nor is it so-called wooden literalism. Historic Protestantism as illustrated by the studies of Luther and Calvin is in this sense literal. There is no doubt that Catholic hermeneutical theory has been moved towards a very healthy respect for the literal meaning of Scripture. The view among so many of the Fathers that the literal and historical senses were for the weak and babes is now no longer defended. At the time of the Reformation, however, the Catholic Church had not picked up its contemporary respect for the literal sense of Scripture although Aquinas and the Victorines did anticipate it. It must also be kept in mind that modern studies of hermeneutics among Catholics still emphasize (i) authoritative interpretation—e.g., papal definitions, the consent of the Fathers, unwritten tradition, and (ii) the validity of the medieval pattern of the four senses (literal and historical, anagogical, allegorical, and tropological). It is still distinc-

---

[6] Craven, *Revelation* (in the Lange *Commentary*), p. 98. Italics are his.

tively Protestant hermeneutics to be especially pledged to the literal interpretation of Scripture.

The major hermeneutical issue is not between a narrow, unimaginative, wooden literalism or a fanciful, imaginative allegorical system. The basic issue is whether the Biblical documents are to be approached in the normal, customary, usual way in which men talk, write, and think; or, whether, that level is only *preliminary* to a second deeper level.[6a] Allegorists do not deny necessarily either the literal meaning of sentences nor the historical reality of events, but they insist that the literal and the historical represent a lower, immature or elementary understanding of the Bible. In defence of the literal approach to Scriptures it may be argued:

(i). *The literal method of interpretation is the usual practice in interpretation of literature.* When we read a book, essay, or poem we presume the sense is literal. This is the only conceivable method of communication. The non-literal is always a secondary meaning imposed upon a previous stratum of language. The previous stratum of language is the literal. This previous stratum is *necessarily* the point of commencement for the interpretation of all literature. If some strange oriental mystical writing be set before us (in translation) we endeavor to make sense out of it by a literal interpretation as our first and necessarily first procedure. In history, for example, when we read of Paul Revere's famous ride we take it as such, and not as conscience riding to the rescue of virtue at the approach of temptation.

Therefore, without prejudging the nature of the Bible one way or the other as to any deeper or profounder sense (typological, allegorical, mythological, existential), we insist that *we ought to commence interpreting it literally.*

(ii). *All secondary meanings of documents depend upon the*

[6a] That Calvin himself rejected a slavish literalism is evident from the following: "To show themselves men of letters, these good doctors prohibit even the least departure from the literal signification . . . If this canon of interpretation be admitted, all the light of faith will be overwhelmed in crudest barbarism." *Institutes,* IV, 17, 23

previous meaning of these documents, namely, upon their literal interpretation. Parables, types, allegories, symbols, and figures of speech (metaphors, similes, hyperboles) presume that the words have a more primitive reference than the sense in which they are used. The parable of the sower depends for its understanding upon the actual practice of farming; the lion as a symbol of strength is derived from real lions who are strong; incense as a symbol of prayer grew out of the observation of a sweet aroma ascending heavenward; and the allegory of Abraham, Sarah, and Hagar depends for its meaning upon these historical personages and their real experiences. If all secondary meanings are additions to a more primitive meaning, then interpretation ought to start at the more primitive meaning, namely, with literal interpretation.

(iii). *A large part of the Bible makes adequate and significant sense when literally interpreted.* The claim of many of the early allegorists that the Scriptures were only *really* understood allegorically is not difficult of refutation. All the great doctrines of the Bible rest clearly on literal exegesis. Practically all of the historical books make sense interpreted literally. Certainly save for the book of Revelation practically all the New Testament yields a *significant* sense when literally interpreted.

Allegorists usually do not realize how much actual literal interpretation they do. The interpretations they impose on Scripture have as their content material which the allegorists have derived from their literal understanding of the New Testament. The inherent insecurity of the allegorical method was made evident in early church history when the gnostics sought to allegorize the New Testament as freely as the orthodox Christians allegorized the Old Testament. This meant a denial of the incarnation and the orthodox fought it, but in principle the gnostics had as much right to allegorize the New Testament as the orthodox did the Old. Perhaps even more so; for would not the fuller revelation of God be filled with even greater mysteries and hidden meanings?

Of course the literal interpretation of Scripture does not blindly rule out figures of speech, symbols, allegories, and types. The *literal* meaning of a figure of speech is its *proper* meaning. "Ephraim is a cake not turned" (Hosea 7:8) means that Ephraim is "half-baked." The literal meaning is not that Ephraim is an actual cake which is semi-cooked. The literal meaning is *the intention of the metaphor*. The same is true of such a saying as "I am the true vine." The literal meaning here is *the intention of the imagery employed*.

(iv). *The literal method is the necessary check upon the imagination of men.* Catholics find their sacramentalism and sacerdotalism by an allegorical interpretation of passages in the Old Testament. Religious liberals so "spiritualized" the teachings of the prophets, our Lord, and the disciples as to fashion them in their own image. The prophets were thus Rauschenbushes' before Rauschenbush, and the disciples were Fosdicks before Fosdick. The hermeneutics of Christian Science, Swedenborgianism, divine science cults, and theosophy is all some form of excessive spiritualizing or allegorizing.

If these secondary interpretations end in hopelessly contradictory theologies, how is the conflict resolved? *They must all give first account to the literal exegesis of Scripture*, and if they fail there we need not believe them when they allegorize. To rest one's theology on the secondary stratum of the possible meanings of Scripture is not interpretation but imagination. That which fills in the details of the imagination is the particular religious system of the interpreter who has derived it from non-biblical sources. In such a procedure the native meaning of the Bible is sure to be lost.

The only sure way to know God's word is to anchor interpretation in literal exegesis. Literal interpretation is to be our *control* in interpretation. Literal interpretation is not the Charybdis of *letterism* nor the Scylla of *allegorism*. It recognizes the value of attention to words and grammar, but knows that human communication is very subtle and complex and cannot be fully sounded by *letterism* in interpretation. It also realizes the human mind is rich in imagination and expression and that interpretation must be awake and adequate to poetry, figures of speech, analogies, types, allegories, and parables. It also knows that flexible literary forms are capable of abuse and so literal interpretation keeps a cautious eye on the literal and primitive meaning of all words and sentences. Hence literal interpretation is not a method followed unimaginatively or woodenly but it is really *a principle of control.*[7]

2. *Cultural*

The word "cultural" is here used in its anthropological sense referring to the total ways, methods, manners, tools, and institutions with which a given people or tribe or nation carry on their existence. It also includes the history of these peoples. If the literal meaning of terms is their *socially designated meaning* then we must of necessity know the culture in which these terms were first used. What a term or word or expression literally means can be determined only from an inspection of the culture of the people who used it. Protestant hermeneutics has insisted that a knowledge of the history and culture of the peoples of the Biblical record is necessary for an adequate understanding of Sacred Scripture.

There is something unusually important involved in this matter. The Catholic Church followed at the time of the Reformation, and still does so today, the rule that the Church is the authoritative interpreter of Scripture. Catholic exegetes do not ignore grammar, culture, and history, but in the final analysis it is the Church which interprets Scripture. Their thesis is that an inspired Book requires an infallible

[7] The Ecumenical Study Conference which brought in a report on "Guiding Principles for the Interpretation of the Bible" specifically brands allegorical interpretation as "arbitrary," (I, f), and in section II makes literal exegesis the necessary basis for all interpretation of Scripture. To be sure it advocates principles which go beyond this, but also to be sure, it *starts* with literal and grammatical exegesis. Cf., Richardson and Schweitzer, *Biblical Authority for Today,* pp. 240–246 where the report is given.

interpreter. When the Reformers broke with the Roman Catholic Church they of necessity broke with dogmatic interpretation (although they did not break with the importance of tradition in understanding the Bible, for none of the major Reformation groups repudiated the Apostles' Creed, Nicean Creed, or Athanasian Creed). In place of dogmatic interpretation they placed *the laws of the understanding of language.* If the major law of the understanding of language is the law of literal interpretation, then the second law is the law of cultural backdrop for the first implicates the second.

This principle is also polemically directed at theosophy, Christian Science, Swedenborgianism, Unity, etc., for all these groups use the language of the New Testament in radical divorcement from its original cultural associations and meanings.

(i). The interpreter must study *Biblical geography.* This is the spatial background of Scripture just as history is the temporal background. He needs to know the data about mountains, rivers, plains, crops, flora, fauna, seasons, and climate. If the interpreter is ignorant of the geography of Egypt he will have a superficial understanding of the significance of the various plagues. A knowledge of geography is indispensable for practically every book of the Old Testament, for the Gospels and Acts, and for many other elements in the epistles and Revelation. Many figures of speech in the Psalms have a geographical referent. To try to interpret the Bible without a basic geographical understanding of Bible lands is like trying to watch a drama with no scenery.

A knowledge of geography is necessary to follow the trek of the Israelites from Egypt to Canaan; to follow the conquest of Joshua of the land; to understand the hundreds of references in the poetic and prophetic books to items of geography; to comprehend many of the Biblical figures of speech; to appreciate many incidents in the life of Christ and the journeys of Paul; and to know the significance of many symbols in the book of Revelation.

(ii). The interpreter must study *Biblical history*. From clay tablets and monuments, from inscriptions and papyri fragments, and from historical documents such as the writings of Josephus and Manetho, we are able to gradually reconstruct much of ancient history. This historical knowledge is indispensable to the best exegesis. The discoveries in Mesopotamia have illuminated the early chapters of Genesis and the life of Abraham. The archeological investigations of Rome, Greece, Asia Minor, Mesopotamia, Palestine, Arabia, and Egypt have all added something to the further understanding of the Sacred Text, both of the Old and New Testaments. A study of Egyptology makes the story of Joseph come to life.[8]

A knowledge of the political intrigues and military campaigns among the Egyptians, Canaanites, Syrians, Assyrians, and Chaldeans is helpful in understanding passages in the prophetic books. The archeological work of Ramsay has done a yeoman's job in revealing how important archeological matters are to the understanding of the book of Acts and the life of Paul.

History (with geography) sets the stage for the Biblical interpreter. A knowledge of the inter-Biblical period sets the stage for the entire New Testament period. It is necessary to know something of the Herodian family to adequately interpret parts of the Gospels and Acts. Greek, Roman, and Jewish history are all necessary for the best comprehension of the book of Acts and life of Paul.

God's revelation is set in a historical context and involves historical personages and events. Rowley is therefore correct in writing:

A religion which is thus rooted and grounded in history cannot ignore history. Hence a historical understanding of the Bible is not a superfluity which can be dispensed within biblical interpretation,

[8] Cf. E. A. Wallis Budge, *The Dwellers on the Nile.*

leaving a body of ideas and principles divorced from the process out of which they were born.[9]

(iii). The interpreter must study *Biblical culture*. Culture is divided by anthropologists into *material* and *social*. Material culture refers to all the things, tools, objects, dwellings, weapons, garments, etc., that people use in their existence. The Scriptures are filled with references to material culture and the wise interpreter makes himself acquainted with the items as he comes across them by referring to Bible dictionaries or specialized treatises on Oriental culture, e.g., E. Rice, *Orientalisms in Bible Lands*.[10] For example, upper-rooms were large rooms and best adapted for group gatherings (Acts 1:13). In the time of Christ people ate by reclining on cots (John 13:23-24). Water was purified by the Jews by letting it stand in huge jugs (John 2:6). Bread was baked in thin sheets over small earthern ovens frequently fired with grass (Mt. 6:30). Grecian lamps (in use in Palestine) were very small and for the foolish virgins to expect them to burn for the three-hour vigil (or longer) was very improvident and therefore foolish (Mt. 25:1 ff.).

Social culture comprises the various customs and practices of people about such matters as puberty rites, marriage rituals, burial rituals, etc. It examines *political* structures of a community to see how it governs itself; its *legal system* and methods of penality; its *religious* practices; and its *economic* structure. The Bible is as replete with references to social culture as it is with references to material culture. Here again the wise commentator will seek to discover the content and meaning of all references to social culture.

The principal purpose of the cultural approach to Scripture (and we are here using culture with reference to this second rule of interpretation after "literal") is to aid us in under-

[9] Rowley, *op. cit.*, p. 8.
[10] Cf. also M. Miller and J. Miller, *Encyclopedia of Bible Life*, and, F. Wight, *Manners and Customs of Bible Lands*.

standing what the normal, usual, customary, and therefore *literal* meaning of the Bible is. Words, sentences, and expressions are meaningful only in terms of a culture, and all discussion of "literal interpretation" is beside the point if it does not reckon with cultural factors. The cultural approach to Scripture is absolutely necessary and essential to the literal approach to Scripture.

The cultural approach is capable of abuse. It is a basis of departure, not the *dominating factor* in interpretation. The form-criticism of the Old (Mowinckel, Gunkel) and of the New (Bultmann) Testaments are examples of an improper use of the cultural approach to the Scriptures (*sitz im leben*). The "Chicago school" with its emphasis on the psychology and sociology of religion is equally aberrant at this score. The cultural approach is (like the literal) a *controlling* principle, and is therefore a flexible tool. If an Old Testament scholar says that a given passage meant so-and-so to the Jews (on the grounds that the passage must have meaning to its contemporaries) *and limits its meaning* to that meaning, he is misapplying the cultural principle and denying the *sensus plenoir* of Old Testament prophecy. If a scholar not only explains some Old Testament passage, but explains it away by an appeal to the cultural, he is again abusing this principle.

The function of the cultural principle is not to do away with Biblical religion or theology, but to serve as a guide to the proper understanding of the Bible. It will save us from the extremes of allegorism and symbolic interpretation by rooting our interpretations in facts. It is not a method to rule out the prophetic and supernatural aspects of the text. The liberal method has been called the critico-historical method, and was a victim of reductive and genetic fallacies. Both orthodoxy and neo-orthodoxy have exposed the inability of this method to handle the Sacred Text.

3. *Critical*

The word *critical* is an abused word. To those who confuse principles of piety with principles of scholarship, the word is equated with scepticism. By critical we mean that *any interpretation of Scripture must have adequate justification.* The grounds for the interpretation *must be made explicit.* We may appeal to *history.* We may say this prophetic passage must mean so-and-so because of the political relations between Israel and Egypt. Or we may argue about some interpretation of the book of Acts on the grounds of some bearing that Roman history might have. It may be *lexical* justification. We may cite lexicons or word-studies or citations from profane authors. It may be *grammatical* and our justification will rest upon evidence supplied by standard Hebrew or Greek grammars. It may be a *theological* justification. We may appeal to the general teaching of Calvinism to interpret some particular passage, e.g., Hebrews 6. It may be *cultural* justification. We may argue that such-and-such was the practice among the Jews at the time of Christ as witnessed by rabbinical writings. For example, Ramsay argues that Paul's advice that women have long hair and wear a veil refers to the complete veiling of women as is practiced in Mohammedan countries today, and that paramours and courtesans were either unveiled or shaven of head. Our justification may be *geographical.* Much of the understanding of the strategy of Joshua and the significance of Joshua's Long Day depend upon adequate geographical information.

In many passages we may not have the measure of justification we desire. We should in all such cases admit our lack of justification and announce our interpretation as a hypothesis.

There is a definite purpose in emphasizing the critical element of interpretation. If our interpretations are critically determined (i.e., justified by the various criteria here suggested), then they are rooted in the sort of fact that scholars can investigate, weighing evidence one way or the other. Thus the critical approach stands in definite opposition to all interpretations determined *arbitrarily*, *dogmatically*, or *speculatively*. When our theology gets top-heavy and starts dictating to exegesis our interpretation is likely to be arbitrary.

The standing protest of Protestantism to Catholicism is that Catholicism may dogmatically define the meaning of a text or the meaning of a doctrine, *and the justification is the claim of the Church to be an infallible teacher*. Can the Scriptures mean one thing when interpreted by adequate criteria of justification and another when made the subject of official interpretation? Is the case so completely closed that forever and ever water in John 3:5 means baptism? Strict Protestant interpretation will never build upon that which is not capable of justification by acceptable canons.

The critical approach is opposed to highly personal interpretations. These highly personal and rather arbitrary interpretations usually are introduced by such expressions as: "Now it is my earnest conviction that . . .," or, "now I know that scholars differ but it seems clear to me that . . .," or, "I put away all books of human origin and read the pure Word and the Holy Spirit showed me [in spite of much grammatical and historical material to the contrary, unfortunately] that . . ." How do we settle differences of deep convictions? A very devout and God-fearing servant of the Lord told this writer that the Lord was sure to come before 1940. (Charles Spurgeon stated in one sermon that the church should not even speculate in what century the Lord would return). Fortunately the sheer duration of time settled this speculation, but what if one should move the date up to the turn of the second millennium after Christ? How do we settle the truth when two people of equal piety and devotion have different opinions? Does the Holy Spirit tell one person the rapture is pre-tribulation, and another that it is post-tribulation?

The very fact that spiritually minded interpreters come to

different conclusions about these matters distresses many people's minds. They have presumed that if a man is yielded to the Holy Spirit his interpretations must be correct. But certain things must be kept in mind. First, the Holy Spirit gives *nobody* infallible interpretations. Second, piety is a help to interpretation but it is not a substitute for knowledge or study or intelligence. Third, all of us are still in the human body and subject to its limitations and frailties and we make mistakes of interpretation in Scripture as well as errors of judgment in the affairs of life. It is the present temptation of at least American evangelicalism to substitute a class of devout Bible teachers for the Catholic pope. To such people the *meaning* of Scripture is that which their favorite Bible teacher teaches. But the Protestant principle must always be this: *the truest interpretations are those with the best justification.*

Finally, the critical spirit in interpretation cuts short all imaginative, fanciful and far-fetched interpretations. Many sermons have been preached on losing Jesus at the Temple. Jesus (as the interpretation goes) is our Saviour; the Temple is the place of communion; we, the people in the pew, are Jesus' parents; the trip home is our daily life; the failure to see if Jesus is in the caravan is our sin of assuming that Jesus is always with us apart from the spiritual exercises of the soul. Although soul-touching sermons are preached following such interpretation the method is absurd from the perspective of a sensible hermeneutics. Such treatment of Scripture borders on trifling.

D. EVALUATION

1. *Advantages*

The merits of the literal-cultural-critical methodology in hermeneutics are:

(i). It seeks to ground interpretations in *facts*. It seeks to rest its case in any given passage on such objective considerations as grammar, logic, etymology, history, geography, archeology or theology. It is thereby loyal to the best in scholarship in our western culture, and in closest sympathy with the rigorous methodology of the sciences.

(ii). It exercises a *control* over interpretation attempting to match the control which experimentation exercises over hypotheses in science. In science a man is free to suggest any hypothesis he may wish but having propounded it, he must make peace with the rest of science. Among other things the hypothesis must have experimental confirmation if it wishes to survive. If not, the hypothesis is weeded out. Thus experimentation exercises a *control* over hypotheses. *So, justification criteria function as controls over interpretations.* All interpretations which do not measure up to these criteria must be rejected or at least held suspect.

This methodology in hermeneutics exercises a check on the constant temptation to place some extra meaning upon the Scriptures. There is not only the Catholic allegorist seeking favorite doctrines in the Old Testament, but there are Bible students who give themselves to an excessive typology, and others to fanciful spiritualizing, and still others to an exaggerated symbolism. Besides these are the numerologists, the Swedenborgians, the Christian Scientists, the mystics, and other cultists all pressing beyond the proper meaning of Scripture. A rigid following of the *criteria of justification* will put a stop to such impositions on the Word of God.

(iii). This methodology has proved itself in practice. The enduring and valuable contributions to Biblical exegesis are the result of grammatical and historical exegesis. It was the methodology of the Syrian school of Antioch, of the Victorines, and of the Reformers. It was the general methodology of such princes among exegetes as Calvin, Bengel, Tholuck, Meyer, Lightfoot, Wescott, and Broadus. It is the methodology which pervades the great exegetical literature of the nineteenth century producing both great Bible commentaries (e.g., the Lange *Commentary*) and exegetical treatises of individual books (e.g., Lightfoot's works on some of Paul's epistles).

This method has enormously enlarged our knowledge of the Bible, and has been a great artesian well of information for systematic theologians. A certain amount of excessive allegorical and typological interpretation remains today but it is under constant scrutiny and check by the grammatical and historical methodology.[11]

2. *Limitations*

This methodology, like any healthy tissue, is subject to attack by some diseases. If not carefully watched it may be afflicted by one or more of the following:

(i). It can become dry, lifeless, and pedantic. It can degenerate into a mere collection of scholarly opinions, and bookish learning. Some interpreters can give twenty opinions of others but not one of their own. People prefer one positive interpretation of a poor variety to the drone of twenty interpretations with discomfiture of the mind as the only reward of patience. Kierkegaard's essay on "Beholding One's Self in the Mirror of the Word" (in *For Self Examination*) exposes this sort of exegetical disease. Just as the little boy pads his britches with a napkin in an effort to take the sting out of a spanking, so the bookish scholar pads his soul with his dictionaries, commentaries, and lexicons so that God's Word never gets through. Such a scholar is so myopic he thinks that *translating* a love-letter is the same as *reading* a love-letter. This sort of scholarly pedantry and calloused bookishness Kierkegaard mercilessly scotches.

(ii). It is likely to stop with exegesis and not press on to the *feeding ministry of the Word of God*. It should result in a truly Biblical teaching and preaching ministry in which relevant application is made to listeners or readers. In its effort to be

[11] Cf. Feinberg's defense of the literal methodology in *Premillennialism or Amillennialism?* p. 49 ff.

accurate and precise it is in danger of missing spiritual relevancy and devotional application.

(iii). It has frequently been distressingly non-committal in matters of prophetic interpretation. It has been our frequent experience to run through the commentaries on some prophetic passage expecting some help as to the locus of fulfilment of the passage only to have commentator after commentator restrict his remarks to grammatical matters. As to the *when* and the *what* they are mute. The deeper problems of prophetic interpretation must await our discussion in that chapter.

Chapter IV

THE PERSPECTIVE PRINCIPLES
OF INTERPRETATION

By *perspective principles* we mean those principles of interpretation which act as a general guide for all interpretation. Such principles have a superintending function. They have a wide generality of application and they serve as guides for every passage of Scripture under interpretation. Hence they form the set of mind for the interpreter as he approaches the several passages of Scripture. They constitute an over-all exegetical orientation. They are general and thereby flexible principles of interpretation. They help the exegete make decisions where a narrower, more restricted principle, offers no help. There is a measure of convention in the interpretation of any document and the perspective principles give guidance at this point.

(1). *The principle of the priority of the original languages.* The purpose of this principle is neither to confine the study of the Bible to the students of Hebrew, Aramaic, and Greek nor to discourage the average Christian from reading his Bible. The average Christian with the proper books and hard work can learn much of the genuine sense of the Scriptures. As long as the interpreter does not work with the original languages he has no method of judging the accuracy of his translation. There is always a veil which separates the interpreter from the original text, and although most of the time this veil is thin if not diaphanous, there are times when it is thick. But there is no method of knowing how thin or thick the veil is, if the interpreter is not a student of the original languages.

We cannot establish the great doctrines of our Faith on any basis less than that of the original languages. In the great debates about the nature of the atonement the theologian is greatly handicapped unless he knows the differences in meanings of the Greek prepositions employed and the verbs used in conjunction with the doctrine of the atonement. The situation is even more acute if the *heretic* professes to know the original language, and the defender of the Faith does not.

Whether it be in matters of great theological concern, or of routine exegesis, the original languages are necessary for accurate, factual interpretation. Some examples are as follows:

The Scripture speaks of "taking away" the fruitless branch (John 15:2). Some have said that the word means "to lift up," that is, the vine is on the ground and needs to be propped up. It is true that the simple meaning of the Greek word here employed is "to raise, to lift up." But this Greek word has many meanings. Thayer's *Lexicon* treats the word under three main headings and thirteen subheadings. The *Lexicon* notes that this word (*airō*) is the customary word for *pruning*. John 15:2 must then refer to a pruning of branches, not to the lifting up of branches.

Hebrews 7:26 reads: "For such an high priest became us." This appears on the surface to be a reference to the incarnation but one glance at the Greek verb used reveals the impossibility of that interpretation. It is the verb, "to be fitting." Hence the verse informs us that we have a high priest who suits us, who fits our needs and situation.

In Hebrews 2:16 the taking on of the seed of Abraham appears again like a reference to the incarnation. A check of the Greek text reveals first of all that the words "on him the nature of angels" is not there; and further, that the verb means "to grasp, to lay hold." The verse is not speaking of Christ's becoming a man rather than an angel, but rather that in redemption He is saving ("laying hold of") men not angels.

Hebrews 7:3 speaks of Melchisedec's having no father, nor mother, and of his being "without descent." The latter means in English, "without children." But the Greek word means, "without genealogy." Hence Melchisedec could have had children, but if their genealogical list were not kept, then Melchisedec would be without genealogy. The verse does not tell us that he had no children, but that no genealogy of Melchisedec is recorded in Scripture.

In the same verse it has been urged that the text teaches that Melchisedec was a Christophany. That cannot be maintained from the close study of the verb. The verb means "to copy, to make a resemblance, to make a facsimile," and has been used with reference to painters making copies of works. The noun derived from this verb actually means "copy, resemblance." The writer of the epistle is affirming that Melchisedec is a copy, a resemblance, a picture of the Son of God, and not literally the Son of God himself.

(2). *The principle of the accommodation of revelation.* The Bible is the truth of God accommodated to the human mind for its proper assimilation. The Bible was written in three *human* languages. The Bible is written in the terms of the *human* environment (physical and social). The truth of God made contact with the *human* mind else it would stand *meaningless.* To be a meaningful and assimilable revelation, the revelation had to come in human languages, in human thought-forms, and referring to objects of human experience. *Revelation of necessity must have an anthropomorphic character.*[1]

The accommodated character of divine revelation is especially obvious in such instances as the Tabernacle and in

---

[1] Cf. the extended discussion of this under the caption, "Does Inspiration Exclude All Accommodation?" by Cellérier, *Biblical Hermeneutics,* p. 266 ff., and in P. Fairbairn, *Hermeneutical Manual,* p. 88 ff. Both agree that there is an accommodation in the *form* of revelation, but not in *matter.*

the parabolic teaching of Christ. In both instances the human and earthly vehicle is the bearer of spiritual truth. Our understanding of the spiritual world is *analogical*. The fact of God's almightiness is spoken of in terms of a right arm because among men the right arm or hand is the symbol of strength or power. Preëminence is spoken of as sitting at God's right hand because in human social affairs, that was the place of honor in relation to the host. Judgment is spoken of in terms of fire because pain from burning is the most intense known in common experience. The gnawing worm is the fitting analogy for the pain that is steady, remorseless, and inescapable. Similarly, the glories of heaven are in terms of human experience—costly structures of gold, silver, and jewels; no tears; no death; and the tree of life. The question as to whether descriptions of hell and heaven are *literal* or *symbolic* is not the point. The point is that they are *valid descriptions* of inescapable realities. The particular character of those realities will become apparent in their own time.

This anthropomorphic character is nothing against the Bible but is necessary for the communication of God's truth to man. This the interpreter will always keep in mind. The point has been excellently stated by Seisenberger:

We must not be offended by anthropomorphic expressions, which seem to us out of keeping with our conception of God. It is with a well-considered design that the Holy Scripture speaks of God as of a Being resembling man, and ascribes to Him a face, eyes, ears, mouth, hands, feet and the sense of smell and hearing. This is done out of consideration for man's power of comprehension; and the same is the case when the Bible represents God as loving or hating, as jealous, angry, glad, or filled with regret, dispositions which apply to God not *per affectum* but *per effectum*. They show us that God is not coldly indifferent to loyalty or disloyalty on the part of man, but notices them well. Moreover we must not forget that man is made in the image and likeness of God, and that therefore in the divine Being there must be something analogous to the qualities of men, though in the highest perfection.[2]

[2] Seisenberger, *Practical Handbook for the Study of the Bible*, p. 466.

The interpreter who is aware of this anthropomorphic character of the divine revelation will not be guilty of grotesque forms of literal exegesis. More than one unlettered person and cultist has taken the anthropomorphisms of the Scriptures literally and has so thought of God as possessing a body.

Before leaving this subject of accommodation of Scripture it is necessary to declare our rejection of the liberals' use of the idea of accommodation. This particular species of interpretation by accommodation stems from Semler. Accommodation to liberalism was the evisceration or enervation of the doctrinal content of the Bible by explaining doctrinal passages as accommodations to the thought-patterns of the times of the Biblical writers.[3] Thus they asserted not only accommodation of form, but of *matter* or *content*. The atonement as a sacrifice was, by way of example, the manner in which first century Hebrew Christians thought of the death of Christ, but it is by no means binding upon Christians today.

(3). *The principle of progressive revelation.* By this principle is not meant the liberal and infidel theory of an evolving religion. By this method a genuine revelation was denied, miracles discarded, and the uniqueness of the religion of Israel destroyed. It received a clear treatment in Fosdick's *The Modern Use of the Bible.*

By progressive revelation we mean that the Bible sets forth a movement of God, with the *initiative* coming from God and not man, in which God brings man up through the theological infancy of the Old Testament to the maturity of the New Testament. This does not mean that there are no advanced elements in the Old Testament, nor any simple matters in the New, but that this is *the general pattern of revelation.* That this is the teaching of the New Testament may be argued from the following:

(a). In the Sermon on the Mount our Lord is not instructing His disciples to *break* the law for he came not to break

---

[3] B. Bacon, *He Opened Unto us the Scripture*, does this sort of exegesis repeatedly throughout the volume.

the law but to fill the law full.[4] That is, he came to bring
out its wider, larger, higher significance. The law was proper
as far as it went, but it did not go far enough. It taught a
basic morality to the children of Israel, but our Lord invites
us to a higher plane in the Sermon on the Mount. No
mere abstinence from killing will do; we must come up to
the full measure of love. No mere refraining from cursing is
adequate; we must have a serious attitude toward the sanc-
tity of a promise. The law of Mount Sinai taught a necessary
but elementary morality; the Sermon on the Mount explains
and develops this morality to its wider and fuller meaning.

(b). In his epistle to the Galatians Paul divides up the
dealings of God into the period before Christ, and after
Christ. The period before the birth of Christ is the period
of childhood and immaturity. It is the period of elementary
education and preparation. In the fulness of time Christ
came and with him comes the full revelation with its maturity
of doctrine and Christian living. The Old Testament was
a period of learning the alphabet, of carnal ordinances and
elementary teaching. In Christ the fulness of revelation
comes, and God's sons are reckoned as mature heirs.

(c). Exceptionally clear in relation to this point under discussion is the teaching of Hebrews 1:1-2. We are told that
God has two great revelations, one of which was given through
prophets to Israel, and the other through a Son to the church.
Three adverbs commence the book of Hebrews (in the Greek
text) and they each describe part of the manner in which
God spoke through the prophets to Israel. First, the Old
Testament was uneven in its progress through *time*. The
revelations came sporadically. The *method* of revelation
greatly varied. We have such a diversity as the law written
with the finger of God, and Balaam rebuked by the voice of
his ass. The *period* of this revelation is the ancient times
(*palai*), that is to say, the time of man's theological infancy

[4] Cf. Broadus' excellent interpretation at this point in his commentary
on Matthew (*The American Commentary on the New Testament*) *in loco.*

and youth. In contrast to the first verse is the second which asserts that God has spoken his final word through his Son. God spoke clearly, directly, and conclusively through the highest possible organ of divine revelation, his Son, and so brought into existence his full revelation, the New Testament.

It is the additional teaching of the book of Hebrews that the Old Testament revelation was a *material* revelation, the spiritual truth being encased in earthly and cultural shells, and one of *types, shadows* and *parables.* Whereas the New Testament is a *spiritual* revelation, and contains the substance, reality and fulfilment of the Old Covenant forms.

This perspective of progressive revelation is very important to the interpreter. He will expect the full revelation in the New Testament. He will not force New Testament meanings into the Old, yet he will be able to more fully expound the Old knowing its counterparts in the New. He will adjust his sights to the times, customs, manners, and morals of the people at any given stage in the Old Testament revelation, and he will be aware of the partial and elementary nature of the Old Testament revelation. He will take Augustine's words ("Distingue tempora et concordabis Scripture"—distinguish the times and you will harmonize Scripture) as a guide so as not to create a contradiction in Scripture by forcing a New Testament standard of morality or doctrine upon an Old Testament passage. Monogamy was a distinct emphasis of the New Testament and must not be urged as a contradiction to the polygamy of the Patriarchs who apparently had no revelation at this point.

Progressive revelation in no manner qualifies the doctrine of inspiration, and it in no way implies that the Old Testament is less inspired. It states simply that the fullness of revelation is in the New Testament. This does not mean that there is no clear Old Testament teaching nor that its predictions are nullified. On the other hand, the heart of Christian theology is found in the New Testament which contains the clearer revelation of God. Christian theology and ethics must take their primary rootage in the New Testament revelation.

(4). *The principle of historical propriety.* Historical interpretation as such is discussed in this book under the division of cultural interpretation in Chapter III. Berkof's chapter on historical interpretation is exceptionally fine.[5] By historical propriety we mean that an interpreter must have some sense as to what men may or may not have believed in any given century of Biblical revelation. As Maas has properly asserted, "The true sense of the Bible cannot be found in an idea or thought historically untrue." [6]

Typical of a lack of historical propriety are efforts to prove baptismal generation from John 3:5, and the "real presence" in the mass from John 6. Certainly the latter was uttered *before* the Last Supper, and if it were a treatise on the same it hardly would have been meaningful to the multitude which heard the words. It is also doubtful if Nicodemus would have understood that the word *water* meant baptismal regeneration. That he could have imagined it meant baptism possibly could be argued from the popularity of John's baptism, but this is only a possibility. Some interpret the *water* to mean the word of God (Ephesians 5:26) but Nicodemus could hardly have read Ephesians!

At least in historical terms water would most obviously mean *cleansing.* Christ would then be making the basic assertion that regeneration is both a *cleansing* and *renewing* experience just as Titus 3:5 calls it "the washing of regeneration."

Lack of propriety in historical perspective is the source of a misinterpretation of Acts 15. The majority of the commentators interpret the speech of James as a summary of the findings of the council which asserted among other things that the Gentiles were *now* being saved. The citation from

---

[5] Berkhof, *Principles of Biblical Interpretation*, Chapter VI. Cf. also Unger, *Principles of Expository Preaching*, Chapter XIV ("The Expositor and Historical Interpretation").

[6] A. J. Maas, "Exegesis," *Catholic Encyclopedia*, V, 698.

Amos used by James is to prove, therefore, that God is *now* saving the Gentiles. Lacking historical perspective at this point some interpreters make the *now*-salvation element of James' speech incidental, and conceive the full force of the Amos quotation to be a description of the *future* salvation of the Gentiles during the millennium. It hardly seems historically proper that James would make the burden of his reply something about the *future* millennium. The question may also be raised as to the degree to which *anything* eschatological had been crystallized in the early church at the time of James' speech. The wisest course in such a situation is to take the advice of Angus and Green:

Of two meanings, that one is generally to be preferred which was most obvious to the comprehension of the hearers or original readers of the inspired passage, allowing for the modes of thought prevalent in their own day, as well as for those figurative expressions which were so familiar as to be no exception to the general rule.[7]

Another interpretation of questionable historical propriety is that one which asserts that Genesis 4:1 contains a reference to the God-man. The text is made to read: "I have gotten a man, *even Jehovah*," as if Eve comprehended the full future meaning of the words of Genesis 3:15. This interpretation presumes far more theological content in the mind of Eve than the record as it stands will allow. The *eth* in the passage more normally means, "with the help of," so the line would read, "I have gotten a man with the help of Jehovah."

(5). *The principle of ignorance.* Farrar cites the Talmudic rule, "Teach thy tongue to say, I do not know." [8] That there are passages that are puzzling and have to date yielded to the skill of no interpreter must be candidly admitted. Lindsay has put his finger on the cause when he wrote: "The obscurity of ancient documents is far more frequently occasioned by our ignorance of multitudes of things, then so familiarly

---

[7] Angus and Green, *Cyclopedic Handbook to the Bible*, p. 180.
[8] Farrar, *History of Interpretation*, p. 474.

known, that a passing allusion only was needed to present a vivid picture, than any difficulties connected with the language itself." [9]

Speech occurs within a context of conversation, and a cultural context. The meaning of a given sentence is dependent upon the context of conversation and the context of culture. When we have Biblical sentences without the full conversational context out of which they arose and where the cultural context is imperfectly known, we can certainly expect some of them to be very puzzling.

We must add to this the observation that language itself is very complex, and it takes a number of occurrences of a word to capture and reflect its diverse meanings. What we say of words also applies to all points of grammar. If we did not have sufficient extra-Biblical materials to supply us with the necessary linguistic and grammatical information we would lack the means of interpreting the Bible as clearly as we would wish. The interpreter must come to the Bible then with the realization that some matters are going to be obscure for the reasons we have just suggested.

Let one who doubts this assertion take some of the commentaries and see their speculations on such verses as Malachi 2:15 or 1 Peter 3:19 or 1 Corinthians 15:29 (with over thirty interpretations) or Hebrews 6:1–9. On the expression "tasted of the heavenly gift" (Hebrews 6:4) there are over ten contending interpretations. Still to be rescued from the obscurity of their meaning are such matters as our Lord's reference to swords (Luke 22:38), or Matthew's reference to the bodies coming out of the grave at the time of the crucifixion (27:52), or the reference of Moses to Azazel (Lev. 16:26).

When there is not sufficient interpretative material on hand the prudent interpreter will admit his ignorance and teach his tongue to say, "I do not know." The interpreter's hope

[9] Lindsay, *Lectures on the Epistle to the Hebrews*, I, 169.

is that archeology will turn up the material which will clear up these obscure references.

(6). *The principle of differentiating interpretation from application.* Another form of this principle is: "Interpretation is one; application is many." A passage of Scripture has one meaning and if it had several (as Cellérier notes)[10] hermeneutics would be indeterminate. But it seems rather clear from Scripture itself that although it has one meaning, there are moral *applications* of the Scripture. For example Paul wrote "For whatsoever things were written aforetime were written for our learning, that we through patience and comfort of the Scriptures might have hope" (Romans 15:4). He further stated that things which happened to the Israelites in the wilderness journey were for our examples (1 Cor. 10:6, 11). In 2 Tim. 3:16 we are told that the Scriptures are for our profit with reference to doctrine, reproof, correction, and education in righteousness.

A given passage in Exodus or Leviticus has one meaning, but the moral principles of the passage may be capable of many applications. We must keep in mind that applications are not interpretations and must not receive that status. We must also be aware of the temptation to misinterpret a passage so as to derive an application from it.

For example, John the Baptist said, "He must increase, and I must decrease," (John 3:30). The strict interpretation of the passage is that John must decrease in *popularity* with the people as our Lord increases in popularity. Only very cautiously may we apply this to our lives, i.e., our plans, programs, and self interests must give way in consecration to Christ. If this application is given as an interpretation, then the one true meaning of the text is lost.

John also mentions that our Lord "needs must go through Samaria" (John 4:2). This was a geographical "must." The

---

[10] Cellérier (*op. cit.*, pp. 35-50) has some sharp but excellent observations about double-sense interpretation.

only convenient way our Lord could go from Judea to Galilee was by way of Samaria. The application is that our lives should be conducted with an eye open to opportunities for personal work, and we must accept certain dispositions as from God for that very purpose.

The point of this principle may be summed up in the judicious words of Todd:

> After the meaning of a passage has been learned one is in a position to apply it to the life of the individual or of a company. The application is, however, quite a distinct thing from the interpretation . . . Much has been lost in the study of Scripture by using them almost entirely by way of application, without inquiring into the literal meaning . . . In devotional study, the important matter is to be able to apply the Scriptures intelligently to the life, so that they may truly affect conduct. Sometimes, however, lessons are drawn which are, to say the least, very farfetched, and not really warranted by the passage. The lesson may be perfectly correct, but it will generally be found that there is some Scripture from which it may be learned without forcing an application which in any way interferes with the interpretation.[11]

(7). *The checking principle.* The purpose of this principle is to check for our own blind spots and peculiarities, to save us from pitfalls of previous erring exegesis, to improve our work with the wisdom of the past, and fill in our imperfect knowledge.

Our results should be checked with *secular* studies if the passage borders on matters of science or history. Whoever comments on Genesis 1 should learn something of contemporary geological, biological, and anthropological studies, and whoever comments on the book of Acts should inform himself of the relevant studies in classics.

Our results should be checked with some great *doctrinal* document to see if we have kept the rule of faith. We may learn that in some matters we have been premature, or that

[11] Todd, *Principles of Interpretation,* p. 24.

our research has been inadequate. It might, on the other hand, reveal shortcomings in our doctrinal symbols.

Our results should be checked with the great *exegetical* labors of the past. Spurgeon, in his customary practical wisdom, wrote that "you are not such wiseacres as to think or say that you can expound Scripture without assistance from the works of divines and learned men, who have labored before you in the field of exposition . . . It seems odd, that certain men who talk so much of what the Holy Spirit reveals to themselves, should think so little of what he has revealed to others." [12]

Such regard for the exegetical literature of the past does not mean slavish conformity nor bookishness in interpretation. However, when men have spent a lifetime studying Hebrew and Greek, and for years have labored on commentaries, it is not the better part of wisdom to ignore such results. On the contrary, it takes a man of extraordinary ability to contribute something genuinely new and fresh in exegetical work. Any interpretation that is quite apart from the commentaries is not necessarily wrong, but it is at least suspect. Too frequently the by-passing of commentaries is done by one whose exegetical labors evidence that he is in the sorest need of helps from commentaries.

(9). *The principle of induction.* In our interpretation of Scripture we must *discover* the meaning of a passage, not *attribute* one to it. Luther wrote that "the best teacher is the one who does not bring his meaning into the Scripture, but brings it out of the Scripture." [13] *Exegesis* is bringing the meaning of a text to the surface; *eisegesis* is reading our ideas into the text. Induction in exegesis means that the Scripture is allowed to speak for itself. Happy is the man who can approach his Bible relatively free from predilections, preju-

[12] Cited by Briggs, *Biblical Study*, p. 360. Briggs himself warns us that the exegetical literature of the past, as helpful as it may be, may also be very confusing.

[13] Cited by Farrar, *op. cit.*, p. 475. "Das ist der beste Lehrer, der seine Meinung nicht in die sondern aus der Schrift bringt."

dices, and biases. Too frequently the Bible is approached with stock-in-trade or mere traditional interpretations. But the task of the interpreter is to determine the meaning of the Bible, not to verify his prejudices.

The parable of the Ten Virgins has suffered from such treatment. It has suffered from the Arminians who wish to prove the amissibility of Christians; from the Perfectionists who wish to prove the second blessing from it; from Calvinists who wish to demonstrate the worthlessness of empty profession; from typologists who wish to make it teach pneumatology; and from eschatologists who have derived timetables from the parable. What senseless questions have gathered about this parable! The more restrained commentators take oil to mean readiness, and Jeremias takes it to mean repentance.[14]

We should take Luther's advice and seek to extract the meaning from Scripture, not import one into it. We should take Calvin's advice and not play with Scripture as with a tennis ball. We should approach the inspired record as humble learners and not as controversialists or dogmatists.

(10). *The principle of preference for the clearest interpretation.* Frequently the interpreter is confronted with two or more equally probable interpretations as far as grammatical rules permit. One is a strain on our credulity; the other is not. One meaning is rather obvious, the other recondite. The rule is: choose the clear over the obscure, and the more rational over the credulous. Or, in the words of Horne, "Of any particular passage the most simple sense—or that which most readily suggests itself to an attentive and intelligent reader, possessing competent knowledge—is in all probability the genuine sense or meaning."[15]

Consider the moot question about the sons of God in

---

[14] Jeremias, *The Parables of Jesus*, p. 132.

[15] T. Horne, *An Introduction to the Critical Study and Knowledge of the Holy Scriptures*, I, 326, italics omitted.

Genesis 6. Are they angels or pious men? Linguistic evidence can be marshalled for both interpretations. By the application of our present convention or rule we would say take the interpretation that interprets the sons of God as pious men, the godly line of Jehovah worshippers. If we interpret *sons of God* as meaning angels then we have on our hands a host of theological and scientific problems. Where do angels get bodies? how are such bodies able to copulate? what is the status of the children produced as far as the question of "in Adam" is concerned? If we take the expression to mean pious men then the verse means that the godly line of Jehovah worshippers was corrupted by inordinate marriages. We are accordingly free from the nest of scientific and theological difficulties the other alternative creates for us.

The same Hebrew word is used for *side* and *rib*. Thus Eve was made either from Adam's rib or side. Those who interpret the word as *side* believe that Adam was bisexual, and that he was subsequently divided into opposite sexes. In the other interpretation the woman is built up from part of man to show their essential physical and spiritual kinship. Certainly the latter is the simpler interpretation and ought to be accepted rather than the grotesque version of a bisexual Adam.

According to Colossians 1:6 and Romans 10:18, the gospel (in the span of Paul's life) was preached in all the world. There are two interpretations possible: (a) we may take the word "world" literally and insist that all the world was evangelized at that juncture in history, or (b) we may take the world in its popular sense of "the then known world."

If the first interpretation is taken, then the question arises how the world was evangelized. The answer given is that the apostles were raptured around the world like Philip was in his ministry. In the second sense, the expression means simply that the major cities and territories of the Roman empire were reached with the gospel. Certainly the latter is the far easier interpretation to accept than the former. Nor can we approve of the notion that it takes more spirituality to believe an extreme interpretation.

But some insist that *verbal* inspiration demands a strict *literal* interpretation at every point. This cannot be defended because no *necessary connection* can be made between verbal inspiration and literal interpretation to the extent that every word or expression verbally inspired can only be literally interpreted. Not only can this connection not be established, but the very data of the Bible forbid such a dictum. First, we would have to take all anthropomorphisms about God literally, which is simply impossible. Secondly, we cannot interpret literally the poetic imagery and figures of speech found so plentifully in the Bible.

Verbal inspiration does not pledge the interpreter to a crude literalism.

A corollary to this principle is this one: *obscure passages must give right of way to clear passages*. The main principle asserted that in any given passage where two interpretations were proposed, the clearest and simplest should be accepted. This corollary principle asserts that when there are two passages dealing with the same topic, the clear passage should interpret the obscure and not the obscure the clear.

There is no question that much mischief has been done with Scripture in the history of interpretation, by interpreters who found more than they should in obscure passages of Scripture. Certainly Saul's encounter with the witch at Endor is an obscure passage from which no great doctrine of the spirit world should be constructed. There is no question that 1 Corinthians 15:29 is exceedingly obscure and no doctrine of proxy baptism can be deduced from it. Our guidance should always be to take the record where it is clear as a guide to doctrine, rather than where it is obscure.

All of the preceding is based upon the proposition that *everything essential to salvation and Christian living is clearly revealed in Scripture*. Essential truth is not tucked away amongst incidental remarks, nor is it contained in passages whose meanings are yet sealed mysteries.

The real doctrinal meat of the Bible is those passages where doctrine is dealt with extensively. For example, the Deity of Christ is explained at some length in John 5; the doctrine of sin in Romans 1-3; the resurrection in 1 Cor. 15; the relationship of law and grace in Galatians. In an extensive discussion of a doctrine we can get our bearings and determine our meanings.

When we use verses as pegs to hang doctrinal beliefs upon we violate this principle. Baptismal regeneration may not be taught in John 3:5 simply because the word "water" occurs. If such a doctrine is taught in Scripture the exegete must be able to turn up an extensive discussion of it, or such a compilation of individual references as to be sufficient evidence that it is taught. The Catholic exegetes are the greatest violators of this principle because according to their views all they require to "prove" one of their doctrines which they have in their traditions is but a passing reference in Scripture, e.g., their doctrine of purgatory or the sacrifice of the mass or Peter's popedom or prayers for the dead.

This is seen in practice so clearly in one passage of Newman's *Apologia pro vita sua* in which on the flimsiest of Scriptural evidence he "proves" the Catholic doctrine of nuns and monks.[16] Newman comes to the Bible with a full-fledged dogma about nuns and monks, he finds a verse which bears a resemblance to the dogmas, and thus the dogma is considered proved. But if we demand *extensive Scriptural references* no such dogmas of nuns and monks is forthcoming.

The same may be said concerning elaborate doctrines of proxy baptism argued from 1 Cor. 15:29. The exegete derives his full-orbed doctrine from his religious tradition, and finding a verse which superficially suggests it, he announces that his doctrine of proxy baptism is Scriptural. Again, the doctrine

---

[16] Everyman's Library edition, pp. 253-54.

would collapse if it had to meet the requirement of *extensive Scriptural references.*

Others who err at this point are those who approach 1 Peter 2:24 ("by whose stripes we are healed") with an elaborate doctrine of divine healing. Again the procedure is the same. A doctrine is formulated within an ecclesiastical tradition, a verse in Scripture is found which sounds like it, and the doctrine is pronounced Scriptural. But an examination of 1 Peter 2:24 reveals no *extensive* discussion on healing in the atonement.

What is essential to salvation and sanctification is treated *extensively* in Scripture either in terms of distinct passages or abundance of references. We are in constant danger of extending our theology beyond the information given in Scripture. This danger can be checked only when we limit our theology to extensive references in Sacred Scripture. We may consider a doctrine Scriptural when there is extensive treatment of it in Scripture, not when we can find only a passing reference to it.

(11). *The principle of the unity of the sense of Scripture.*[17] There are two basic reasons for urging this principle. The first is that hermeneutics is possible only if it is determinate, and it is determinate only if the meaning of the Scripture is one. The second is that when more than one sense is imposed on Scripture the meaning of the word of God is obscured. Some check must be put upon the uninhibited exegesis of many of the early Fathers which is representative of all improper spiritualizing, symbolizing and typifying. The temptation which overtook these Fathers is not as far removed as it would appear.

It is not uncommon to hear sermons which allegorize the healings in the Gospels and the book of Acts. Nor is it uncommon to encounter studies in types which are far beyond any sober exegetical defense. Certainly, too, many historical

---

[17] We are indebted to Berkhof for elements of this discussion (*Principles of Biblical Interpretation,* p. 57 ff.).

Old Testament passages are indefensibly allegorized by one who is seeking something to edify or inspire.

Rahab's cord is taken as a type of redemption because it was red in color—an interpretation springing from the allegorical interpretation of the Fathers! These early Fathers saw baptism in every Old Testament reference to water, and the crucifixion in all references to wood. Studies in the Tabernacle may at times be more appropriately called "studies in religious imagination." There can only be confusion of the meaning of the Word of God, and even obscuration, when under various pretexts the unity of the sense is abandoned.

The unity of the sense of Scripture does not intend to deny that there is figurative language in the Bible. The *literal* meaning in such cases is the *proper* meaning as determined by the specific form or type of the figure of speech. Nor does this principle deny typology nor multiple fulfilment in predictive prophecy. There is a *connection* between type and anti-type, prediction and fulfilment, so that the anti-type and the fulfilment are expansions of the original meaning of the text, not new additional meanings. When connections cannot be made between immediate meaning and the expanded meaning, then we are on insecure exegetical ground.[18]

(12). *The principle of the analogy of faith.*[19] The origin of this notion is in the Reformation during which period it was used hundreds of times. It has also appeared as "scripture

---

[18] This general theme must again be discussed with reference to typology and prophecy. Berkhof admits that there is a deeper sense to Scripture and uses the word "hyponoia"—the word used by allegorists to indicate the secret meaning of text—for he realizes this is essential to preserve the unity of Scripture. Old Testament passages must have a deeper meaning by which they anticipate the New Testament church.

[19] The expression, "the analogy of faith" is derived from Romans 12:6. Most scholars believe that theologians and expositors who make this mean, "the system of theology contained in Scripture," misinterpret the passage. It really refers to the amount of faith the believer possesses. Some still insist it means the system of doctrine taught in Scripture. Cf. J. H. Blunt, "Analogy of Faith," *Dictionary of Doctrinal and Historical Theology*, pp. 18–19.

interprets scripture," or, "scripture is its own interpreter" (*scriptura sacra sui ipsius interpres*). It was aimed at refuting the special place the Roman Catholic Church had assumed in the interpretation of Scripture. The Catholic Church had insisted that it had the power to interpret Scripture, and it could by this power make the obscure Scripture clear. The Reformers countered by stating that the guidance in understanding the obscure Scripture is to come *from other Scripture* where the given doctrine is treated with clarity. It was, as Torm notes,[20] a move not only to rebut the Catholic position at this point, but to give the Bible to the laity. The principle has been subsequently expanded to mean that the Bible is to be interpreted as one whole, one harmonious system of doctrine.

Horne defines the analogy of faith (as a principle of interpretation) to be "the constant and perpetual harmony of Scripture in the fundamental points of faith and practice deduced from those passages in which they were discussed by the inspired penmen either directly or expressly, and in clear, plain, and intelligible language." [21]

As indicated the principle moved on from the assertion that the clear passages of Scripture were to hold priority over the obscure passages to the assertion that there is one Faith in the Scriptures, and no passage may be interpreted out of keeping with this one Faith. The problem of "this one Faith," is the problem of the unity of the Bible.[22] The unity of the Bible may be a *formal theological unity*. The assumption here is that there is one counsel of God underlying the Scriptures and with diligent exegesis and theological interpretation it can be recovered. The result would be a systematic theology. The unity of the Bible may be in its *perspective*.

---

[20] Fr. Torm, *Hermeneutik des Neuen Testaments*, p. 230. The term, "analogy of Scripture," is used as equivalent to the "analogy of faith."

[21] Horne, *op. cit.*, I, 342. Italics omitted.

[22] For a recent thorough study of this problem with excellent bibliographical materials see Rowley, *The Unity of the Bible*.

Lutheran theologians find it in a Christological unity.[23] Torm finds it in the identity of the God of revelation ("Und das ist er, insofern die Bible von Anfang bis Ende ein Bericht über die Offenbarung des einem und selben Gottes ist").[24] It is the same self-revealing God in all parts of the Bible. Others find the "one Faith" in the *dogmatic teachings of the Church* e.g., Anglicans and Catholics.

Most theologians would settle for a measure of formal theological unity centering around the Person of Christ as the "one Faith" of the Scriptures.[25] Students of hermeneutics have further indicated that this principle of analogy of faith must be carefully understood. (i) It must not efface the difference between the Old and New Testaments. There is "one Faith" but it has been progressively revealed which grants a priority of weight to the later revelation. (ii) It must allow for the rich individuality of the personalities of the writers and the literary forms they employed. Paul must not be made to speak like Luke, nor can we speak in the same breath of the prose of James and the poetry of Isaiah. (iii) It must allow for help from the contemporary literature of the Scriptures for its interpretation.[26]

In actual practice the analogy of faith expresses itself in several corollary maxims: e.g., the obscure passage must always give way to the clear one; no doctrine may be founded on one verse or a few miscellaneous verses; points of doctrine not settled by specific reference may be settled by "the general tenor of Scripture"; doctrines are more secure as they are taught in much Scripture or which are taught in several

[23] "Hermeneutics," *The Lutheran Cyclopedia*, p. 221. Cf. Torm's remarks: "Das alles führt Luther dazu, das Schriftganze mit 'Christus' zu identifizieren. Die Einheit der Schrift sei in Christus gegeben; dagegen sei keine 'schriftstellerische Einheit' vorhanden." *Op. cit.*, p. 230.

[24] Torm, *op. cit.*, p. 232.

[25] Exemplified by Kuyper, *Principles of Sacred Theology*, pp. 297, 429, 477, and 527.

[26] Cf. Torm, *op. cit.*, p. 229 ff.

different parts of the Scripture; if two doctrines are clearly taught which apparently contradict, accept both of them (e.g., predestination and free will, and, depravity and re-,sponsibility); [27] and passages marked by brevity of treatment should be expounded in light of passages of greater length which deal with a common matter.

The analogy of faith principle is a good principle if it does not get out of hand.[28] It is out of hand when dogma dictates to Scripture, and not Scripture to dogma. Properly used the analogy of faith is of great service. It binds all our interpretation and theological thinking into one well-knit system.

By following the analogy of faith we part with the critics who constantly oppose one writer of the Bible to another. Typical of this is opposing Jesus to Paul. Further, liberals claim there is no *one* theology of the Bible—only theologies.[29] They speak of Johannine, Petrine, and Pauline theologies. That there are peculiar emphases in these writings would be foolish to deny. To claim that these emphases fracture the unity of Scripture must be challenged. The principle of the analogy of faith forbids such a fragmentation of the Bible.

The analogy of faith thus prevents any glaring theological contradictions from appearing in our interpretations. It would forbid interpreting Romans 8 to mean the security of the believer, and then interpreting Hebrews 6 as teaching the amissibility of salvation. The Bible cannot teach many millennial doctrines at one time. The principle of analogy of the faith or the harmonious interpretation of the Bible is rooted in the conviction that if the Scriptures are inspired of God they contain only one true system of theology, even though that system might not be easy to reconstruct.

[27] Cf. Berkhof, *Principles of Biblical Interpretation*, pp. 163–166.

[28] Behm speaks of it as follows: "In dem reformatorischen Grundsatz *scriptura sacra sui ipsius interpres* ist auch das A und O aller hermeneutik enhalten, dass exegetisches Verständnis nur auf dem Weg lebensvoller historischer Erfassung der Zusammenhänge zu gewinnen ist." *Pneumatische Exegese?* p. 19.

[29] Cf. Parsons, *The Religion of the New Testament*, pp. 1–4.

CHAPTER V

THE SPECIFIC PRINCIPLES OF PROTESTANT
INTERPRETATION

HAVING enunciated the basic theory of Protestant hermeneutics, and given its panoramic principles, we must now
clearly show how the theory expresses itself in exegesis. It
is assumed at this point that the inspiration, canon, and text
of the books of the Bible have been established. Suppose now
we have a definite passage of Scripture before us. What is
our procedure?

(1). *The principle of the study of words.* Words are the
units of thought, and the bricks of conceptual construction.
Any study of Scripture, therefore, must commence with a
study of words, and words may be studied different ways.

(a). Words may be studied *etymologically.* This study is
best done with a lexicon. Such investigations into words add
to our insight into the meaning of words. For example, *hell*
(as derived from *hades*) literally means *invisible*, being composed of the alpha privative (prefix of negation) and the verb
to see. It is, therefore, the place that is invisible, the abode
of departed spirits. But the word *hell* (derived from *Gehenna*)
has no etymological derivation in the Greek coming from
the Hebrew. In that it refers to a locality it is of little help
to further trace its etymology in the Hebrew. When we track
down the word *paradise* we find it comes from the Persian
so there is no help to be derived here from its etymology.
A steward is a *ruler of a household*, the word being composed
of *household* and *to rule.* A bishop is an overseer, the word
composed of *over* or *upon* and *to look.* Such a study can be
followed throughout the vocabularies of both Testaments.

Etymology helps further in understanding how words are constructed. From primitive roots both Hebrew and Greek have methods of constructing several possible other words. For example, from the Hebrew verb *to rule* may be derived *king, queen,* and *kingdom.* From the Greek root *krin* we may add a verb ending and get *krino,* "to judge"; or we may add the instrumental ending *tēs* and get *kritēs,* "the judge"; or the noun ending *ma* and get *krima,* "judgment."

To the student with the books, time, and training, many profitable hours of such study are awaiting, although we must be reminded that frequently the etymology of a word offers no help in exegesis. The etymology of the word may be obscure (*diakonos,* for example), or the meaning of the word may have shifted far from its original etymological sense.

(b). Words may be studied *comparatively.* This is best done with concordances in the original languages. This study reveals how many times a word is used, what writers in the Bible use it, and the various meanings of the word evident from its usage. A comparative study of the word *spirit* reveals that it has several meanings. In some instances it means an evil spirit; in others, the human spirit; in others, the proper inner attitude; and in still others, The Holy Spirit.

The same is true of the word *soul.* Sometimes it means person; other times it means enthusiastically like our expression "from the heart"; and again it may mean the spiritual and immortal part of our being. Such a flexibility of usage of word justifies Kuyper's observation that "a sharply drawn distinction of conceptions and a constant usage of words is foreign to the Scripture." [1]

Another feature of the comparative study of words is the study of *synonyms.* Fortunately we have in hand Girdlestone's *Synonyms of the Old Testament* and Trench, *Synonyms of the New Testament.* There is also some material on synonyms in Thayer's *Lexicon.* Such studies reveal the shades of meaning in similar words. These studies also help us discover

[1] Kuyper, *Principles of Sacred Theology,* p. 496 fn.

what words are used as equivalents. For example, in the synoptic Gospels there are scores of instances where one writer uses one word or expression, and the next one another, and yet they are used so as to leave the clear impression that they are equivalents. Matthew 20:21 speaks of Christ's being seated "in his kingdom," and Mark 10:37 of His being seated "in his glory." Hence, to be seated in His kingdom, and to be seated in His glory are equivalent. Matthew uses the expression "to enter into life" (18:9) whereas Mark uses the expression "to enter into the kingdom of God," (9:47). Evidently the two terms are considered equivalent.

(c). Words may be studied *historically*. Sometimes a word has a history, or has historical or cultural reference, and such information enriches our understanding of the word. When it is said that our Lord offered *supplications* (Hebrews 5:7), the word used is associated with the custom of bringing an olive branch to a dignitary from whom one is requesting a favor to assure him of the sincerity of the appeal. When our Lord mentioned that if we were *compelled* to go one mile, we should go two (Matt. 5:41) He was referring to a well-known Persian custom. When a Persian messenger carried the message of the empire he could compel inhabitants of a locality to carry his baggage one mile, or to perform any service the messenger commanded. Such historical studies of words not only enrich our understanding of words, but supply interesting illustrative material for preaching.

Information of this sort may be had from the better commentaries and lexicons. In addition to this are studies in archeology which specialize in linguistical and lexical matters such as Deissmann, *Light from the Ancient East* or Cobern, *The New Archeological Discoveries*.

In connection with the historical studies of words, the principle of *usus loquendi* may be mentioned. This rule calls for the interpreter to try to discover the meaning of the word to the people at the time and locality in which the document being interpreted was written. Illustrative of this is the change of mood among New Testament scholars. Previous generations of New Testament scholars moved too easily from classical studies in Greek to the meanings of the New Testament. Abrahams registered a protest to this in 1909 in his essay in the *Cambridge Biblical Essays*. Recent studies have emphasized that Palestinian Jewish literature forms the real basis for the *usus loquendi* of New Testament words, and not the Greek classics. We are thankful to Doeve who has summarized for us the history of the use of rabbinical studies in New Testament exegesis in his *Jewish Hermeneutics in the Synoptic Gospels and Acts.*

Another violation of *usus loquendi* is to read our own theological meanings into words rather than investigating the meaning of these words during Old or New Testament times.

(d). Words may be studied in terms of their equivalents in *cognate languages*. Studies in the Arabic and Aramaic languages clear up some of the obscurities in the Hebrew. Tablets from Egypt to Babylon have created a new chapter in Semitic and Old Testament philology. The Septuagint is of great importance in discovering what Greek words the translators considered as parallel to Hebrew words. The Vulgate gives us some appreciation of what was considered the Latin equivalents to Hebrew and Greek words in Jerome's time. Similar assistance can be had from the Syriac Peshitta, Old Italia, Coptic, and Armenian versions.

A thorough study of the word *to baptize* would take us through the Greek classics, then over to the Septuagint, then to the Targums, then to rabbinic literature, then to the New Testament, then to the versions. Extra information might be garnered from the papyri or Patristic writings. This would then give us the best possible basis for ascertaining the *usus loquendi* of the word at the time the New Testament was composed.

Most interpreters of Scripture have neither the linguistic training nor the library facilities to carry on such an extensive inquiry. Most of us are shut up to the best possible secondary sources such as grammars, lexicons, concordances, journals, Bible dictionaries, and commentaries. An interpreter sensitive to these finer points will build his library to make it a good interpretative tool. The student who knows the languages of the Bible will find much material in lexicons and critical commentaries. All students may glean much from such works as Vincent's *Word Studies in the New Testament;* Robertson's *Word Pictures in the New Testament; Cambridge Greek Testament,* etc.

(2). *The principle of grammatical interpretation.* Although words are the bricks of thought, a sentence is a unit of thought. Basic notions only are conveyed by single words. The complexities of thought must be expressed in sentences. Grammar states the principles which arrange the formation of words into meaningful sentences.

First of all, much of that which has been said of words applies to grammar. Secondly, one must be fully aware of the entire routine of grammar—verbs, nouns, adjectives, prepositions, adverbs, pronouns, etc. He must have clearly at his finger tips grammatical concepts as number, gender, case, mood, tense, state, participle, infinitive, etc. Some training or understanding in the science of linguistics can greatly help the interpreter. It will sharpen his understanding of grammar and translation problems very much.

Having mastered the words of the sentence, the interpreter must then give attention to grammar and note the construction of the sentence giving special attention to idioms. For this study he may use Hebrew and Greek grammars, critical commentaries, and reliable translations. Granted a modicum of intelligence and a good hermeneutical sense, the interpreter is then ready to pronounce a reasonably accurate judgment of the meaning of the sentence.

The larger portion of the exposition in exegetical and critical commentaries is concerned with grammatical exegesis.

Word studies and historical studies are valuable as they are made to contribute to grammatical exegesis. As a guiding principle capable of modification only by larger and more theological considerations we may assert that *nothing should be elicited from the text but what is yielded by the grammatical explication of the language.*

There is great value in paying attention to grammatical details. Tense generally refers to location in time, or state of completion or of existence in time. In John 1:1 we read, "In the beginning was the Word." *Was* is in the imperfect tense. Now the imperfect tense implies a previous state and its continuance. If John 1:1 were interpreted to bring out the full force of the imperfect it would be translated: "In the beginning the Word had been existing, and is still existing." The theological point is that it so nicely indicates the eternal existence of the Son. He was already existing before the dawn of creation. In John 1:14 we read, "And the Word became flesh." *Became* is an aorist, which means the completion of an event in historical time. If the imperfect were used, then the incarnation would have been a process enduring over a period of time. Nor could the present or future be used as the event is accomplished in history. Thus the aorist clearly indicates the point-event in historical time of the incarnation of God in Christ.

In Hebrews 1:1 the King James Version states "God spake" but in the Greek it is an aorist participle, and should be rendered "God having spoken." The import of this is that in the next verse with reference to the New Testament, the Scriptures says "has spoken to us," the verb being an aorist indicative. The meaning then is this: God commenced speaking in the Old Testament but He did not speak all his mind; then in the New Testament he finally finished what he had to say.

The Greek preposition also deserves careful attention. Hebrews 6:1 mentions faith *toward* God. The word *toward* is the preposition *epi*. The Jews had believed *in* God but had rested their salvation *upon* the law.[2] But in the Christian faith they must learn to put faith *upon* (resting upon) God for salvation, in the same sense that they had rested upon the law.

Some of the crucial points in the theology of the atonement are concerned with the different meanings of the prepositions: *peri* (with reference to), *hyper* (for the benefit of), and *anti* (in place of).

Atkinson's *The Theology of Prepositions* is an interesting and charming study revealing the importance of the study of the Greek preposition.

In any language there is a long list of grammatical rules which the interpreter applies from his knowledge of that particular language. Special attention must be given to those grammatical constructions known as *idioms*.[3] Both the Hebrew and the Greek have many of them which are important for the proper interpretation of the Bible. Many of the details about the time of our Lord's death, burial and resurrection must be understood in terms of idioms about time reckoning.[4]

(3). *The principle of contextual interpretation.* Todd has correctly observed that "The Bible is no mere collection of good texts or verses put together without any relation to one another, but careful study very soon shows that each verse or passage has a very real relation to that which immediately precedes as well as what follows," [5] and Barrows aptly states that "To interpret without regard to the context is to interpret at random; to interpret contrary to the context is to teach falsehood for truth." [6] Both of these writers speak to the point that an understanding of the contexts of sentences is important for their proper interpretation.

[2] Cf. *epanapaue nomō* of Romans 2:17.

[3] Cf. Angus and Green, *Cyclopedic Handbook to the Bible*, p. 181 ff. Young, *Analytic Concordance* (twentieth edition) has a list of 71 Biblical idioms (p. vii). C. F. D. Moule, *An Idiom Book of New Testament Greek*.

[4] Cf. A. T. Robertson, *A Harmony of the Gospels*, notes 11, 12, 13, and 14. Pp. 279-91.

[5] Todd, *Principles of Interpretation*, p. 20.

[6] Barrows, *Companion to the Bible*, p. 531.

Just as words are not properly understood until seen in the prospect of the sentence, so sentences are not properly understood until they are seen in the prospect of their context. For example, the English word *nature* has several major meanings and its meaning in a given sentence can only be determined by the sentence as a whole. Parallel to this is the truth that a *thought* expressed in a sentence can only be properly deduced when that *thought* is set in the light of the thoughts which precede it and which follow after it. The study of the context of a passage takes its place with the study of words and grammar as absolutely basic to the interpretation of Scripture. There are several *circles* of context which a good interpreter notes.

(i). Every writer of the Bible writes in a given *culture* and hence a vital part of the context of any passage is the cultural background of the writer of the passage. When we interpret Judges we are sure of a very different cultural background than that of John when he wrote Revelation. Revelation was written after the coming of Greece and Rome and the supremacy of the west. Judges is located in the Palestinian bronze-age culture. It is this *cultural circle of context* which supplies the clue for matters of history and social and material culture mentioned in the text.

(ii). The second *circle of context* is the Bible itself. Every volume of Scripture is within the boundary of inspired writings. Hence every volume has its own unique contribution to the great history of sin, redemption, and salvation. It is a segment of a body of literature inspired for our edification, instruction, and doctrinal learning. Because a given volume is part of Sacred Scripture it is treated with reverence and studied with prayer. Further, its place in the total plan of God in Sacred Scripture is noted, and its peculiar contribution to that plan is studied. If any of its teachings are qualified by subsequent revelation, this too must be noted.

(iii). The third *circle of context* is the specific book in which the passage occurs. It is either a book in the Old Testament or New Testament, in either case demanding a special approach due to the very Testament it is situated in. The interpreter realizes that he has one mental set if he interprets Isaiah 12 and another one if he interprets Romans 12.

Further, the interpreter notes *the general intent of a book* as a clue to the meaning of the particular passages within the book. Hebrews endeavors to prove that what a Jew gives up in Judaism he receives again in an exalted spiritual form in Christianity. Galatians is Paul's defense of his gospel, apostleship, and doctrines of grace. Matthew is a concerted effort to demonstrate the Messiahship of Jesus. The better we know the theme of a book, the motivation of the author, the goals intended, the better we can handle the individual passages and sentences.

(iv). The fourth *circle of context* is the material which immediately precedes and follows the passage under consideration. If we know the flow of thought leading to a passage, and the flow of thought away from it, we can predict with some certainty the flow of thought within the passage. Clues to the meaning of a passage are frequently found in such preceding or following materials. Paul uses the word *law* over sixty times in Romans and with different meanings. A most careful study of the context is necessary to determine the meaning of the word *law* in each of its uses.

Some examples to illustrate the necessity of observing context are as follows: (i) In Luke 15 are given the parables of the lost sheep, the lost coin, and the lost son. Luke introduces the parable by stating that the publicans and sinners drew near to hear our Lord. The Pharisees then murmured and said, "This man receiveth sinners, and eateth with them." The three parables then are our Lord's justification for his eating with sinners and are parables about sinners finding the Saviour and not of backslidden Christians. (ii) In Matthew 16:28 our Lord says that "There be some standing here, which shall not taste of death, till they see the Son of man coming in his kingdom." Then if the reader follows through into the seventeenth chapter he will find the fulfilment of this is the transfiguration of our Lord, which interpretation is verified by Peter's subsequent remarks on this event (2 Peter 1:15–18). (iii) In 2 Peter 2, Peter mentions the dog which returns to its vomit, and the sow that returns to the mire. Some have regarded this as a reference to believers, and have so urged the amissibility of salvation. However, by noting what Peter says in verse 1 of this chapter we realize he is discussing false teachers bringing in damnable heresies and not believers. (iv) In Colossians 2:18–23 Paul discusses the futility of a barren asceticism. But the true nature of spirituality is discussed in the next chapter and unless the reader follows through he does not grasp the totality of Paul's thought. The marvelous invitation at the beginning of the third chapter must be interpreted in view of the context, namely, as a description of the true spirituality in contrast to the false spirituality which he is attacking in the second chapter.

In view of the frequent abuse of the principle of considering carefully the context, we may fully understand and sympathize with Robertson's remark that "The first step in interpretation is to ignore the modern chapters and verses." [7]

(4). *The principle of interpreting according to the literary mold.* The Spirit of God in the inspiration of Scriptures chose to use a variety of types of literature. In that the type of literary form employed governs the attitude and spirit in which a document is approached, it is necessary for the interpreter to recognize literary forms *as necessary to the interpretation of Scripture.* The principle of strict literal interpretation needs sufficient qualifications to be able to adequately interpret varieties of literature.

Many parts of Scripture are *poetic.* Poetry has some rules to itself, and Hebrew poetry has a genius of its own. The structure of Hebrew poetry has received considerable atten-

[7] Cited by Miller, *General Biblical Introduction*, p. 11.

tion since the times of Bishop Lowth and the interpreter should have some familiarity with the subject.

A strict literalistic approach to the poetic language of the Scripture is certainly not adequate. "Poetic license," and the rich imagery of language must be handled with the requisite measure of insight into poetic language.

Some parts of the Scripture are *dramatic* in form. This is certainly true of Job. In truth, Job is a combination of the poetic and dramatic, and a wooden approach to Job will yield nothing but an inadequate understanding of its contents. Bowman has recently argued that the book of Revelation is very dramatic in character being divisible into acts and scenes, and that even some of the accoutrements of dramatics of that period may be noted.[8]

We may note in passing that some books of Scripture are historical in form, e.g., Acts; some are biographical, e.g., the Gospels; others are letters or epistles. We also have in the Old Testament the chokmatic or wisdom literature. Job, Ecclesiastes, and Proverbs are typical of this literature.

The point to be noted is this: *the literary form governs the meanings of sentences* and therefore the interpreter must be sensitive to the implications of the literary form for the interpretation of the passage of Scripture.

(5). *The principle of interpretation by proper use of cross references.* The same topic may occur two or more places in Scripture, and the interpreter may gather information from one reference to guide his interpretation of another. Such cross references may be verbal, or, conceptual, or, parallel.

(i). A *verbal cross reference* is a reference which contains the same word or expression occurring in the passage being interpreted. Not all verbal cross references are valid for exegetical purposes, hence they must be divided into *real* verbal cross references, and *apparent* cross references.

[8] J. W. Bowman, "The Revelation to John: Its Dramatic Structure," *Interpretation*, 9:436–453, October, 1955.

An *apparent* cross reference is a reference which contains the same word or expression used in the passage being interpreted, but the relationship is that of pure verbal coincidence and nothing is gained by comparison. One writer may use such words as *sacrifice, fat, wood,* or *save* in such a way as to be of no interpretive help for their occurrences in other passages. An uncritical listing of word-occurrences can lead an interpreter to some silly mistakes and superficial generalizations.

A *real* cross reference is a reference in which the words used in one instance aid in the understanding of the same word used in another instance. A study of the word *soul,* or *spirit,* or expressions such as *son of man* or *flesh* may lead to some very helpful conclusions.

The most valuable tools for this sort of study are the *Hebrew* and *Greek* concordances.

(ii). *Conceptual* cross references are those references which, although not containing the same words, contain the same substance. For example, Hebrews 2 and Philippians 2 discuss the incarnation. Romans 3 and Hebrews 10 both treat the atonement. 1 Cor. 15 and Revelation 20 discuss the resurrection from the dead. Conceptual cross references enable one to see a given passage in greater depth and detail. What one passage omits the other contains. On the other hand what we would be tempted to read into a passage is checked by what a conceptual cross reference contains. It is well to note, for example, that Paul apparently considers *the filling of the Spirit* and *letting the word of Christ dwell in us richly* (Eph. 5:18 and Col. 3:16) as equivalent expressions.

(iii). *Parallel* cross references are those passages in one book of the Bible which recount the same events or material in another part of the Bible. To get the full account and the necessary facts before us, it is necessary to have all parallel passages examined. The four Gospels contain much material common to each other and the faithful interpreter will work with a Greek harmony of the Gospels to be sure he has all the necessary data at hand to interpret any given passage in the Gospels.

The life of Paul may be patched together from the book of Acts, and from biographical remarks in the Epistles. These two sets of data must be compared and contrasted in writing the life of Paul.

Other passages of the Scriptures which exhibit this sort of parallelism are: Kings and Chronicles; Exodus and Deuteronomy; and various Psalms which treat of similar themes.

For such a study the student has available a number of harmonies of the Gospels in both English and Greek. For the life of Paul he may consult Goodwin, *A Harmony of the Life of St. Paul* and for Old Testament historical books he may use Crockett, *A Harmony of Samuel, Kings and Chronicles*.

(6). *The principle of the interpretation of figurative language*. The literal interpretation of Scripture readily admits the very large place which figurative language has in the Scriptures, and Feinberg is correct when he writes that "It is not true that [the literalists] require every single passage to be interpreted literally without exception." [9] Literal interpretation does not mean painful, or wooden, or unbending literal rendition of every word and phrase. The literal meaning of the figurative expression is the proper or natural meaning as understood by students of language. Whenever a figure is used its literal meaning is precisely that meaning determined by grammatical studies of figures. Hence figurative interpretation does not pertain to the spiritual or mystical sense of Scripture, but to the literal sense.[10]

[9] Feinberg, *Premillennialism or Amillennialism?* (second edition), p. 27.
[10] Cf. Unger's remark that "Figurative language is, therefore to be thought of as an ally and not an enemy of literal interpretation, and as a help to it and not a hindrance." *Principles of Expository Preaching*, p. 176.

The careful exegete notes quite a number of figurative elements in the Scriptures.[11] The Scriptures employ the *simile* (a comparison of two things in one or more aspects usually employing the words "as" or "like"); the *allegory* (where a moral or spiritual truth is told in terms of a narrative or segment of history); the *ellipsis* (the condensation of the meaning of a sentence by the omission of elements supplied by the reader usually gathered from the context); the *metaphor* (the comparison of two things without the use of the words "as" or "like"); the *paradox* (the assertion of two propositions as true which seem to be contradictory but may in fact not be); *irony* (a method of criticizing or judging by seeming to praise or congratulate); the *hyperbole* (the intentional use of exaggeration for effect); *synedoche* (a form of expression in which the whole is spoken of for the part, or the part for the whole); *zeugma* (the yoking together of two nouns in association with another word in which the other word applies to just one of the nouns), and the *euphemism* (a soft or moderate expression for a more direct and perhaps shocking one). This does not exhaust the list of figures of speech but the student may check the following in an unabridged dictionary: *brachylogy*, *litotes*, *meiosis*, *oxymoron*, *personification*, *paranomasia*, and *metonymy*.

The student of Scripture also notes the longer type of figurative expression: the allegory, the fable, the parable, the symbols, and the proverb. In all of these his interpretation is guided by a thorough grammatical, historical, and contextual study of each, and an effort is made to derive all the light possible from other Scripture references, from archeology, from history, and from customs of the times. With reference to these figurative elements in the Bible the serious student of Scripture concurs with the opinion of Barrows

[11] Both Unger (*op. cit.*, Chapter XVI), and Berkhof (*Principles of Biblical Interpretation*, p. 82 ff.) have full discussions of figurative language, and cite examples from Scripture. Horne, *An Introduction to the Critical Study and Knowledge of the Holy Scriptures*, has a full discussion of figurative language. I, 359–372.

that they are "no less *certain and truthful* than its [the Bible] plain and literal declarations. The figures of the Bible are employed not simply to please the imagination and excite the feelings, but to teach *eternal verities*." [12]

BIBLIOGRAPHY FOR CHAPTERS IV AND V

Horne, *An Introduction to the Critical Study and Knowledge of the Holy Scriptures.*

Angus and Green, *Cyclopedic Handbook to the Bible.*

Todd, *Principles of Interpretation.*

Farrar, *History of Interpretation.*

Dana, *Searching the Scripture.*

Terry, *Biblical Hermeneutics.*

Seisenberger, *Practical Handbook for the Study of the Bible.*

Chafer, *The Science of Biblical Hermeneutics.*

Fairbairn, *Hermeneutical Manual.*

Jowett, *The Interpretation of Scripture.*

Hartill, *Biblical Hermeneutics.*

Cellérier, *Biblical Hermeneutics.*

Barrows, *Companion to the Bible.*

Warren, "By What Authority: Pitfalls in Pulpit Interpretation," *Interpretation*, I, 207–18, April, 1947.

The Ecumenical Study Conference, "Guiding Principles for the Interpretation of the Bible," *Interpretation*, 3:450–59, October, 1949.

Dobschutz, "Interpretation," *Hastings Encyclopedia of Religion and Ethics*, VII, 390–95.

Young, "Biblical Idioms," *Analytic Concordance.*

Torm, *Hermeneutik des Neuen Testaments.*

Berkhof, *Principles of Biblical Interpretation.*

Unger, *Principles of Expository Preaching.*

Briggs, *Biblical Study.*

[12] Barrows, *Companion to the Bible.*, p. 557.   Italics are his.

CHAPTER VI

THE DOCTRINAL USE OF THE BIBLE

PART of the task of hermeneutics is to determine the correct use of the Bible in theology and in personal life. The doctrinal interpretation of the Bible is the work of the theologian. It is advancing beyond the grammatical and the historical sense to the fuller meaning of Scripture. Grammarians may differ over grammatical points in exegesis which may or may not influence theology, but the differences among theologians are sharper and more profound because theologians are dealing with the full implications of Biblical truth. A strictly grammatical and exegetical study may never discuss the problem of the Trinity, but the problem is inescapable to the synoptic method of the theologian.

Theological interpretation is thus characterized by: (i) an extension of the grammatical meaning to discover its fuller theological significance, and (ii) a synoptic view of all the Biblical data on a given subject.

The justification for doctrinal hermeneutics is the claim of Scripture to contain a knowledge of God which may be expressed as teaching (*didachē*). Biblical religion is not merely religious experience, nor are its teachings religious speculations. Biblical religion is grounded in the objective knowledge of God. It is in philosophical language a *revelational theism*. The constant allegations that the Bible is treated by the orthodox as a "theological Euclid" or as a storehouse of "intellectual propositions about God" are not true. Belief in an objective revelation in Scripture is not immediately reducible to dry intellectualism in religion. Certainly the Reformers and the great Reformed theologians are not so guilty. But neo-orthodox writers have stated that orthodoxy represents intellectualism in religion (i.e., faith is assent to dogma or creed), and this has become the "standard" interpretation of orthodoxy by their followers without the followers taking the trouble to see if this really represents orthodoxy. Intellectualism is a disease which can infect *any* theological system including neo-orthodoxy.

Belief in a genuine revelation of God in Scripture, then, leads the conservative Protestant to believe that the Scriptures are capable of theological interpretation. Our Lord Himself made *teaching* one of the great items of the Great Commission. He was in His own ministry a *doctrinal* teacher. We note that people were astonished at His teaching (Matthew 7:28); He claimed His doctrine was from God (John 7:16); and He invited men to discover its divine origin (John 7:17).

Paul speaks of obeying doctrine from the heart (Romans 6:17) and warns us of false doctrines (Eph. 4:14). He warns Timothy to be careful of sound doctrine, referring to doctrine at least twelve times in the books of Timothy. In 2 Timothy 3:16–17, *the first profit of the Scripture is doctrine.*

Doctrine gives the Christian faith its substance and form. If there has been no disclosure of God in Scripture then there can be no doctrine, but if there has been a disclosure then doctrine is possible. From the divine disclosure doctrine is educed, thereby giving the Christian faith its substance and content.

That the Scriptures contain a valid revelation of God in the sense that the Fathers and the Reformers so understood was repudiated by Schleiermacher, Ritschl, and religious liberalism in general. Now that liberalism's beliefs have been pounded out quite thin on the anvil of criticism, it is apparent how mistaken they were. Orthodoxy and neo-orthodoxy concur in believing that religious liberalism is theologically bankrupt.[1]

In that neo-orthodoxy so vigorously attacks propositional revelation, and accepts revelation as inward encounter, and reduces the Bible to the level of "witness" or "instrument," it is to be questioned if it has escaped what liberalism did not. How a non-propositional revelation gives rise to a *valid* propositional witness is the unsolved problem of neo-orthodoxy. It is our prediction that when neo-orthodoxy passes from the evangelistic stage to the critical stage a "propositional wing" will develop. As yet it is not clear how a contentless revelation (non-propositional) gives rise to a propositional witness (Scripture).

All forms of orthodoxy (Eastern, Roman Catholic, Protestant) have historically accepted a divine revelation which forms the grounds of a valid theology. For this reason we can give assent to Newman when he wrote:

> I have changed in many things: in this I have not. From the age of fifteen, dogma has been the fundamental principle of my religion: I know no other religion; I cannot enter into the idea of any other sort of religion; religion, as a sentiment, is to me a dream and a mockery. As well can there be filial love without the fact of a father, as devotion without the fact of a Supreme Being.[2]

Doctrinal hermeneutics commences where exegetical hermeneutics leaves off. It works with the understanding that it is to be very much guided by *general hermeneutics*. Therefore a theologian builds upon general hermeneutics. The principles we suggest to govern doctrinal studies of the Bible are:

[1] See two very shrewd and important critiques of liberalism at this point in C. W. Dugmore, editor, *The Interpretation of the Bible*. T. W. Manson, "The Failure of Liberalism to Interpret the Bible as the Word of God" (pp. 92–107); and John Lowe, "The Recovery of the Theological Interpretation of the Bible," (pp. 108–122).

[2] *Apologia pro vita sua* (Everyman's Library edition), p. 65. This is in contrast to the modernists' position as defended by Sabatier in *Outlines of a Philosophy of Religion*, and, *Religions of Authority and the Religion of the Spirit*. Also, Harnack, *What is Christianity?*

(1). *The theologian is a redeemed man standing in the circle of divine revelation.* He is a changed man; he has undergone regeneration. He is a committed man; he has found the truth in Jesus Christ and in Scripture. He comes not as a religious speculator but as a man with a concern. He seeks the fullest explication he can of the meaning of the divine revelation and his personal experience of the grace of God. His motivation to engage in theology stems from his experience of the gospel, and he seeks the meaning of that Book from which the gospel is preached.

This has cardinal significance with reference to the way the entire Bible is treated. It is fundamentally a record of divine love, divine redemption, and divine salvation personally received. We are dealing with a dimension of truth in addition to that of symbolic formalism (mathematics, logic), and more than the problems of causal connections (science). In theology we deal with the personal, the moral, the ethical, the spiritual, and the invisible. Theological science must then be carried on within this circle of faith and commitment, and not as dry, abstract or impersonal investigation.

Further, this means that the main themes of theology will be the great truths about God (His love, His grace, His divine action), about man (his creation, his sin, his future), and about Jesus Christ (His birth, His life, His death, His resurrection, His ascension, His ministry as a priest, His return).

The Bible is mistreated when it becomes a handbook of prophecy and world politics (pyramidism, British-Israelism, Russellism) for such an approach misses the heart of the Bible: namely, *the Christological-soteriological nexus.*

The Bible is mistreated by hyperdispensationalism (and dispensationalism if it is not careful) when it spends its energies in delineating the unfolding of a plan of numerous and discrete periods. The chief task of the interpreter is to assign the various passages of Scripture to their correct periods. If this is not done then wrong doctrines and practices, it is claimed, are taught and enforced at the wrong times.

Such a pigeon-hole method of interpretation is far short of the great evangelical and conservative tradition in exegesis.[3]

This is not to eliminate prophetic nor dispensational interpretation, but it does assign to them their correct proportion in the divine revelation.

(2). *The main burden of doctrinal teaching must rest on the literal interpretation of the Bible.* In our treatment of general hermeneutics we maintained that the literal meaning of the Bible was the first and controlling principle for the understanding of the Bible. This principle is to be carried over into doctrinal interpretation.

This does not deny that substantial doctrinal truth is conveyed symbolically, parabolically, typically, and poetically. But as previously indicated, the symbolic *et al.* (i) depend on the literal sense for their very existence, and (ii) are controlled by the literal. For example, the effort to spiritualize the Levitical priesthood and so make it a justification for a clergy-priesthood, is to be rejected as it lacks New Testament verification.

The great doctrines of the faith should be those which can be determined by the literal approach to the meaning of Scripture. A theology which ignores this *control* could well bring us back to the confused labyrinth of so much patristic and medieval exegesis.

(3). *The main burden of our theology should rest on the teaching of the New Testament.* Although the Old is prior in time the New is prior in method. The New Testament is the capstone of revelation, and God's word through the supreme instrument of revelation, His Son (Hebrews 1:2). Because it is the *final, full,* and *clear* revelation of God, it would be foolhardy to make the New revolve around the Old.

In the New Testament is the life of Jesus Christ, God in the flesh (John 1:1, 14). In its pages are recorded His birth,

[3] Cf. J. C. O'Hair, *The Unsearchable Riches of Christ.* For an examination of the system cf. John B. Graber, Ultradispensationalism (unpublished doctoral dissertation, Dallas Theological Seminary, 1949).

ministry, death, resurrection, and ascension. In the epistles are the full revelation of ethical, spiritual, and theological truth. Christian theology must then plant itself squarely within the New Testament. Whatever divergences there might be among the Eastern Orthodox, Roman Catholic, and Protestant theologians, they have agreed to this point: *the worth of the Old Testament to the Christian Church is that it is in seed and preparatory form a Christian document.*

This is by no means to be construed minimizing the Old Testament, nor is it a detraction from its divine inspiration. It is the recognition of the truth taught in Scripture itself that the full light of revelation shines in the New Testament. The great doctrines of faith, sin, atonement, Christ, sanctification, resurrection, heaven, hell, and the new earth with its new Jerusalem are all most clearly developed in the New Testament.

This means that a theologian must have a historical sense in his use of cross-references and proof texts. Otherwise his Scriptural evidence is collated without any sense of proportion or relative importance. This sense of proportion of importance is indispensable in Biblical theology.

(4). *Exegesis is prior to any system of theology.* The Scriptures are themselves the divine disclosure. From them is to be derived our system of theology. We can only know the truth of God by a correct exegesis of Scripture. Therefore exegesis is prior to any system of theology.

Great mischief has been done in the church when the system of theology or its framework has been derived extra-Biblically. Pantheism was the bed-rock of Schleiermacher's theology. Logical pantheism was the pole around which Hegel interpreted Christianity. Kant's notion of Christianity was guided by his theory of ethics. Ritschl's theology is predicated on Kant's philosophy. Much of neo-orthodoxy is inspired by Kierkegaard, Heidegger, Ebner, Kant, and Buber.

If the grounds of Christian theology is the revelation of

God, then theology must be grounded in revelation and not in philosophy.

The historic Protestant position is to ground theology in Biblical exegesis. A theological system is to be built up exegetically brick by brick. Hence the theology is no better than the exegesis that underlies it. The task of the *systematic* theologian is to commence with these bricks ascertained through exegesis, and build the temple of his theological system. But only when he is sure of his individual bricks is he able to make the necessary generalizations, and to carry on the synthetic and creative activity that is necessary for the construction of a theological system.

Philosophy does have a role to play in theological construction but it is not in itself either the *data* or the *principium* of theology. Its function is ancillary. It provides the theologian with what Kuyper in his *Principles of Sacred Theology* calls "the logical action." The theologian uses the principles of formal and applied logic in hammering out his system. He familiarizes himself with the problems philosophers and theologians have had in common during the history of both philosophy and theology. He learns the validity of various types of argumentation. He discovers the criticisms by philosophers of theologians, and learns to judge wherein the philosopher has been right and wrong.

The exegetical theologian and systematic theologian seek to determine the content of the divine revelation. The philosophical theologian is the watch-dog and detective.

He keeps his eye on contemporary philosophy to see what is developing there and its possible relationship to Christian theology for good or evil. He scans the writings of the scientists to see the implications and importance of contemporary science for Christian faith. He scrutinizes theological publications to see what ancient heresy might be here disguised in modern dress, or what philosophical system or assumptions are presupposed.

The church needs both the exegetical and the philosophical

theologian, and she suffers when she is in want of either. The exegetical theologian protects the church from the misinterpretations of the heretics, and the philosophical theologian protects the church from the improper intrusion into Christian theology of non-Christian principles.

(5). *The theologian must not extend his doctrines beyond the Scriptural evidence.* A scientist is at liberty to spin as many hypotheses as he wishes. In weeding out the true from the false he is guided by logic and experimentation. He has no right to claim truth till these two judges have handed in their decision in the affirmative. All scientific speculation is controlled by logic and experimentation, and speculation is not treated as fact till it passes these two monitors.

What answers to this in theology? What is the control we use to weed out false theological speculation? Certainly the control is logic and evidence. The *evidence* is the Scriptures themselves. It is our conviction that many of our troubles in theology are due to the fact that theologians have extended themselves beyond the data of Scripture and have asked questions about which no answer can be given. There are many points about the atonement on which we can render no precise decision because the Scriptures are silent. What was the relationship *precisely* of the two natures at the moment of sin-bearing? In what *exact* sense were our Lord's sufferings penal? To what *exact* degree did He suffer? Similar such questions can be asked of the Incarnation and of the Trinity. So lacking are we of information of such pin-pointed questions that much of our theological definition is by negation, i.e., we may not know what the *exact* truth of the doctrine is, but we know what *cannot* be true.

Every sentence has implications. The sentences of the Scriptures have implications, and the sentences we say about the Scriptures themselves have implications. Science uses logic and experimentation to weed out the true implications test an implication's truthhood or falsity. The very creative and synthetic task of theology drives us beyond exegesis.

The theologian must use all the care and intelligence and learning he has to fill out *correctly* what is implied in Scripture. Therefore he must be aware of his predicament and keep as close as he can to his Biblical data.

Many are the questions asked about heaven—will we eat? Will we wear clothes? Will we know each other? Will we remember loved ones who are lost? Will family ties be reunited? Will we see the Trinity or just the Son? Will babies become adults? Will we speak Hebrew or Greek? The *best* answer will not be the most clever nor the most sentimental, but the one within the *limitations* of the Biblical data on these subjects. Where Scripture has not spoken, we are wisest to be silent.

Certainly great care must be used in formulating statements about the relationship of the divine sovereignty to human freedom. Perhaps much of our trouble in this regard is due to the posing of questions to which there is no Scriptural material for answers. The importance of the great Calvinistic-Arminian debates of the past are not to be minimized but something of the *spirit* of Faber's remarks ought to color our thinking in this regard, and could well be extended to other theological problems.

It may not be the most philosophical, but it is *probably the wisest opinion which we can adopt*, that the truth lies somewhere between the two rival systems of Calvin and Arminius; though I believe it to exceed the wit of man to point out the *exact* place where it *does* lie. We distinctly perceive the two extremities of the vast chain, which stretches across the whole expanse of the theological heavens; but its central links are enveloped in impenetrable clouds and thick darkness.[4]

Training in logic and sciences forms an excellent back-

[4] Faber, *Discourses*, I, 478–79 (cited by Horne, *op. cit.*, I, 423. Italics are in Horne's statement). The differences between Calvinism and Arminianism are not meaningless and are capable of some decision. We accept the general system of Calvinism in theology, but we do not believe that the precise relationship of sovereignty and freedom can be dogmatically stated.

ground for exegesis. It will give the interpreter the requisite background in the general rules of logic, the principles of induction and evidence, and the practical uses of the same in laboratory work. So much of exegesis depends on the logic of implication and the principles of induction and evidence, that it is unwise not to have a working knowledge of the same. Laboratory work which is properly supervised can inculcate into the student a reliable sense of what is evidence and what is not.

Ministers, Bible students, and interpreters who have not had the sharpening experiences of logic and science may have improper notions of implication and evidence. Too frequently such a person uses a basis of appeal that is a notorious violation of the laws of logic and evidence, yet may have a tremendous appeal to an uncritical Christian audience. *The pursuit of a blessing should never be at the expense of truth.*

In summary, there is no simple rule which tells us that we have gone beyond our Scriptural data. The dangers of so doing ought always be in the mind of the interpreter and the theologian so that they may be ever so careful to keep their exegetical and theological work within the limitations of the Biblical data.

(6). *The theological interpreter strives for a system.* A system is a corpus of *interrelated* assertions. A telephone book or a catalogue is not considered a system in the proper sense of the word for they are nothing more than convenient classifications of data. The theologian strives to present the *system of truth* contained in Sacred Scripture. This involves: (i) a systematic formulation of each individual doctrine of the Bible with the data gathered intelligently from the entire range of Scripture. This results in exegetical-theological studies of such topics as God, man, sin, redemption, and Christ. All the important references will be treated exegetically. Then the individual references will be used to forge the unified Biblical doctrine of the subject matter. (ii) The individual doctrines will be interrelated into a coherent systematic theology. How we understand the divine Person bears directly on how we think of the plan of redemption. Our doctrine of sin in many ways determines how we formulate our notion of salvation. This interplay and interrelation among doctrines is inevitable. The goal is a formulation of all the great doctrines of Scripture into one grand edifice of Christian Theology.

We concur with Hodge[5] that this is to be an inductive procedure. The theologian to a degree imitates the scientist. The theologian is the scientist; the "facts" to be examined are in Scripture; and the procedure is inductively directed. The theologian is to be a careful collector of facts. He tries to be as thorough and systematic as any scientist. His rules of evidence, however, are not experimentation and observation but Biblical hermeneutics. Just as the scientist strives for a systematic formulation of his knowledge, so the theologian strives for *systematic* theology.

It is true that the theologian does more than what we have here outlined. Into the formulation of any doctrine must go what may be learned from the history of both theology and philosophy. The history of philosophy is important because many of the problems of theology have been problems of philosophy; and many attacks on Christian doctrines have been made by philosophers. For example, it would be rather foolhardy to discuss the immortality of the soul without a glance at the Platonic literature on the subject, or the existence of God without taking into account the criticisms of Kant. The great schoolmen were both theologians and philosophers as were the two greatest minds of the early church —Origen and Augustine. Systematic theology demands a minimum acquaintance with the history of philosophy if systematic theology is to be written with competence.

The history of theology is indispensable for the theologian because no man is wise enough to ignore the great men of the past who have literally slaved on the great theological prob-

[5] Charles Hodge, *Systematic Theology*, I, 9 ff.

lems. The major doctrines of systematic theology have been under discussion for almost two millennia, and every theologian must also be a historical theologian, if he is to properly find his way around in systematic theology.

It has been the faith of orthodox theology in all its expressions that there is one great system of truth taught in Sacred Scripture. It is true that the Lutheran theology does not press for a system as much as the Reformed theology does, but to claim that the Lutheran theology is indifferent to system in theology is to go contrary to the nature of the theologies they have produced. However, religious liberalism and neo-orthodoxy have challenged the very existence of *systematic* theology.[6] Both agree that the Bible contains a medley of contradictory theologies. It was under this belief that there emerged such studies as Pauline theology, Petrine theology, and Johannine theology. Such theologies are even taught in some orthodox schools without a realization of their birth in religious liberalism.

Liberalism claimed the unity of the Bible to be the unity of the religious experience it proffered. What each generation has in common is not the same theology, but the same religious experience.

Neo-orthodoxy claims that the unity of the Bible is the *unity of perspective* (Aulén, Barth, Brunner). What each generation has in common with every other generation is the same theocentric attitude in faith, or the same Christological orientation to all theology.

The question is of course the nature of the unity of the Bible. Is it a unity of religious experience (liberalism), or a unity of perspective (neo-orthodoxy), or the unity of doctrine (orthodoxy)? Certainly it is not the claim of orthodoxy that we can *completely* systematize the teaching of the Bible. The

[6] Tillich's use of the word systematic in his work, *Systematic Theology*, does not refer to the traditional notion of systematic theology but to his method of the correlation of all methodological knowledge with theology.

very character of the Bible as a *historical* revelation prevents that. But the *ideal goal* of theology is to attain to a systematic theology which faithfully represents the teaching of Scripture. Some neo-orthodoxy reasoning is that because it is difficult of achievement it is impossible of achievement, but we do not believe that you can deduce impossibility from difficulty.

Nor are we to forget the *historical progression* of revelation. Systematic theology takes into account this process, and so claims that systematic theology is not the effort to harmonize all the teaching of the Bible as if it were all on the same flat level, but that the systematic teaching of the Scripture *is in its final intention.*[7]

We do not believe that any neo-orthodox theologian or even liberal theologian would baldly say that theology is to consist of *completely discrete doctrines.* Even Kierkegaard who affirmed that an existential system is impossible with man developed a series of interrelated propositions. The mere listing of doctrines is no more theology than chronicling is the writing of history. Although the determination of the system of theology as contained in Scripture may be difficult, we do not believe that either liberalism or neo-orthodoxy has given sufficient reason to give up the quest for unity, nor have they themselves engaged in the opposite canon—a mere listing of discrete, unrelated doctrines.

(7). *The theologian must use his proof texts with proper understanding of his procedure.*

The use of proof texts is perfectly legitimate. Both liberalism and neo-orthodoxy have strongly castigated the orthodox use of proof texts, and not with good reason. There

---

[7] For the important recent literature on the unity of the Bible see the excellent bibliographical references in H. H. Rowley, *The Unity of the Bible.* Davies (*The Problem of Authority with the Continental Reformers*) claims that one of the glaring weaknesses of Calvin's theological method was that he failed to employ the principle of progressive revelation. The result was that he treated all verses in the Bible as having the same value in theological construction.

is no doubt that the Scriptures quoted closely yield the doctrines of orthodoxy, not liberalism nor neo-orthodoxy. Neither liberalism nor neo-orthodoxy can hold their positions if held to a strict citation of Scripture.

That both liberalism and neo-orthodoxy are inconsistent at this point is evident to anyone who will take the care to read their works and see how they too cite proof texts—when the honey is to their taste. A proof text is used even to prove that one should not use proof texts! "The letter killeth, but the spirit giveth life," (2 Cor. 2:6). The writings of Barth and Brunner are replete with proof texts, but with no justification why one verse is not admitted to theological debate, and another one is. We may cite the Bible in general but not in particular. But how is a general truth known apart from being forged from particulars? The method of religious liberalism to pick and choose verses to taste is now admitted even by the neo-orthodox as a wretched method of treating the Scripture. Speaking of the liberals' treatment of Scripture Lowe writes that "Those who could not bring themselves to disregard what was said by our Lord or by St. Paul or John, unconsciously read into their texts the modern views they liked best. It was the nineteenth century substitute for the discarded allegorical method." [8]

The conservative insists the citation of Scripture is nothing more than a special application of "foot-noting" which is standard scholarly procedure. It would be a rare work of scholarship which cited opinions of authorities without indicating the passages in which these opinions were expressed. If a scholar claims that Anaximenes taught this, or Socrates

[8] *Op. cit.*, p. 115. Burrows (*An Outline of Biblical Theology*) cites enough Scripture to require an index of twenty-nine pages. Evidently proof texting is not as bad as we were told. He does say the older method of citation without regard to historical background was mechanical and therefore wrong. But evidently proof texting correctly done is proper. The objection against orthodoxy at this point must then be against *how* it was done, not *that* it was done. Brunner, in his *Dogmatics*, I, cites more than 400 verses in 353 pages of text. Barth cites over 2,000 in his *Dogmatik*, I/2.

that, or Aristotle something else, he is expected to cite the evidence in terms of the writings of these men as contained in the critical editions of their works, or in writings of contemporaries or near-contemporaries who are commenting on the beliefs of these men. If a scholar claims Aquinas held a certain position about man's creation he is expected to give the reference or references. The liberal and neo-orthodox objection to the use of proof texts reflects a deep theological prejudice (both against a valid revelation of God in Scripture) rather than a rebuttal of a false method of scholarship.

There is no doubt that the proof text method is capable of serious malpractice. The mere listing of proof texts is of no value unless each verse is underwritten by sound exegetical work. It is disconcerting to discover how many verses set down in a book of theology to prove a point melt away when each is examined rather vigorously from the standpoint of exegesis. Not only does it appear that many verses are used that have no relevance but frequently a verse is used whose meaning is actually very different from the one intended by the inspired writer.

For example, Zephaniah 3:9 refers to God returning to the Jews a *pure language*. Many have taken this to mean that the Jews will speak Hebrew in the millennium. The actual meaning of the text is that God will give the Jewish people a *clean* language (morally and ethically) in contrast to an impure language.

Many of the older theologians were guilty of citing a verse in the Old Testament to prove something with reference to salvation and justification, and treating it as if it were as clear and lucid as something in Romans and Galatians. This is one of the most unhappy features of the older theologies which has been happily corrected by a much better sense of historical and progressive revelation, nor can the beneficial influence of dispensationalism be gainsaid at this point.

It is almost instinctive with conservatives to grant a point in theology if a proof text is given. Sometimes the array of texts to prove a point is rather imposing. *But there must be a sound exegetical examination of every text cited* or else we are guilty of superficial treatment of Scripture. The use of proof texts is only as good as the exegesis undergirding their citation. No theologian has a right merely to list verses in proof of a doctrine unless in his own research he has done the requisite exegetical work. It means that every theologian must be of necessity a philologian. Part of the greatness of Charles Hodge as theologian was that he was an able expositor before he was a professional theologian.[9] There is no question that the heart of the striking power of Calvin's *Institutes* is that Calvin was a great expositor and he brought the richness of his expositions into magnificent use in his theological writing.

Furthermore, the theologian must use his texts in view of their context, and in view of their place in the Scriptures. His textual evidence must have a sense of proportion, so that they will have the proper weight of evidence assigned to them. For example, the doctrines of original sin, Satan, the Holy Spirit, and the resurrection are far more dependent for their explication on New Testament passages than on Old Testament ones.

(8). *What is not a matter of revelation cannot be made a matter of creed or faith.*

It is the heritage of the Reformation that only what is taught in Scripture is *directly* binding to conscience. We can loose and bind only as we are in accord with Sacred Scripture.

We thereby object to Catholicism which adds to the revelation of Scripture the moral unanimity of the Fathers, the ecumenical creeds, the decisions of the ecumenical councils, and the *ex cathedra* utterances of the papacy. The Roman Catholic Church does not add these as additional revelation, but as authoritative interpretations of the revelation (the

[9] Note the wonderful tribute paid to Hodge's commentary on *Romans* by Wilbur Smith (*Profitable Bible Study*, p. 174).

deposit of faith in Scripture and Tradition), *and binding to the conscience.*

We thereby object to cults and sects which add to Scripture the voice of man in the form of official handbooks (Mormonism, Christian Science, Russellism, Seventh Day Adventism—with its veneration of the writings of Mary Ellen White), or the writings of their leaders which possess for all practical purposes the authority of an official handbook.

We thereby object to men who would equate their interpretations with the Word of God. To believe that one has an acceptable interpretation of Scripture is not objectionable; to forget humility and human imperfection and so to equate one's interpretation as identical with the divine revelation is objectionable.

We thereby object to speculations about matters in Scripture which lead men beyond the Scriptures themselves. Many of the older sermons on hell were far in excess of the teaching of Scripture, e.g., Jeremy Taylor's sense-by-sense description of the torments of the damned. Precise statements as to who the anti-Christ is, are not matters of faith, even though the *Westminster Confession* stated it was the pope. If the Scriptures affirm he is to be revealed (*apokaluphthē*, 2 Thess. 2:3), how are we to know who he is till he is revealed?

We thereby object to infringement on Christian liberty by men who make their own moral judgments with the certainty and authority of Scripture. What is specifically condemned in Scripture, we have the right to condemn today. What is condemned directly in principle in Scripture we may condemn today. For example, dope is not directly condemned in Scripture, but certainly the principle which condemns drunkenness condemns the use of dope. What is not directly condemned in Scripture, or what is not condemned by immediate application of a principle, must be judged by Christian conscience, but cannot be made as binding as things directly condemned or directly condemned in principle. We must apply the truth of Scripture to life today; otherwise we are not true to our trust. But in so doing we must be ever so careful not to put our interpretations of matters in our culture on the same level as Holy Scripture. The more debatable items are to Christian consciousness, the more tentative should be the spirit of our interpretation. When we brashly identify our interpretations of problems in morals, ethics, and separation with Sacred Scripture, we are making something a matter of faith which is not by its nature a matter of revelation.

There is no system of politics, economics, or culture taught in the New Testament. We may believe some system of economics, etc., is more Christian than another, but we cannot artlessly equate this system with the New Testament teaching. The surprising thing of the Church is its apparent vitality which enables it to live through a variety of political, economic and cultural systems.

The encroachment of the word of man upon the Word of God is a danger we should constantly be alert to, and with all our strength we should maintain the freedom of the Word of God from the word of man.

(9). *The theological interpreter must keep the practical nature of the Bible in mind.*

The Scriptures are not a handbook on all there is to know. They are not a handbook on *all* there is to know about God or religion. The Scriptures do not profess to be a *complete* body of knowledge. The intention of Scripture is to supply man with the knowledge of salvation (2 Timothy 3:15), and what is necessary for a godly Christian life (3:16–17). Only what is in some way related to these two themes is discussed in Scripture.

Much that our speculative appetite would desire is not there. The Scriptures do not contain typical Greek expatiations on epistemology and metaphysics. The problem of evil is not discussed in the abstract but in the concrete. The book of Job is a theodicy not about how evil exists in a good God's universe but how it is that the God of Job permits this specific man of godly character to undergo such sufferings. Habakkuk wants to know why the law is slack and judgment does not go forth (1:4). Why is it that the God of the Torah with eyes too pure to behold evil tolerates Torah-breakers in Israel? Malachi speaks of those who say there is no value in serving God (3:14) because the wicked are prospering, not the righteous.

- The Scriptures do not treat of everything because their content is controlled by their central purpose, the story of divine love and redemption. Human curiosity asks more than this. But we must stay its demand and keep our attention centered on the central message of Scripture.

The oldest saw in this regard is: "where did Cain get his wife?" Where Cain got his wife contributes nothing to the movement of the Bible, so that romantic sideline is ignored. The science of historiography informs us that no history can be exhaustive. All history writing is selective, and the principle of selection is determined by the historian. This accounts for the history of music, the history of theology, the history of art, etc. Biblical history is then that special selection which in some measure—infinitesimal or great—contributes to the story of salvation.

(10). *The theological interpreter must recognize his responsibility to the church.*

The issues proposed in the Scriptures are the greatest in man's entire range of knowledge. The Scriptures speak of an eternal penitentiary, hell, man's greatest disvalue; they speak of heaven, man's greatest bliss; and they speak of salvation, man's most wonderful experience. Further, the Scriptures profess to teach this with the authority of God, underwritten with supernatural credentials by its writers. There are no greater issues before the human race than these.

Whatever the variations in detail might be, it is nevertheless true that the Eastern Church, the Roman Catholic

Church, and the Reformers agree that: (i) the Scriptures are the truth of God; (ii) the Scriptures do teach the unspeakable woe of hell, and the indescribable bliss of heaven; and (iii) salvation from one destiny to the other was wrought by the birth, death, and resurrection of Jesus Christ, God manifest in the flesh.

All Biblical criticism and theological writing should be done in the light of these sobering considerations. This is not meant to put any check on the quest for truth, nor to impose any sort of ecclesiastical control in theological matters. But millions of people now believe the historic Christian gospel, and no man should dare shake their confidence in their belief without taking the full measure of the significance of his act.

Such a stricture applies to the critic, the theologian, and the man who would reinterpret Christianity and bring us the "true" gospel. James informs us that there should be few teachers (3:1) because the condemnation of a teacher—if he lead the flock astray—is great. All such proposed changes should be seriously pondered before being offered to the Church.

After carefully stating that the Bible is to be read and interpreted by each believer for himself, and that no priestly caste is to be the official interpreter of the Bible, Hodge says:

It is not denied that the people, learned and unlearned, should not only compare Scripture with Scripture, and avail themselves of all the means in their power to aid them in their search after the truth, *but they should also pay the greatest deference to the faith of the Church.* If the Scriptures be a plain book, and the Spirit performs the functions of a teacher to all the children of God, it follows inevitably that they must agree in all essential matters in their interpretation of the Bible. And from that fact it follows that for an individual Christian to dissent from the universal Church (*i.e.,* the body of true believers), is tantamount to *dissenting from the Scriptures themselves.*[10]

---

[10] *Op. cit.*, I, 184. Italics are mine.

(11). *No doctrine should be constructed from an uncertain textual reading.*

Doctrine should be established solely from those passages about which textual criticism has raised no doubts. The copyists made many mistakes in copying the New Testament. Sometimes they copied the same line twice or made other such mistakes of dittography. Sometimes they took a part of a later verse and for some reason or other inserted it in a former verse (cf. Romans 8:1 and 8:4). Sometimes a liturgical usage of later times is added to a verse (cf. "for thine is the kingdom, and the power, and the glory, for ever. Amen," of Matthew 6:10). The numerous types of mistakes have been collected in the various books on textual criticism, and no Bible student or minister should seek to express himself on matters of textual criticism till he has familiarized himself with the subject.

The fact is that there are textually insecure passages in the New Testament, and doctrine should not be based on that which might potentially be the voice of man and not the voice of God. The ending of Mark's gospel is a case in point. We are certain of the text through Mark 16:8. But from verse 9 on, the text is not certain. Some scholars are rather certain that the text originally ended with verse 8. Others offer reasons for the retention of the long ending. But until scholars are able to settle the text more certainly no doctrine may be built from this passage about baptismal regeneration, speaking in tongues, casting out of demons, picking up serpents, drinking poison, or divine healing.

BIBLIOGRAPHY

Cellérier, *Biblical Hermeneutics*, p. 217 ff.

Angus and Green, *Cyclopedic Handbook to the Bible*, p. 358 ff.

L. S. Chafer, *Systematic Theology*, I, pp. 114–119.

T. Horne, *Compendious Introduction to the Study of the Bible*, pp. 148–151.

E. Brunner, *Dogmatics*, I, 12, 46, 62, 72, 76 (for a repudiation of a true doctrinal unity of the Bible, and an attack upon *systematic* theology).

E. W. Parsons, *The Religion of the New Testament*, Chapter I, for a recent liberal opinion as to the lack of a doctrinal unity of the New Testament.

A. Kuyper, *Principles of Sacred Theology*.

Connolly Gamble, "The Method of Theology," *Interpretation*, 9:91–99, January, 1955.

Chapter VII

THE DEVOTIONAL AND PRACTICAL USE OF THE BIBLE

A. The General Use of the Bible for Christian Living

The first purpose of the Holy Bible is to make men "wise unto salvation through faith which is in Christ Jesus" (2 Tim. 3:15). After a man has received this salvation, then we are told that "All Scripture is given by inspiration of God, and is profitable for doctrine, for reproof, for correction, for instruction in righteousness that the man of God may be perfect, throughly furnished unto all good works" (2 Tim. 3:16, 17). Most of the material of the Bible is for the Christian, and specifically for his growth in knowledge, holiness, and spirituality. Doctrine and theology are in primary intention aimed at making sinners into saints, and immature Christians into Christian men. The Bible and its study is one of the prime requisites for every Christian in order that he may lead an effective and genuine Christian life.

In using the Bible for moral, ethical, spiritual, and devotional purposes aimed at our spiritual growth, we suggest the following principles:

(1). *All practical lessons, all applications of Scripture, all devotional material, must be governed by general Protestant hermeneutics.*

More pointedly it could be stated this way: all such usages of the Bible must be based upon sound exegetical principles. The notorious dictum: "The ends justifies the means," is frequently baptized into the Christian fold under the guise of: "The blessing justifies the means.'

If a blessing is derived from an improper interpretation of Scripture, the blessing has come not because of improper interpretation, but in spite of the misinterpretation. If a passage does not yield the help and strength the interpreter is seeking, he ought not to distort it until he does get a blessing from it, but he ought to go elsewhere in the Scripture where a blessing can be derived from the native meaning of the text.

In the intense desire to find something practical or devotional in Scripture, we are in danger of obscuring the literal or genuine meaning of the passage. It may sound harsh to so speak, but not too infrequently a very devotional message is conjured up from the Scriptures by a method of interpretation which is nothing short of trifling or tampering with Scripture.

Never should we handle a passage of Scripture in such a way as to distort its original meaning simply because we feel under pressure to find something devotional or spiritual or especially edifying in *every* passage we are called upon to teach or explain. Let the truth of God be its own blessedness.

(2). *The Bible is more a book of principles than a catalogue of specific directions.*

The Bible does contain an excellent blend of the general and the specific with reference to principles for Christian living. If the Bible were never specific we would be somewhat disconcerted in attempting a specific application of its principles. If the Bible were entirely specific in its principles, we would be adrift whenever confronted with a situation in life not covered by a specific principle. The *emphasis* in Scripture is on moral and spiritual principles, not upon specific and itemized lists of rules for moral or spiritual conduct. There are two very important reasons for this:

(i). If it were entirely specific in its practical teachings, then it would be provincial and relative. If Paul had classified sin solely in terms of specifics and therefore in terms of the culture of his day, then as new ways of sinning were devised by man, and as culture changed, Paul's teaching would no longer be relevant. As we study the terminology of Paul we are amazed how he was able to put his finger on the universal element of human sin, and so provide every generation in all cultures with a reliable guide to moral and spiritual behaviour.

(ii). If it were a legal code of rules, then the Bible would foster an artificial spirituality, and indirectly sponsor hypocrisy. If the directions were all specific, a man could live up to the letter of the rules, and yet miss the spirit of true godliness. Real spiritual progress is made only if we are put on our own. Unless we must take a principle and interpret its meaning for a given situation in life, we do not spiritually mature. It is this general nature of New Testament ethics which helps prevent hypocrisy. As long as there is a specific code to obey, men can conform without change of heart. Obedience to a moral code with no change of heart may result in the discrepancy between inner life and outward conduct which is one of the characteristics of hypocrisy. But inasmuch as we must govern ourselves by principle, we are put on our own mettle. In each important decision we shall ask ourselves: *what is the spiritual principle involved?* From this consideration we may then proceed to: *what ought I do?* If we so treat our moral and spiritual decisions we develop in spiritual insight and moral strength. Such development is central to a mature spirituality.

(3). *The Bible emphasizes the inner spirit rather than the outward religious cloak.*

The moral teaching of the Old Testament contains many rules about kinds of food permitted and banned; types of clothing which may be worn, and types prohibited. The basic purpose of these *material* regulations was to inculcate in the Jewish people a sense of *discrimination*. Right and wrong had to be learned on the obvious level of the material to help the mind to learn to discern right and wrong in the more subtle level of the spiritual. In the New Testament morality and spirituality are lifted to a higher level by being inward and spiritual.

The New Testament does not, however, condemn only improper motives, but it also condemns external acts. Gluttony, drunkenness, and revelling are specifically forbidden, and chaste, honorable behaviour before men is taught. But the *emphasis* is upon the inner spiritual life rather than upon a mere social circumspection.

Measuring spirituality entirely by outward appearances is not just to the person being judged. Judging spirituality by external matters (diet, dress, sanctimonious acts) fails to consider that our Lord taught that true spirituality was a secret activity. The external parade of piety as made by the Pharisees is specifically condemned. Prayer is to be in the secret of the closet. Giving is to be such that the right hand does not know what the left hand is doing. Fasting is to be hidden by grooming one's self before one appears in public and so to appear as if one were not fasting.

Negations ("touch not, taste not, handle not," Col. 2:21) do not measure piety; they prepare the way for true piety. True piety is faith, hope, and love. The church has had a constant battle with asceticism. If man is born a legalist in soteriology, he is a born asceticist in sanctification. Asceticism is the belief that the body and the material world are in some sense evil and that victory over them is both by abstinence from the world and by bodily suffering. That there is a measure of truth to asceticism is evident from the Biblical teaching about fasting and sexual abstinence (1 Cor. 7:5). But that asceticism as practiced at times in the history of the church is unscriptural is also evident from the words of our Lord (Luke 11:24 ff.) and of Paul (Col. 2:20 ff.).

The Bible is to be used to develop a true inner life. The Beatitudes inform us that happiness is an *inner* quality of life. Spirituality is striving toward correct attitudes, spiritual graces, the fruit of the Spirit (Gal. 5:22-23). The emphasis on outward religious show and manifest badges or banners of religious profession is not in keeping with the Biblical perspective on spirituality.

(4). *In some statements it is the spirit of the statement that is to be our guide.*

We are enjoined to cut off our hands and pluck out our eyes if they offend (Matt. 5:29, 30). People who have had the courage to conform to this literally do not impress their contemporaries with their spirituality but with their foolhardiness. Is not the *spirit* of the command that we should not pamper or nurse our sins, but deal with them with the utmost severity? If life and death are the issues, then sin certainly must be treated with the greatest dispatch and severity.

Certainly when our Lord told Peter to forgive his brother seventy times seven he was not prescribing the number of times we are to forgive a brother, but he was prescribing the *spirit* of forgiveness (Matt. 18:21 ff.). The same holds true for commands to turn the other cheek, to go the second mile, to yield the second garment. Certainly, if taken literally they become mechanical or external guides to conduct—the very thing they are intended to correct. But if the inner spirit of the command be taken, these passages teach us lessons of generosity, of kindness, of helpfulness. Rather than being covetous we ought to be generous; rather than being goaded by a spirit of vengeance we should be prompted by a spirit of love; rather than being tightfisted we should be merciful to the destitute.

(5). *Commands in terms of one culture must be translated into our culture.*

When our Lord and his apostles gave exhortations and teachings they spoke in terms of the prevailing culture. Otherwise they could not have communicated effectually with their audience. Paul's statements about women (e.g., 1 Tim. 2:9) must be reinterpreted for our culture. The same applies for Paul's statements about cutting the hair and wearing the veil. Cutting the hair was associated with paramours, and wearing a veil (not some modern perky hat) was the sign of a decorous woman. In modern terms this means that Christian women should avoid all appearances of immodesty, and should be chaste and dignified in dress and behaviour.[1]

B. GUIDANCE FROM EXAMPLES

The lives of the great men of the Bible provide a great story of spiritual guidance, and the great events of the Bible provide a vast amount of practical wisdom for godly living. We learn, too, by the mistakes of good men or by the sinful careers of bad men.[2] Events in the lives of great men are often recorded without an express comment by the Biblical writers. Therefore guides are necessary so that we may benefit from their examples without making needless mistakes.

(1). *We must make a distinction between what the Bible records and what it approves.*[3] Men frequently make the mistake of assuming that whatever is written in the Bible is thereby approved. Therefore, there is a rather uncritical justification of their activities on the basis that they parallel the activity of men in an inspired document. The *fact* of divine inspiration does not mean that *all* which is in the Bible is the will of God. The Bible no more morally approves of all that it records than an editor approves of all that he prints in his newspaper.

Records of lying, adultery, incest, cruelty,[4] and deceit are

---

[1] Cf. Paul Woolley, "The Relevance of Scripture," *The Infallible Word*, pp. 201–204.

[2] "When we read of the failings, as well as the sinful actions of men, recorded in Scriptures, we may see what is in our own nature: for there are in us the seeds of the same sin, and similar tendencies to its commission, which would bring forth similar fruits, were it not for the preventing and renewing grace of God. And as many of the persons, whose faults are related in the volume of inspiration, we should learn from them, not only to 'be not high-minded, but fear' (Rom. xi:20); but further, to avoid being rash in censuring conduct of others." Horne, *op. cit.*, I, 427. Italics are omitted.

[3] Miller, *General Biblical Introduction*, p. 19.

[4] Jephthah's cruel vow has been euphemized into a pledge of perpetual virginity, because it is felt that the Bible approved his act. Although the Bible nowhere condemns it, by the same token it nowhere approves

found in the Bible, but on each occasion the sacred writer does not necessarily add his word of condemnation. There are not only sinful acts but erroneous notions recorded. The voice of the devil is heard, the voice of Judas, the voice of demons, the voice of the opponents of Christ, and of the enemies of the apostles. Inspiration here extends only to fidelity of recording. Such words do not constitute either the will of God or the approval of God. Therefore, in every example from a man's life or from Israel's history it must be determined if in any Scripture there is approval or disapproval of this specific situation. If there is none, then we must analyze the passage to see if it is approved or disapproved by other clear teaching of the Bible.[5]

(2). *We may take direct application from all of those incidents that the Bible directly censures or approves.* The woman who poured out the valuable incense was censured by Judas but approved by Christ, and made an example for all church history (John 12:1 ff.). The equivocal behavior of Peter at Antioch was expressly condemned by Paul writing under inspiration, and is a lesson to all not to be guided by opinion but by principle (Galatians 2:11 ff.). Certainly the rebellion of Saul, the immorality of David, the pride of Absalom, the treachery of Judas, the denials of Peter, and the lying of Ananias and Sapphira stand as examples of what not to do. So the faith of Abraham, the obedience of Moses, the loyalty of Elijah, and the love of John the Apostle stand out as great examples to follow.

(3). *Express commands to individuals are not the will of God for us.* Abraham was commanded to offer up his son;

it. The apology to be made at this point is not to distort the very clear meaning of the vow, but simply to indicate that in an inspired record, not all the deeds of even good men are approved by the mere token of being included in the inspired book.

[5] "We should carefully distinguish between what the Scripture itself says, and what is only said in the Scripture, and, also, the times, places, and persons, when, where, and by whom anything is recorded as having been said " Horne, *op. cit.*, I, 426. Italics omitted.

that is not a standing order for each father. Joshua was commanded to slay all in his military campaign; that is not instruction for Christian soldiers. A passage of great instruction is found in the closing part of John's Gospel. Our Lord tells Peter that he will suffer a violent death (John 21:18–19). Misery loves company, so looking at John Peter said, "what shall this man do?" (v. 21) as if to say "haven't you something equally as painful for him?" Our Lord says that if He wills it, John might never die! Two disciples are offered utterly contrasting experiences, yet both within the will of Christ. It behooves us to be unusually careful that we do not try to apply uncritically the commands given to good men of the Bible. Paul's trip to Arabia is not the will of God for some, nor is Peter's call to the apostleship the will of God for others, even though both of these activities were the will of God for Paul and Peter respectively.

(4). *In the lives of men in the Scriptures determine what the outstanding spiritual principle is.* Hebrews 11 is a remarkable example of going through the Old Testament and isolating from the lives of its great men a great spiritual virtue for our benefit. There is a danger of becoming too particular in our lessons from great men, and unconsciously engaging in double-sense interpretations. But if the essential spiritual principles are the goal of our investigations, we derive positive food for the soul, and avoid the mistakes of trying to find too much meaning in trivial details.

(5). *In the application of examples to our lives we do not need a literal reproduction of the Biblical situation.* Baptism need not be done in the river Jordan nor in the land of Palestine to be Scriptural baptism. Neither do we need to go to an upper room in Jerusalem to have the Lord's Table.

C. Promises

"Every promise in the book is mine" is one of the overstatements of the century. Few Bible promises partake of such universality. In applying the promises of the Bible to our specific situations we need to exercise great care. If we apply promises to ourselves that are not for us, we may suffer severe disappointment. Also, promises must not be used to tempt God. A reserve and a patience should temper all our usages of promises.

(1). *Note whether the promise is universal in scope.* The classic example of a universal promise is "and whosoever will, let him take the water of life freely" (Rev. 22:18). General invitations to salvation are for all men, but invitations to prayer or to special blessings are only for the company of the saved.

(2). *Note whether the promise is personal.* When God said to Paul, "Be not afraid, but speak, and hold not thy peace: for I am with thee, and no man shall set on thee to hurt thee" (Acts 18:9–10), that was personal to Paul and may not be used generally. Missionaries in difficult situations may hope for this type of deliverance but may not command it.

(3). *Note whether the promise is conditional.* When it says "Draw nigh unto God and he will draw nigh to you" (James 4:8), there is a human condition to be fulfilled before the promise is received.

(4). *Note whether the promise is for our time.* Some promises pertain just to the Jews in their land and have ceased with the coming of the New Testament. Some promises refer to future conditions that shall prevail upon the earth at the close of the age. Evidently, in Revelation 2 and 3 certain promises were restricted to different churches.

In connection with the use of promises some have used the Bible on the same principle of animistic divination. Divination is the means whereby primitives decide whether they should undergo a proposed adventure such as hunting, fishing, or battle. Common methods among primitives to decide the portent of future events are to read the entrails of pigs or chickens; to crack a bone in the heat of the fire and decide what to do from the nature of the crack; to throw an egg on a grass roof to see if it breaks or not; to use the fire-test to determine guilt. On the sillier level divination is predicting one's future by the reading of cards or tea leaves.

Whenever we force the Bible to say something on specific items of our life, we are in danger of divination. If we do this we leave the sensible, intelligent use of the Bible for that which borders on primitive divination. Most notorious is the custom of opening the Bible and putting the finger on a verse and taking that verse as divine guidance. This method dishonors the intelligence of God, the sobriety of the Bible, puts the Christian faith in a ridiculous light, and places the method of determining the will of God on a superstitious, magical basis. It ought to be added: *no promise of the Bible is to be used that is not in keeping with sane, exegetical principles.*

The type of divination mentioned above exists on a more sophisticated level with those who every day try to find specific guidance from the Bible—not guidance in the sense of getting truth, soul-food, and principles, but in finding one particular verse that tells them exactly what to do that day, or how to resolve a given situation. To do this they have to admit that God can give a message through the Bible that is completely divorced from the native, grammatical meaning of the verse. If this is permitted, then what is to prevent the interpreter from finding anything he wishes in the Bible?

To be specific, at the outbreak of World War II, a certain individual could not decide what his course of action should be—enlist? join the merchant marine? get a theological waiver? He went to his Bible and, finding a reference to those who go down to the seas in ships, he took it as his orders from God to enlist in the United States Navy. The action could not be based upon any sensible exegetical principle, nor upon any spiritual principle; it was a haphazard coincidence between the verse that had the word *seas* in it and the United States Navy.

The will of God is determined from the Bible only in terms

of what it says in its first grammatical sense, or what can be derived from it in terms of great spiritual principles. To use the Bible as in the above example is in direct violation of the nature of inspiration and of the character of the Bible. God does not "double-talk" when He speaks in Scripture, i.e., He does not have a historical, common-sense meaning, *plus* some special message to us in a given situation. If God speaks to us in a given situation, it must be in terms of the sound exegesis of the passage.[6]

D. THE USE OF THE BIBLE IN PREACHING OR TEACHING

The preaching and teaching ministry in the church is applied hermeneutics and exegesis and comes under the discussion of the practical use of the Bible. The *basic theory* of the ministry must be understood if the correct ministry of preaching will be done by the preacher or teacher. The preacher is *a minister of the Word of God.* He is not a person who has a full and free right of sermonizing before a group of people. If he is a true minister of God *he is bound to the ministry of the Word of God.* He has only one claim to the right to preach and demand decision, and that is that he is *declaring the truth of God.* It is impossible to separate the man from his calling, but as much as possible the minister must realize preaching is not *his* opportunity to express *his* religious views. His fundamental task in preaching is not to be clever or sermonic or profound but *to minister the truth of God.* The apostles were called *ministers of the word* (Luke 1:2). The apostles were ordained as *witnesses of Jesus Christ* (Acts 1:8). Their task was to preach what they heard and

[6] "The only way of ascertaining the will of God . . . is to learn it by zealous application as students of the revelation of that will contained in the Scriptures. Short cuts as pulling verses out of boxes, getting guidance by daily motto books, and letting the Bible fall open like a casting of dice are not only useless; they are deceptive." Paul Woolley, "The Relevance of Scripture," *The Infallible Word*, p. 195. His entire refutation of the magical use of the Bible is good.

saw with reference to the life, death, and resurrection of Jesus Christ. The elder (pastor) is to labor *in word and doctrine* (1 Tim. 5:17). What Timothy is to hand on to others is not apostolic succession but *the truth of Christianity* which he heard from many Christians (2 Tim. 2:2). Paul instructs Timothy not to sermonize but to "preach *the message*" (2 Tim. 4:2. Grk: *kērukson ton logon*). Peter says he is an elder by virtue of having *witnessed* the sufferings of our Lord (1 Peter 5:1).

The New Testament servant of Christ was not one free to preach as he wished, but one bound to minister the truth of Christianity, to preach the word of God, and to be a witness of the Gospel. This is very far removed from much of our contemporary preaching which is hardly more than popular, superficial, and personal discourses on religious themes.

One of the mighty issues of the Reformation was the nature of the Christian ministry. Martin Luther and John Calvin both opposed the notion of the ministry as a priesthood. The doctrine of justification by faith alone meant the end of Catholic priestcraft and sacerdotalism. What then was a minister? He was according to both Luther and Calvin *a minister of the Word of God*. In place of the liturgy and sacrament was put the singing of hymns and the preaching of the Word of God. No longer was the altar the focal point of attention, but the open Bible with the man of God preaching forth its meaning and content. The magnificent and thrilling singing of hymns was the spirited way in which the Reformed movement expressed its new joy in Jesus Christ and its freedom from the ritual and liturgy. The mass, so central to Catholic piety and ministry, was replaced by *the preaching of the Word of God*.

Again it is painful to note how these great Reformation convictions have been forgotten, and how the great emphasis on the ministry of the Word of God as God's supreme method of blessing His people has given way to popular, ephemeral sermonizing.

The rules for the practical use of the Bible in preaching are basically derived from (i) general hermeneutic theory, and (ii) the conviction about the nature of the Christian ministry.

(1). *The minister must realize he is a servant of the Lord and bound to the word of the Lord.*

His basic motivation in preaching must be to convey to people the truth of God's word. This means he should publicly read the Bible which is evidently the meaning of "give attendance to reading" (1 Tim. 4:13). He should teach God's word for one of the requirements of a pastor is "apt to teach" (1 Tim. 3:2). He should *herald* or *preach* the word of God.

(2). *The preacher must use all Scripture in accordance with the rules of hermeneutics.*

It is felt too frequently by preachers that preaching is of such a nature as to exempt the preacher from close adherence to the rules of exegesis. Proper exegesis is necessary for commentators and theologians but preachers—it is argued—have a 'poetic license' with reference to Scripture. This is most unfortunate reasoning. If the preacher's duty is to minister the Word of God, hermeneutics is the means whereby he determines the *meaning* of the Word of God. *To ask for exemptions from the strict rules of hermeneutics is then to ask for an exemption from preaching the true meaning of the Word of God.* This is precisely a repudiation of what a man is called to preach, namely, the truth of God's Word.

This does not mean that preaching is nothing but public exegesis or drab commenting on the Sacred Text. There must be energy, life, imagination, relevancy, illustration, and passion to all preaching. Bookish, dry, technical exposition is not necessarily preaching the Word of God. But whenever Scripture is used, it must be used according to sound rules of hermeneutics.

The principal mistakes in preaching in violating the meaning of Scripture are:

(i). Taking a phrase from a text because of its attractive wording. The preacher does not actually expound the meaning of the text, but uses the felicitous wording of it as the basis for his own sermonizing. Broadus says that this is not preaching Scripture, but merely the words of Scripture.[7] No matter how literary the expression nor how catchy to the ear, a phrase must not be wrenched from its content and preached upon with no real interpretation of its meaning. This is not preaching the Word of God.

(ii). A preacher may choose a text but rather than explaining it sermonize on it. The remarks in a sermon need not be as narrow as the text, but if a text or passage is employed then the preacher is under holy obligation to explain its meaning. Either the preacher ignores the text save for the topic it suggests, or else he misinterprets it altogether. This is not a wilful perversion of Scripture but a negligent or careless or ignorant method of treating the inspired Text. Broadus is not too strong when writing on this sort of an abuse of a text when he says: "It is a mournful fact that Universalists, Romanists, Mormons, can find an apparent support for their heresies in Scripture, without interpreting more loosely, without doing greater violence to the meaning and connection of the Sacred Text than is sometimes done by orthodoxy, devout, and even intelligent men."[8]

(iii). A preacher may "spiritualize" a text or a passage and so impose a meaning on the text that is not there. This is usually done under the sincere pretense that the preacher is seeking a deeper meaning of the Bible. It is actually a species of patristic allegorization, and it is astounding how many of the patristic allegories are taught in Protestantism under the guise of typology.

One of the primary causes of this Protestant allegorizing is the proper motive to be edifying. Some Scripture is plain historical narrative and it is not especially edifying for the

[7] John A. Broadus, *A Treatise on the Preparation and Delivery of Sermons* (thirtieth edition), p. 33. Broadus has a learned and unusually wise discussion of the sermon and the interpretation of the text. Part I, Chapter II, "The Text—Interpretation."

[8] *Ibid.*, p. 47.

preacher to summarize so many historical incidents. But i
he can read into the passage something about Christ, or th
gospel, or spiritual life, then he can make the passage very
interesting. But he does so at the expense of its true meaning.
He then is no longer preaching the Word of God but engaging
in allegorization. Again we cite with much approval the
judgment of Broadus about this sort of treatment of the
Sacred Text:

Among Baptists, for instance, the influence of Fuller, Hall, and
others, and the wider diffusion of ministerial education, have
wrought a gratifying change. But there is still much ignorance to
overcome, and too many able and honored ministers continue sometimes to sanction by their potent example the old-fashioned spiritualizing [really, allegorizing]. It is so easy and pleasant for men of
fertile fancy to break away from laborious study of phraseology
and connection, to cease plodding along the rough and homely
paths of earth, and sport, free and rejoicing, in the open heaven;
the people are so charmed by ingenious novelties, so carried away
with imaginative flights, so delighted to find everywhere types of
Christ and likenesses to the spiritual life; it is so common to think
that whatever kindles the imagination and touches the heart must
be good preaching, and so easy to insist that the doctrines of the
sermon are in themselves true and Scriptural, though they be not
actually taught in the text,—that preachers often lose sight of their
fundamental and inexcusable error, of *saying that a passage of God's
Word means what it does not mean.* So independent, too, one may
feel; so original he may think himself. Commentaries, he can sneer
at them all; other preachers, he has little need of comparing views
with them. No need of anything but the resources of his own
imagination, for such preaching is too often only building castles
in the air.[9]

The proper and improper limits of typological exegesis will
be discussed in the chapter on typology. But the proper
alternative to spiritualizing the Old Testament is to *principlize* the Old Testament. To *principlize* is to discover in
any narrative the basic spiritual, moral, or theological prin-

[9] *Ibid.*, p. 52. Italics are his.

ciples. These principles are latent in the text and it is the process of deduction which brings them to the surface. It is not an imposition on the text. Allegorizing is the imputation to the text of a meaning which is not there, but *principling* is not so guilty. By principlizing we are able to obtain devotional and spiritual truth from Scripture and avoid the charge of eisegesis.

When David repeatedly refuses to slay Saul we see the principle of obedience to powers that be. When Saul is not patient with God's prophet we see the principle of disobedience. When Isaiah prays for the shadow to retreat on the sundial we see the principle of great spiritual courage. In truth, Hebrews 11 is a magnificent example of principlizing. The great faith of a multitude of men is set before us as the true principle of their lives.

BIBLIOGRAPHY

Angus and Green, *Cyclopedic Handbook to the Bible*, Chapter X. The best general account in the literature.

Terry, *Biblical Hermeneutics*, Part Second, Chapter XXIV.

Chafer, *The Science of Biblical Hermeneutics*, Chapter IV.

Pierson, *Knowing the Scriptures*, Chapter I.

Manley, editor, *The New Bible Handbook*, p. 72 ff.

Horne, *An Introduction to the Study and Critical Knowledge of The Holy Scriptures*, I, 425 ff.

Broadus, *Treatise on the Preparation and Delivery of Sermons*, (thirtieth edition), Part I, Chapter II.

Baughman, "Books on Biblical Preaching," *Interpretation*, 5:470–477. An annotated bibliography.

Chapter VIII

THE PROBLEM OF INERRANCY AND SECULAR
SCIENCE IN RELATION TO HERMENEUTICS

A. The Problem of Infallibility and Inerrancy

Judged by their official creeds and confessions, all the
major churches of Christendom have accepted the divine inspiration of the Bible. They are agreed that the Bible is a
book brought into existence by the special grace of God, possessing a quality which books of purely human production
do not have. Judging further from official creeds and confessions the churches have accepted the *infallibility* of the
Bible in all matters of faith and morals. Men may depend on
the doctrines and morals of the Bible with complete certitude
of their truthfulness. Going yet another step, these churches
have accepted the *inerrancy* of all the historical and factual
matters of the Scriptures which pertain to matters of faith
and morals. This is demanded by the very historical nature
of the Biblical revelation, and the plan of redemption. Some
men have tried to defend infallibility of the faith and morals
of the Bible, but not the inerrancy of the Bible.[1] What is
actually proposed is that the major historical features of the
Scriptures are reliable. The Bible is errant in historical, factual, and numerical matters which do not affect its faith and
morals.

To accept the infallibility of the faith and morals of the
Bible is *mutatis mutandis* to accept the historical trustworthi-
ness of the historical elements in redemption. The Christian

[1] For example Gore (*Lux Mundi*) and Briggs (*The Bible, The Church,
and Reason*).

faith has taught the infallibility of the faith and morals of Scripture, and the inerrancy of all matters of history pertaining to faith and morals. No lower ground than this can be held. It is true that extremes can be found in orthodoxy in this matter. J. Paterson Smyth (*How God Inspired the Bible*) does not wish to admit more than infallibility of faith and morals. The Buxtorffs defended the inspiration of the Hebrew vowels.[2]

Careful conservative scholarship has indicated that the inerrancy of the Bible must be judged by the very nature of the divine revelation. The revelation came to men speaking human languages and living in a cultural context. To be meaningful it had to come in the language of the prophets and apostles, and employ the cultural background for figures, illustrations, analogies, and everything else associated with linguistic communication. No artificial or abstract theory of inerrancy is to be imposed on the Scriptures.

To impose a precise literalness to the number usages of the Bible is an illustration of an artificial theory of inerrancy. Some interpreters have insisted that Jesus had to be in the grave exactly seventy-two hours because he said he would be buried for three days and three nights. But the expression "three days and three nights" *must be determined by Jewish usage.* In fact to insist on exactly seventy-two hours creates confusion. If Jesus were crucified on Friday, as practically all competent scholars agree, then the resurrection would not be till late Monday afternoon. In fact, if the burial were in the afternoon—as is stated in the Scriptures that it was before sundown—the resurrection had to be just seventy-two hours later in the afternoon. If one insists that the crucifixion were on Wednesday then the seventy-two hours ends before sundown on Saturday, and not on the Lord's day.

[2] Hebrew was originally written with consonants (radicals) only. When it ceased to be a spoken language, Jewish scholars added vowels (vowel points) to indicate its pronunciation. It is now universally admitted that these vowel points are a late insertion and not part of the autographs.

In 1 Cor. 15:5 Paul says our Lord was seen after his resurrection by "the twelve." An artificial notion of inerrancy would demand twelve apostles, but Judas was dead and his successor was not appointed till after the ascension. But "the twelve" had become a regular expression for "the group of disciples."

Two other illustrations may be given to show that inerrancy must be judged by *usus loquendi* of the times and not artificially. In Mark 1:2 a citation is made from Malachi and Isaiah. Isaiah's name does not appear in the King James, but it does in the best critical editions of the Greek text. Mark attributes both citations to Isaiah. The Jewish custom in citing two or three prophets in a brief catena of Scripture was to name only the leading prophet. In Matthew 27:9 a verse from Zechariah is cited as coming from Jeremiah. The Jewish tradition was that the spirit of Jeremiah was in Zechariah and such a method of citation would not offend their historical sense.

We can sum up what we have been trying to say as follows: *in judging the inerrancy of the Scriptures we must judge them according to the customs, rules, and standards of the times the various books were written, and not in terms of some abstract or artificial notion of inerrancy.*

To those who accept the infallibility and inerrancy of Scripture, the problem of inerrancy presents a special problem to the interpreter. In dealing with this important and difficult problem we suggest the following principles:

(1). *A belief in the inerrancy of the Bible does not mean that all the Bible is clear.* The inspiration of the Bible does not guarantee its lucidity. The apostle Peter indicates that the prophets themselves were puzzled about what they wrote (1 Pet. 1:10 ff.). He further admits that Paul said many things which are hard to interpret (2 Peter 3:16, *dysnoētos*, difficult to understand). The writer of Hebrews tells his listeners that his exposition about Christ and Melchisedec is lengthy and difficult to interpret (Hebrews 5:11). Our Lord

Himself puzzled his own disciples with many of his utterances. The inerrancy of the Scriptures does not mean that it is possible to give a clear interpretation of every passage.

Above the express statements of the Scriptures to their own partial obscurity is the very nature of the Bible. We must expect obscurities from the very fact that the Bible is written in ancient languages, in a strange culture, and that the Bible refers to persons, places, and events for which no other source for corroboration exists. The Bible was composed over a vast geographical territory—from Egypt to Babylon to Rome—and written over a span of some fifteen centuries.

A considerable source of encouragement is the findings of archaeology which are clearing up some obscurities. The reference to seething a kid in its mother's milk has been a puzzler since patristic exegesis (Exodus 23:19). It is now known to be part of heathenish idolatry.[3]

The older commentators spent much time trying to unravel the meaning of the expression "daily bread" in the Lord's prayer. Deissmann has discovered the expression in the papyri and it refers to the provisions given to laborers and soldiers for the following day's work. Deissmann[4] translates it: "Give us today our amount of daily food for tomorrow."

(2). *When we assert the inerrancy of the Bible, we do not assert that the Bible speaks all its mind on a subject in one place.* It is the total Bible in historical perspective which is inerrant. The monogamous ideal of marriage is not clearly set forth till the pages of the New Testament. What is not even mentioned to a two-year-old is reprimanded in a ten-year-old. So God tolerated much in the Old Testament period while mankind (specifically Israel) was in its ethical and theological

[3] Cf. J. Finegan, *Light from the Ancient Past*, p. 148. The rite is referred to in the Ras Shamra texts.

[4] Deissmann, *The New Testament in the Light of Modern Research*, p. 86. For the better understanding of the grammar of the New Testament from research in papyri see A. T. Robertson, *A Grammar of the Greek New Testament in the Light of Historical Research* (fifth edition), pp. 1–139.

swaddling clothes. The full light of revelation burns in the New Testament. It is not proper to pit the earlier part of the Bible against the later as if they contradict. M'Intosh has argued repeatedly in his work, *Is Christ Infallible and the Bible True?* that the immature or preliminary does not exist in a state of contradiction with the mature and final, and with this we agree.

The complete mind of God on a subject matter is given (as far as revelation contains it) by a historico-synoptic view. No charge of errancy can be made against the Bible by isolating a doctrine from its complete Biblical development.

(3). *Belief in the inerrancy of the Scriptures leads us to affirm there are no contradictions in the Bible.* As much as is made over the proposed contradictions in Scripture, it is surprising how few examples of any possible merit can be supplied, and it is further surprising how difficult it is to make a successful case out of these examples. To be specific Marcus Dods lists six contradictions in the Gospels as his basis for not accepting their inerrancy, and Frederic Kenyon supplies us with another list of contradictions which prove the errancy of the Scriptures.[5] In both cases it will be discovered that in the conservative commentaries there are plausible explanations of every one of these alleged contradictions. The burden of proof is on the accuser. The believer in the Scriptures needs only to show that the evidence of errancy is not conclusive. A contradiction to be valid must be unequivocal, and as long as the proposed contradiction is alleged on ambiguous grounds no charge of errancy is valid.

Archeology has again supplied some help at this point. The difficulties about Luke's census that were once so formidable have now practically vanished, thanks to archeology. Certain other embarrassments in the Gospel accounts have been relieved.[6]

---

[5] Dods, *The Bible: Its Origin and Nature*, pp. 136–37. Kenyon, *The Bible and Archaeology*, p. 27.

[6] Cf. A. T. Robertson, *A Harmony of the Gospels*, p. 71 fn.

In considering so-called contradictions many matters must be weighed: (i) We must be sure of our original text. In the healing of the maniac of Gerasa it was assumed incredible that the pigs could run thirty-five miles to the lake and plunge in, for the town of Gerasa was so situated. Textual critics have come to the conclusion that the correct reading of the original text should be Gerasenes. To supplement this has been the work of Thompson who has found the ruins of a town named Khersa right at the edge of a steep place by the sea.[7]

(ii) Some problems, especially those dealing with numbers, may easily be corruption of the text; e.g., 1 Sam. 13:1 and Acts 13:21; 1 Kings 4:26 and 2 Chronicles 9:25. Paul declares that twenty-three thousand died in a plague (1 Cor. 10:8), whereas Numbers 25:9 records twenty-four thousand. That Paul records how many died in a day and Moses in the entire plague is a thin explanation because how would Paul know such a breakdown of the figures? A corrupt text seems to be the better accounting of this. It could also be argued that Paul contradicts Moses only if he intended to be giving the exact number. If he had *in mentis* the intent of only supplying a round number no contradiction exists. The same is true for 1 Kings 7:23 where the value for *pi* is three. It has been argued that with a flange the circumference could be reduced to 30 cubits, but if the numbers are general and not intended to be to the decimal point no contradiction can be said to exist. Further the susceptibility of numbers to corruption in ancient texts is well known.

(iii). We may misinterpret one or both of two conflicting passages. The two genealogies of Christ present a real problem. That they are contradictory has never been unequivocally established.[8] Further, the scheme of Matthew to give

[7] Robertson, *loc. cit.*
[8] Cf. Robertson's discussion. *Op. cit.*, p. 259. We prefer Machen's solution to Robertson's, however. *The Virgin Birth of Christ*, p. 229 ff.

his genealogy in compressed form and in units of fourteen each is his specific intent, and not to be made thereby contradictory to a fuller account. Much care must also be used in correlating the Gospel narratives. In the healing of blind Bartimaeus, Matthew mentions two blind men, whereas Luke and Mark mention only one. In the healing of the Gerasene demoniac Matthew again mentions two, and Luke and Mark, one. Mark and Luke pick out the more notorious of the two and limit their account to him. The healing of blind Bartimaeus is stated to be while leaving the city, and while entering the city. There was a new Jericho and an old Jericho. If the healing took place between the two cities both expressions are true.

(iv). We may identify two similar events that are really different. There is the possibility of two cleansings of the Temple (John 2; Matthew 21). The Sermon on the Mount might have been given several times (Matthew 5; Luke 6). Many of the healings evidently followed similar patterns even to the conversation.

(v). The fuller account is to be used to explain the shorter account. No contradiction is to be construed if the writer condenses an account or speech for economy of space or time. What God said to Ananias in Acts 9:10–19, Paul puts in the mouth of Ananias as speaking to him (Acts 22:12–16). Acts 9 is the full account of Paul's conversion, and Acts 22 the abbreviated account.

(vi). In a given instance one writer may give direct discourse, and the second either indirect discourse or a simple statement of the content of what was said. This is a constant phenomenon in the synoptic Gospels. This is standard and accepted methodology of prose composition and not to be taken as contradictory.

(vii). Inerrancy does not mean *literalness* of detail. All of the speeches in the book of Acts are very short, and we are persuaded that Peter and Paul talked for more than one or two minutes. We have in Acts a faithful digest of these speeches and not the *ipsissima verba* of Paul and Peter.[9]

(4). *Belief in the inerrancy of the Bible does not demand the original manuscripts nor a perfect text.* That original manuscripts of the Bible existed cannot be doubted although sometimes critics of inspiration argue as if original manuscripts never existed. The Biblical writers began with copies, so it seems! Nor can it be doubted that errors of transmission took place when the autographs were copied. It is therefore entirely proper to assert that a given reading in a text might not exist in the original text. We have not by so reasoning proved the autographs to be inerrant, but on the other hand we have argued that corruptions do exist and that there may be a difference between present-day manuscripts and autographs. The fact of textual corruptions is not a denial of inspiration, but a *problem* of inspiration. It is a logical *non sequitur* to argue from a corrupted text to a denial of inspiration. There is nothing inherently contradictory in the notion of an inspired text imperfectly transmitted.

Obviously we have no autographs of either Testament. The oldest manuscript of the New Testament is the John Rylands Papyrus fragment of the Gospel of John dated by some as early as A.D. 125, although usually about A.D. 150. Until the discovery of the Dead Sea Scrolls our oldest Old Testament manuscript was the Leningrad Codex, dated A.D. 916. Now we have manuscripts of Isaiah and Daniel dated a hundred years or so before the birth of Christ, and fragments of many of the other Old Testament books.

All orthodoxy needs to claim in this regard is that errors of transmission touch nothing vital in Scripture. There is no question that the most faithfully transmitted manuscripts from antiquity are the Old and New Testaments. For proof

---

[9] *Verbal* inspiration does not mean *exact literal reproduction* of what is said or done. A study of parallel passages with a Greek harmony of the Gospels reveals how many words and expressions the Spirit considered synonymous; and it is also interesting to note variation in detail and difference of length of accounts.

of this assertion with reference to the Old Testament we cite Green: "It may be safely said that no other work of antiquity has been so accurately transmitted." [10]   The texts of Daniel and Isaiah in the Dead Sea Scrolls are substantially Masoretic and so further confirm this claim of Green.

As far as the New Testament is concerned, the situation is just as satisfactory.   In the first place the number of Greek manuscripts for critical work is now over 4000.   If Latin and other early versions be admitted, then the figure moves up over the 13,000 mark.   Further, practically the entire New Testament can be culled from citations in the Fathers.   There is nothing in classical documents which even comes close to this.   Hort claims that less than one thousandth of the New Testament text is corrupt.   In the remarkable providence of God the text of the Bible in the original languages forms the most reliably transmitted texts known to classical scholarship.

B. The Problem of Science

If we accept the divine inspiration of a Book which was written several centuries before the discoveries of modern science we are faced with the very acute problem of relating its statements about creation to those of modern science.   To claim that the Bible is a book filled with anticipations of modern science does not seem to accord with the cultural conditioning of any revelation, and to declare all its statements about nature as invalid does not seem to accord with its inspiration.   What canons of interpretation should we follow in regard to this important and knotty question? [11]

(1).   *When we assert the inerrancy of Scripture we do not*

---

[10] Green, *General Introduction to the Old Testament: The Text*, p. 181. Cf. also remarks of the same commendatory nature by Kenyon, *Our Bible and the Ancient Manuscripts*, pp. 38 and 47.   For the conservative position clearly and lucidly explained see John H. Skilton, "The Transmission of Scriptures," *The Infallible Word*, pp. 137–187.

[11] We have treated this more extensively in our volume, *The Christian View of Science and Scripture*.

assert that the Bible uses scientific language. Classical scholars, historians, and students of the history of philosophy make a conscious effort to find modern counterparts to ancient terminology. This is not considered as depreciating the validity of these terms. Thomists insist that if present scholars would take the pains to make accurate correlations between Thomas' vocabulary and modern terms, present day scholars would find much more significance in Thomas. Others have said that much of Newton's genius goes unheralded because scholars will not bother to learn the scientific Latin jargon of Newton's day and transpose it into our contemporary language. The popular nature of the Biblical statements about nature is no argument against the validity of these statements.

The Bible is a book adapted for all ages of the human race and therefore its vocabulary about nature must be popular. It is no objection against inerrancy that the Scriptures are in popular language.

(2). *No objection can be brought against inerrancy because the language of the Bible is phenomenal.* A language which is phenomenal is restricted to terms of description and observation. Its language about astronomy, botany, zoology, and geology is restricted to the vocabulary of popular observation. What can be seen through microscope or telescope is not commented on. Phenomenal language is true because all it claims is to be descriptive. One is not deceived when he sees the sun rise and the sun set. One is deceived only if he artlessly converts his observations into theories.

The corollary to this is that the Bible does not theorize as to the actual nature of things. It does not contain a theory of astronomy or geology or chemistry. It does not seek to present knowledge which could be formed into a science text. The words of Paul Woolley are very relevant at this point:

The Bible, then, should not be approached with a view to finding it a comprehensive treatise on, for example, natural science. A great many statements in the realm of natural science are to be found in the Bible, and they are true statements. But the Bible offers no information as to the validity of the various modern theories concerning the nature of matter and the constitution of the physical world. There is nothing in the Bible with which to test the theories of relativity . . . One could not write a biological textbook from the Bible alone.[12]

(3). *No objection can be brought against the inerrancy of the Bible because it is a culturally conditioned revelation.* The Bible uses the terms and expressions of the times of its writers. Any revelation must be so accommodated to the human mind. The interpreter who seeks for modern relativity theory in the Bible is mistaken as he asks the Bible to speak on a subject it *ex hypothesi* will not. When the religious liberal renounces much of the Bible because it is culturally conditioned he fails to understand that inspiration uses cultural terms and expressions to convey an infallible revelation.

The mustard seed is not the smallest seed known to botanists, but among the Semites it was considered to be the smallest of seeds. Its phenomenal growth became the basis for an analogy for the growth of anything unusually small to something very large. For our Lord to have given the Latin terms of the smallest seed would have been grotesque.

John 1:13 states that the Christian is born of God, not of "bloods." It was the Jewish opinion that the seeds of inheritance were carried in the blood-stream. Does John argue that the seeds of reproduction are in the bloodstream? What John intends to teach is that a man is born of God, not on the basis of his Jewish ancestry. He had to use the culturally current terms to make his theological point. The same is true of much of the psychology of the Bible, e.g., attributing psychic properties to bowels, kidneys, heart, liver, and bones. The divine revelation came in and through these modes of expression and the infallible truth shines *through* them.

(4). *It is not proper to attempt to find numerous correlations*

[12] Paul Woolley, "The Relevance of Scripture," *The Infallible Word,* p. 190.

of Scripture and modern science. The careful interpreter will
not try to find the automobile in Nahum 1, or the airplane
in Isaiah 60 or atomic theory in Hebrews 11:3 or atomic
energy in 2 Peter 3. All such efforts to extract modern scientific theories out of Scripture eventually do more harm
than good.

(5). *It must be kept in mind that Genesis 1 is in outline form.*
Contemporary works which endeavor to sketch the salient
facts of the universe run up to five hundred pages. Genesis
sums up creation in thirty-four verses (Gen. 1:1 to 2:3). The
extreme brevity of the account must temper all our exegesis
of it. Trying to read too much specific detail into this sketch
can cause needless conflict with science. It is always prob-
lematic to go from the "let there be" of Genesis to the *modus
operandi.*

It is the province of the sciences to fill in the details of
what is in outline form in the Bible. Science should not
preëmpt to itself *the first principles* of the Biblical account,
nor should theologians endeavor to dictate to the scientists
empirical details about which Genesis 1 is actually silent.
The Church has suffered much because (i) what theologians
have said about what Genesis 1 has not been clearly differ-
entiated from (ii) what Genesis 1 actually says. A. J. Maas
has stated very acceptably the relationship which science
should bear to interpretation, and interpretation to science.

It would be wrong to make Scripture the criterion of science, to
decide our modern scientific questions from our Biblical data. . . .
It is well, therefore, to temper our conservatism with prudence;
prescinding from 'matters of faith and morals' in which there can
be no change, we should be ready to accommodate our exegesis to
the progress of historians and scientists in their respective fields,
showing at the same time that such harmonizing expositions of
Scripture represent only a progressive state in Bible study which
will be perfected with the progress of profane learning.[13]

[13] "Hermeneutics," *Catholic Encyclopedia*, VII, 275.

Maas suggests in this citation that our interpretations about science and Scripture should be kept fluid. Exegesis and science are both developing and progressing. It would be improper to make hard and fast interpretations if this is the situation. Just as history gives us clues to the meaning of prophecy, so our knowledge of science gives us greater insight into the Biblical statements about natural things. No interpretation of Genesis 1 is more mature than the science which guides it. To attempt to interpret the scientific elements of Genesis 1 *without* science is to attempt the impossible for the concepts and objects of the chapter have meaning only as they are referred to nature, and the subject matter of science may be called simply "nature."

One more observation must be made, however, before we conclude this chapter. The older polemic against the inspiration of the Bible was directed at specific contradictions. One unequivocal contradiction could, it was urged, bring down the doctrine of inerrancy. The critics thought they could produce examples but the orthodox felt the examples to be equivocal. The attack has taken a new, drastic and serious turn. It is not so much directed at finding contradictions or discrepancies in Scripture as it is in finding deep-seated contradictions in the very nature of the record.

One example of such an alleged deep-seated contradiction is the assertion that the historical record of the Old Testament does not contain the true order. The prophets were actually before the law. The Jewish canon which governs the order of the books in the Bible is the reverse order of history.

Further, the discussion over this or that fact in Scripture and science gave way to a new problem. The allegation was that the Scriptures represented the cosmological schemes of antiquity and were in very violent contrast to the world as understood by modern science. To attempt to reconcile Genesis to geology was repudiated because in the eyes of the critics it amounted to trying to harmonize some ancient Babylonian cosmology with the cosmology of modern science.

A third deep-seated contradiction alleged by the critics is that there was a moral contradiction between the Old and the New Testaments. Some of the practices of the Old Testament are primitive or barbaric or cruel and in stark contradiction to the ethics of the New Testament.

Finally, the critics have proved to their satisfaction at least that the Bible represents no theological unity, but is a veritable congeries of theologies. The Old Testament books reflect a variety of religious beliefs, and several main strands of divergent theological thought can be found in the New Testament. Priest is set against prophet, the New against the Old, Paul against Peter, and John against James.

This is where the older problem of "discrepancies and contradictions" have moved and evangelicalism must reply in kind to maintain the unity of the divine revelation.

BIBLIOGRAPHY

Angus and Green, *Cyclopedic Handbook to the Bible*, p. 259 ff.

R. A. Torrey, *Alleged Discrepancies in the Bible.*

H. E. Guillebaud, *Some Moral Difficulties in the Bible.*

J. R. Van Pelt, "Discrepancies," *International Standard Bible Encyclopedia*, II, 852–54.

Terry, *Biblical Hermeneutics*, p. 404.

W. Arndt, *Does the Bible Contradict Itself?*

Barrows, *Companion to the Bible*, p. 543.

T. Horne, *An Introduction to the Critical Knowledge and Study of the Holy Scriptures*, I, Bk. II, Chapter VIII.

J. Urquhart, *The New Biblical Guide*, Vol. VIII, Part II, "The Question about the Inerrancy of Scripture."

C. A. Briggs, *The Bible, The Church, and Reason*, Chapter IV, "Is Holy Scripture Inerrant?"

J. W. Haley, *Alleged Discrepancies of the Bible.*

C. Daniel, *The Bible's Seeming Contradictions.*

G. Dehoff, *Alleged Bible Contradictions Explained.*

Bernard Ramm, *The Christian View of Science and Scripture*, "A Classified Bibliography," pp. 355–60.

CHAPTER IX

THE INTERPRETATION OF TYPES

THE content of special hermeneutics is rather large. Terry (*Biblical Hermeneutics*, revised edition) has a large list of subjects comprising special hermeneutics, e.g., Hebrew poetry; figurative language such as tropes, metonym, personification, synedoche, apostrophe, interrogation, hyperbole, irony, simile, metaphor, fables, riddles, and enigmas; parables; allegories, proverbs, and gnomic poetry; types; symbols (actions, numbers, names, colors); dreams; prophecy (general, Messianic, apocalyptic); Old Testament quotations in the New; accommodation; progress of doctrine and analogy of faith; and the doctrinal and practical use of the Bible. Out of this list there are three items in particular which need special attention due to their importance, namely, typology, prophecy, and parables.

A. JUSTIFICATION OF TYPOLOGY AS A BIBLICAL DISCIPLINE

It has been the contention of critics that typology is forced exegesis rather than an interpretation rising naturally out of the Scriptures. Some exegesis of the Old Testament in the name of typology is forced, to be sure. However such excesses—past and present—do not destroy the Christian contention that the typological method of interpretation is valid. The justification for typological interpretation is as follows:

(1). The general relationship which the Old Testament sustains to the New is the very basis for such a study. The strong *prophetic element* in the Old Testament establishes a real and vital nexus between the two Testaments. The fact of prophecy establishes the principle that the New is latent in the Old, and that the Old is patent in the New. The form of prophecy may be either verbally predictive or typically predictive. The former are those prophecies which in poetry or prose speak of the age to come (e.g., Psalm 22, Isaiah 53); the latter are those typical persons, things, or events which forecast the age to come. Thus a type is a species of prophecy and should be included under prophetic studies. Typological interpretation is thereby justified because it is part of prophecy, the very nature of which establishes the nexus between the two Testaments.

Torm makes it even stronger than this. Torm prefers to speak of the typological method of thinking (*Betrachtungweise*) rather than the typological method of interpretation (*Auslegung*). The reason for this is two-fold: typological interpretation is based on the unity of the Testaments. It shows that the divine revelation is of one piece.[1] We are thus able to relate part to part and understand their places in the divine revelation. Torm claims, secondly, typological interpretation is really a philosophy of history! He writes: "Typological interpretation is not so much an interpretation as a historical consideration, a method and manner of judging historical events and relations—a sort of philosophy of history, if you please." [2] It is the special Christian perspective on a very special segment of human history.

(2). Our Lord's own use of the Old Testament is His invitation to us to find Him in the Old Testament. In Luke

[1] "Die Bedeutung der typologischen Betrachtungweise ist die, dass sie uns den Blick für die Einheit in der Offenbarung Gottes öffnet und gerade dadurch uns die bleibende Bedeutung, die jeder kleine Teil der Offenbarung für die Gesamheit hat, erkennen lässt." F. Torm, *Das Hermeneutik des Neuen Testaments*, p. 224.

[2] "Die 'typologische Auslegung' ist also nicht so sehr eine Auslegung als eine historische Betrachtung, eine Art and Weise, die geschichtlichen Ereignisse und Verhältnisse zu beurteilen,—eine Art Philosophie der Geschichte, wenn man will." *Ibid.*, p. 223.

24:25–44 Christ teaches the disciples about Himself, beginning at Moses and following through *all* the Scriptures. Luke 24:44 mentions the divisions of the Jewish canon (Moses, Prophets, Psalms) thus making the reference as wide as the Old Testament canon. In John 5:39–44 Christ invites men to search the Scriptures for *they testify to him* inasmuch as Moses wrote of Him. Paul uses the sacrificial language of the Old Testament in speaking of the death of Christ (Eph. 5:2) thus showing that Christ is in the offerings. Hebrews clearly teaches that the Tabernacle which was, is now realized in a present heavenly tabernacle of which Christ is the minister of the sanctuary (Hebrews 9:9–11, 23–24). Thus Christ is to be found in the Tabernacle. And certainly from Paul's reference in 1 Cor. 10:4 Christ was in the wilderness wanderings. It is the conviction of many scholars that the Christian interpretation of the Old Testament stems directly from the teachings and example of our Lord.

(3). Even more specific is the vocabulary of the New Testament with reference to the nature of the Old.[3] The following words are used in the New of the Old. *Hypodeigma* means a sign suggestive of anything, a representation, a figure, a copy, an example. *Typos* and *typikos* (from the verb, *typtō*, "to strike") mean the mark of a blow, the figure formed by a blow, an impression, a form, a letter, a doctrine, an example, a pattern, a type. *Skia* (from *skēnē*, a tent) means a shade, a sketch, an outline, an adumbration. *Parabolē* means a placing by the side, hence a comparison, a likeness, a similitude. *Eikon* means an image, a figure, a likeness. *Antitypon* means a repelling blow, an echoing, a reflecting, a thing formed after a pattern, a counterpart, an antitype. *Allegoreō* means to tell a truth in terms of a narrative.

These New Testament words referring to the nature of the Old Testament establish the typical character of the Old Testament. In addition to this is the weight of the entire

---

[3] Cf. H. S. Miller, *The Tabernacle*, p. 19 ff.

book of Hebrews, for it is almost completely devoted to a study of the typical character of the Old Testament.[4]

The fact that the Old Testament prophecy includes the typical, the invitation of our Lord to find Him in all the Old Testament which includes the typical, and the vocabulary of the New Testament indicating the typical element of the Old, is adequate justification of the theological study of typology.

B. SCHOOLS OF TYPOLOGICAL INTERPRETATION

In the history of typological exegesis certain schools of interpretation are discovered.[5] As a preparation for a discussion of the rules of typological interpretation we shall briefly note these schools.

(1). One group of interpreters *saw too much as typical.* The motivations of the various subgroups of this family are diverse. The apostolic Fathers and early apologists were apologetically motivated. Part of their proof for the divinity of Christianity was its antiquity, and its antiquity could be demonstrated by a typological interpretation of the Old Testament. Other fathers were motivated to see Greek philosophy taught in the Old Testament (Origen and Clement) and at this point the typological loses itself to the allegorical as Darbyshire observes.[6] Others, following the rules of Philo, sought to obviate supposed difficulties in the literal interpretation of the text. The medievalists and other Catholic theologians realized that typical interpretation of the Old Testament could strengthen the Biblical evidence for many of the Church's doctrines. The Protestant schools of Cocceius and Hutchinson regarded the Old Testament as a larder

---

[4] Note also 1 Cor. 10:6, and 10:11 for the typical character of some Old Testament history. Davidson (*Old Testament Prophecy*) has two excellent chapters on typology (XIII, XIV).

[5] The subject is treated historically in Fairbairn, *The Typology of Scripture*, I, pp. 1–40; and in Darbyshire, "Typology," *Hastings Encyclopedia of Religion and Ethics*, XII, 501 (Part 3, "History of Typology").

[6] *Op. cit.*, 502.

richly stored with New Testament teachings. In the effort to find devotional and edifying truth in all Scripture, and to find Christ veritably in *all* Scripture, some dispensationalists have pressed typological interpretation beyond its proper measure.

Although the motivation of these different subgroups is varied, and their emphases different, and even their procedures divergent, they yet agree to this one point: *the Old Testament is a rich mine of New Testament truth and the spiritual interpreter can dig it out.*

(2). Directly opposite to this group are those *rationalists and critics* who see the entire typological method of interpretation as a case of forced exegesis. These men have broken with the doctrine of special revelation, denied the doctrine of plenary inspiration, and accordingly renounced the supernatural world view of Biblical religion. In that prophecy as prediction is obviously a case of supernatural inspiration, it must be denied in either the form of didactic prediction or typical prediction. Thus to the rationalistic critics there are two types, and hence there can be no typological interpretation. Darbyshire's judgment is that "modern writers of the critical school have unduly ignored the importance of typology."[7] It is really more than this. They have not only ignored it; they have denied it.

(3). Bishop Marsh proposed in his *Lectures on the Criticism and Interpretation of the Bible* his famous principle that a type is a type only if the New Testament specifically so designates it to be such. This is a very strict principle and was advocated to curtail much of the fanciful and imaginary in typological interpretation. Because it is a stern and precise formula it has exerted a great influence on theological thought. Many Protestant exegetes if not adhering to the very letter of Marsh's principle certainly follow it very closely.

(4). Salomon Glassius propounded in his *Philogia Sacra*

(5 vols., 1623–36) that types were of two sorts, *innate* and *inferred*. He has been followed in basic theory by such typologists as Cocceius, Keach, Horne, Fairbairn, and Terry. This school we may designate as the *moderate school.* The moderate school agrees with Marsh that the New Testament is the point of departure in typological studies, but insists that Marsh did not dig out the full teaching of the New Testament on the subject. An *innate* type is a type specifically declared to be such in the New Testament. An *inferred* type is one that, not specifically designated in the New Testament is justified for its existence by the nature of the New Testament materials on typology.

The most able defender of the moderate school has been Fairbairn and he is supported by Terry.[8] Fairbairn's criticisms of Marsh are as follows: (i) The relationship in Marsh's system between type and antitype is too artificial. The Old Testament and New Testament contain the same basic system of theology. They run side by side like two parallel rivers. Their parallelism is indicated by occasional channels (types) which connect them. These channels (types) are possible only because the two rivers run parallel. The Marshian principle fails to realize that other channels may be cut through which are not specifically named in Scripture, otherwise the relationship of the two Testaments is rather mechanical. Terry criticizes this principle when he writes: "But we should guard against the extreme position of some writers who declare that nothing in the Old Testament is to be so regarded as typical but what the New Testament affirms to be so." [9] (ii) In order to escape from the lawless aberrations of other schools the system of Marsh limits itself to too meagre a field. (iii) As we do not wait for the fulfilment of prophecy to declare a passage to be a prophecy, so we do not need the New Testament to declare everything a type that is a type. (iv) The very implication of Hebrews itself is that only a

[8] Terry, *Biblical Hermeneutics* (revised edition), pp. 255–56.
[9] *Ibid.*, p. 248.

fraction of the great parallels between the two Covenants is considered, and that it is left to our Christian maturity to draw the other parallels. (v) If the whole (e.g., the Tabernacle, the wilderness journey) is typical, then the parts are typical. (iv) The avoidance of extravagances in typology is not to be accomplished by narrowing typology mercilessly to a small field, but by establishing typology from an empirical investigation of Scriptures themselves.

At the present time typological interpretation is undergoing a revival. To be sure we still have the rationalists who deny the very existence of types, and to be sure we have extremists.[10] Some scholars would adhere rather closely to Marsh, and more to Fairbairn. But due to the new interest in theology, Biblical theology, and exegesis we have a new interest in typical interpretation. The revival in Old Testament theology has produced a new interest in typological interpretation. It is through the typological interpretation of the Old Testament that these recent scholars preserve the Christian character and value of the Old Testament. It must also be noted that Catholic scholars have been thinking seriously of typological interpretation and they have tried to rescue the study from the excesses to which the Fathers seem to have committed it. This new sober spirit of typological exegesis among Catholics may be noted in such works as *A Catholic Commentary on the Holy Scriptures;* the articles on "Exegesis" and "Hermeneutics" in *The Catholic Encyclopedia* (by A. J. Maas); and in the writings of Dean Daniélou (e.g., *Origen*, Part II, Chapter II, "The Typological Interpretation of the Bible").

C. TYPOLOGICAL AND ALLEGORICAL INTERPRETATION

In the history of interpretation the question has been occasionally asked whether allegorical and typological interpreta-

[10] A very remarkable and blessed work is C. H. M., *Notes on the Pentateuch* (6 vols.). Although filled with much insight and spiritual truth, yet, from the strict hermeneutical standpoint, it abounds in allegorisms and excessive typological interpretations. Its redeeming worth is its emphasis on Christ, grace, salvation, and Christian living.

tion are one method of interpretation mistakenly called by
two different names, or actually two different methods of interpretation.[11] One group insists there is but one method of
spiritual interpretation but that it passes under other names
such as typological, allegorical, or mystical. Jewett's contention is that there is but one such method but that among
evangelicals it is called typological if proper, and allegorical
if improper. Those who insist that the typological and the
allegorical are two different methods of interpretation maintain that the genius of each method is peculiar enough to
separate it from the other.[12]

Although to some theologians the problem might be academic, to others it is vital. A dispensationalist is anxious to
preserve the distinction, for one of his strongest charges
against amillennialism is that it uses the improper method
of allegorizing, yet the dispensationalist must retain the
typological method as valid. The amillennialist finds it to
his advantage to efface the difference. He would assert that
there is a mystical or spiritual sense to Scripture, and such
mystical interpretations are valid if they conform to New
Testament truth and invalid if they do not.[13]

The issue should be settled apart from these vested theological interests, on purely hermeneutical considerations. Is
there a genius peculiar to each of these methods calling for a
valid distinction, or do we have two words describing essen-

[11] Cf. the discussion by Darbyshire, *op. cit.*, p. 500; by Jewett, "Concerning the Allegorical Interpretation of Scripture," *The Westminster
Theological Journal*, 17:1–20; by Torm, *Hermeneutik des Neuen Testaments*, p. 223 f.; by Horne, *Introduction*, I, 364; by Angus and Green,
Cyclopedic Handbook to the Bible, p. 221; by Dana, *Searching the Scriptures*, p. 38; by Meyer, *Critical and Exegetical Handbook to the Epistle
to the Galatians*, p. 201, fn. 7.

[12] Thus the etymology of the two words would indicate their respective genius: "allegory"—one story in terms of another, and "type" an
impression made on a material by the master-copy.

[13] Berkhof actually uses the word *hyponoia* for the mystical sense of
Scripture which is the word used in the classics for allegorical interpretation. (*Principles of Interpretation*, p. 59.) Note this classical use
of *hyponoia* in Geffcken, "Allegory, Allegorical Interpretation," *Hastings Encyclopedia of Religion and Ethics*, I, 328.

tially one method of interpretation? We believe it is possible to find a specific genius for each of these methods calling for their separation.

Allegorical interpretation is the interpretation of a document whereby something *foreign, peculiar,* or *hidden* is introduced into the meaning of the text giving it a proposed deeper or real meaning. Geffcken notes that in allegorical interpretation "an entirely foreign subjective meaning is read into the passage to be explained," [14] and Hoskyns and Davey note that the "allegory expresses the relationship between certain persons and things *by substituting a whole range of persons or things from an entirely different sphere of experience.*" [15]

Typological interpretation is specifically the interpretation of the Old Testament based on the fundamental theological unity of the two Testaments whereby something in the Old shadows, prefigures, adumbrates something in the New. Hence what is interpreted in the Old is not foreign or peculiar or hidden, but rises naturally out of the text due to the relationship of the two Testaments.

To find Christ or the atonement in the sacrificial system, or to find Christian salvation or experience in the Tabernacle follows from the character of the divine revelation. If the problem could be rested at this point, all would be well, but such is not the case. When Philo or Origen or Clement find Platonic philosophy in the Old Testament we might cite this as clearly allegorical interpretation; and when the writer to the Hebrews finds Christ in Old Testament institutions we may cite this as a clear example of typological interpretation. But what sort of interpretation is it when the Fathers find all sorts of adumbrations in the Old Testament with reference to the New? Each piece of wood is discovered to be a reference to the cross, and every pool of water speaks of baptismal regeneration! Here scholars admit that the typical and the

[14] *Op. cit.,* I, 328.
[15] *The Riddle of the New Testament,* p. 127. Italics are ours.

allegorical methods are difficult to differentiate.[16] Should this be called improper typological interpretation, or straight allegorical interpretation?

Jewett's case for the identity of the two methods is based on Wolfson's definition of the allegorical method: "The allegorical method essentially means the interpretation of a text in terms of something else, irrespective of what that something else is." The critical words in this definition are: "in terms of something else." Our impression of Wolfson's treatment of Philo and the allegorical method is that the *something else* means something foreign, secret, hidden, imported—which was the burden of our previous citation of Geffcken. But if typological interpretation rises *naturally out of the text* then it is not an interpretation of *something else* and is therefore a method of interpretation within its own rights. Or as Fairbairn puts it, the typical meaning "is not properly a different or higher sense [as allegorical interpretation demands], but a different or higher application *of the same sense.*" [17]

The history of allegorical interpretation has brought to the surface the emphasis on the hidden, secret, and imported meaning. Further, the list of rules for the detection of an allegory (e.g., Philo and Origen) reveals that an entirely different spirit is at work in allegorical interpretation than in typological interpretation.

Attention to the literature on the subject reveals that many scholars do believe that a genuine distinction obtains between the two methods of interpretation. Dana states that the difference is that the typological method is based on the theological connectedness of the two Testaments, whereas allegorical interpretation is "assigning to Scripture an as-

---

[16] Cf. Darbyshire, *op. cit.*, pp. 500–501. Darbyshire notes that in such instances it is arbitrary whether the interpretation is allegorical or typological. Jewett (*op. cit.*) is able to make one of his strongest points with this problem.

[17] *Op. cit.*, I, 3. Italics are ours.

sumed meaning different from its plain literal meaning, derived deductively from some abstract or philosophical conception. It takes the events and ideas of Scripture as symbols beneath which are concealed profound or hidden meanings." [18]

Darbyshire reviews the attempts to define the two methods apart.[19] Marsh finds the difference that in typology the facts and circumstances of one instance are *representative* of other facts and circumstances; whereas in allegorical interpretation they are emblematic. Mildert indicates that that which makes a type a type is *divine intention* (and presumably there is no divine intention in allegorical interpretation). Wescott notes that typology presupposes a purpose of God being accomplished from age to age so that matters in one age may represent a subsequent age, whereas in allegorical interpretation the imagination of the interpreter supplies the connection between the two levels of meaning.

Torm also discusses this problem and finds a difference between the two. In allegorical interpretation the interpreter finds alongside the literal sense of the text a different and deeper meaning which may even completely exclude the literal meaning. ("Man versteht unter dieser Auslegung, die— auch wenn nach dem Textzusammenhang kein bildische Rede vorliegt—neben dem buchstäblichen Sinne des Textes ober bisweilen auch unter vollständigem Ausschluss deselben eine andere hiervon verschiedene und vermeintlich tiefere Bedeutung findet.")[20] And in speaking directly to the problem of their difference he states that the allegorical meaning goes alongside the literal meaning of the text, and that it is independent of the literal meaning, and may even exclude it; whereas the typological interpretation proceeds directly out of the literal explanation. ("Der Unterschied zwischen der typologischen Auslegung [oder Betrachtungweise] und der

[18] Dana, *Searching the Scriptures*, p. 38.
[19] *Op. cit.*, I, 500–501.
[20] Torm, *op. cit.*, p. 213.

allegorischen ist m. a. W. der: Die allegorische Auslegung geht neben der buchstäblichen Erklärung ihren Weg [ist von ihr unabhängig, ja kann sie sogar auschliessen], während die typologische Auslegung [Betrachtungweise] gerade von der buchstäblichen Erklärung ausgeht.")[21]

It would seem that an investigation of Gal. 4:24 would settle the issue but it does not. The following interpretations have been put on this text: (i) that it is an *illustration* and therefore says nothing in justification of allegorical interpretation; (ii) that it is a page out of rabbinical exegesis and therefore improper and indefensible; (iii) that it is a page out of rabbinical exegesis, to be sure, but it is a proper form of interpretation which the rabbis abused; (iv) that it is an *argumentum ad hominem* and therefore does not constitute a justification for allegorical interpretation; (v) that it is one instance of an inspired allegorical interpretation; Paul definitely makes note that he is departing from usual methods of interpretation, and it therefore constitutes no grounds for allegorical interpretation in general; (vi) that it is an allegorical interpretation and thereby constitutes a justification of the allegorical method; and (vii) that it is in reality a typological interpretation, or similar to one, regardless of the use of the word allegory in the text.

Lightfoot[22] says Paul uses the word *allēgoria* in much the same sense as he uses the word *typos* in 1 Cor. 10:11. Meyer[23] believes that by *allēgoroumena* Paul really means *typikōs legomena*. Findlay claims that "in principle the Pauline allegory does not differ from the type." [24] Lambert[25] thinks that Gal. 4:24 is part of the general typology of the New Testament and thinks that this particular example is a blend-

[21] *Ibid.*, p. 223, fn. 2.
[22] J. B. Lightfoot, *The Epistle of Paul to the Galatians* (first edition), p. 180.
[23] *Op. cit.*, p. 201, fn. 7.
[24] Findlay, *The Epistle to the Galatians*, p. 289. He also speaks of "legitimate" and "illegitimate" allegories.
[25] Lambert, "Type," *Dictionary of the Apostolic Church*, II, 623, 624.

ing of the allegorical and typical. Vincent presses for a distinction of type and allegory while commenting on Gal. 4:24:[26] whereas Robertson does not.[27] Lenski thinks that any connection between Paul's use of the word *allegory* in Gal. 4:24 and what is understood by the expression "allegorical interpretation" is purely verbal and not real. "What Paul presents is akin to type and antitype, but only akin," he writes. "Hence also he does not speak of a type. All types are prophetic; Paul is not presenting prophecy and fulfilment. Paul does not go a step beyond the Scriptural facts; what he does is to point out *the same nature* in both." [28]

An appeal to Gal. 4:24 to settle the issue is inconclusive for it is evident that the expression Paul used is not capable of unequivocal interpretation. Interpreters evidently have settled their minds on the proposed difference or lack of different between the allegorical and typological methods of interpretation on other grounds than Gal. 4:24.

D. NATURE AND INTERPRETATION OF TYPES

The interpretation of a type depends upon the nature of a type. Terry quoting Muenscher defines a type as: "In the science of theology it properly signifies the *preordained representative relation which certain persons, events and institutions*

[26] Vincent, *Word Studies in the New Testament*, IV, 149.

[27] Robertson, *Word Pictures in the New Testament*, IV, 306.

[28] Lenski, *The Interpretation of St. Paul's Epistles to the Galatians* (etc.), p. 237. Italics are his. It is also interesting to note that the outstanding French Biblical scholar, Daniélou thinks there is a difference between typological and allegorical interpretation (*Origen*, pp. 139 and 174). Burton (*A Critical and Exegetical Commentary on the Epistle to the Galatians*) believes that "which things are allegorical utterances" refers to Paul's interpretation of the passage, not to the original meaning intended by the writer of Genesis. He is not sure if the argument is *ad hominem* or if Paul is really giving us an example of spiritual exegesis. Pp. 253–56. Johnson (*The Quotations of the New Testament from the Old*) finds no objection in taking this as an allegory. Paul does not impugn the historicity of the passage. Allegorical interpretation is part and parcel of all great literature and the Biblical allegories are closer to the literary allegories of the classics than the allegories of the Jewish rabbis. P. 118 ff.

of the Old Testament bear to corresponding persons, events, and institutions in the New." [29] Miller's definition is: "Typology is the doctrine of symbols and types; the doctrine that persons and things in the New Testament, especially the person and work of Christ, are symbolized, or prefigured, by persons and things in the Old Testament." [30] Moorehead says that types are "pictures, object lessons, by which God taught His people concerning His Grace and saving power." [31]

By analyzing these definitions the following *elements* of a type are manifest: (i) In a type there must be a *genuine resemblance* in form or idea between the Old Testament reference and the New Testament counterpart. The connection between type and antitype must not be accidental nor superficial but real and substantial. (ii) This resemblance must be *designated*. The problem of designation is the crux of the Marshian principle. In fanciful systems of typology designation springs from the imagination of the interpreter either on arbitrary or superficial grounds. Previously in this work we have defended the principle of Fairbairn that types are *innate* and *inferred*. A type is properly designated when either it is so stated to be one in the New Testament, or wherein the New Testament states a whole as typical (e.g., the Tabernacle, and the Wilderness Wanderings) and it is up to the exegetical ability of the interpreter to determine additional types in the parts of these wholes. (iii) *Dissimilarity* is to be expected. There is no one-to-one correspondence between type and antitype. Great care must be taken to lift out of the Old Testament item precisely that which is typical and

[29] Terry, *op. cit.*, p. 246. Italics are his.
[30] Miller, *The Tabernacle*, p. 15.
[31] Moorehead, "Typology," *The International Standard Bible Encyclopedia*, V, 3029. Ludwig Koehler's definition of a type is: "Typus ist eine Gestalt, eine Begebenheit, ein Zusammenhang, der nicht um seiner selber willen Gewicht und Bedeutung hat, sondern dessen Zweck und Wert darin besteht, dass er eine andere Grösse auch sie eine Gestalt, eine Begebenheit, ein Zusammenhang, andeutet, vorbildet, weissagt." "Christus im Alter und im Neuen Testament," *Theologische Zeitschrift*, 4:252, July–August, 1953.

no more. There are points of pronounced similarity and equally so, points of pronounced dissimilarity between Christ and Aaron or Christ and Moses. The typical truth is at the point of similarity. One of the cardinal errors in typology is to make typical the elements of dissimilarity in a type.

The heart of typology is the similarity between the two Testaments. If the two covenants are made too dissimilar then the justification of typology is either weakened or broken. The Old Testament system is complex and care must be taken in treating it. The New Testament stresses the contrast of law in its legislative elements with the gospel, but sees marked similarities between the gospel and the ceremonial part of the law.

It is also apparent that there is a fundamental harmony between the Old Testament theology and the New ("Novum Testamentum in Vetere latet; Vetus in Novo patet"). It is shown by Paul that the act of faith is the same in both Testaments (Romans 4); that the process of justification is the same (Romans 4:22–24); that the same basic system of sacrifice underlies both Testaments (Hebrews 9, 10); that the life of faith in the Old Testament is the model for the New Testament saints (Hebrews 11); that the doctrine of sin is the same as Paul proves by his catena of Old Testament quotations in Romans 3; that the Messiah of the Old Testament is the Savior in the New (Hebrews 1). It is this profound similarity of the two Testaments which makes predictive prophecy and typology a possibility.

Returning to our central subject we note that *types are prophetic symbols* or as Davidson puts it, "Typology is a species of prophecy." [32] We suggest the following rules of interpretation:

(1). *Note the typology of the New Testament and see how it treats the subject.* This much immediately is apparent: *the New Testament* deals with the great facts of Christ and redemption; with the great moral and spiritual truths of Chris-

[32] A. B. Davidson, *Old Testament Prophecy*, p. 210.

tian experience, when it touches on typology. It does not deal with minutiae, and with incidentals. We should then learn that in typology we should restrict our efforts to major doctrines, central truths, key spiritual lessons and major moral principles. A typology which becomes too fascinated with minutiae is already out of step with the spirit of New Testament typology.

(2). Note that the New Testament specifies the *Tabernacle* with its priesthood and offerings, and the *Wilderness Wanderings* as the two major areas of typical materials. This indicates the wholes which have typical parts. By no means is typology restricted to these areas, but these are the areas where most of the typical material is to be drawn.

It is of course a matter of convention to affirm whether some passages are types or predictions. Is the flood a type of coming judgment or a prediction? Is Jonah a type of Christ or a prediction? Are the children of Isaiah types of believers (Hebrews 2:13)? Or were they analogies of believers? Is the call of Israel out of Egypt a type of Christ, or an analogy of Christ, or a prediction of Christ? (Matt. 2:15).

It should go without saying that if an interpreter proposes a typical interpretation, he should search the New Testament to see if it has any reference at all to the Old Testament passage under consideration. Obviously anything so treated as a type in the New Testament is proper for us to treat likewise.

(3). *Locate in any given type the typical and the accidental.* What is typical must be judged from New Testament considerations and the general hermeneutical skill of the interpreter. Hence a good exegete will restrain his imagination when he discusses the Tabernacle. Much about the Tabernacle has no typical significance and this ought to be clearly apprehended. Not all the actions of the priests, nor all the elements of the sacrifices have precise New Testament counterparts. The interpreter who presses beyond the typical into the accessories of the text, then brings forth what is not there *by designation.*

Temptations to be novel, clever, original or shocking should be resisted. Typology is not always appreciated as it should be because some students of it have gone to extremes and thereby soured the subject to other students. Certainly a teacher of the Bible should not boast of finding more types than other teachers because he is more spiritual than they. To be spiritual minded is not a license to abuse the rules of hermeneutics.

(4). *Do not prove doctrine from types unless there is clear New Testament authority.* Hebrews plainly proves some theological points from typological considerations, but we may not do the same because we are not inspired. Types may be used to *illustrate* New Testament truth. The central rod of the construction of the Tabernacle wall cannot properly be used to prove the unity or security of believers, but it may be used to illustrate the same.

In general a humble spirit should characterize our interpretations of typology. What is clearly taught in the New Testament may be asserted with confidence, but beyond that restraint should be the rule. Typology involves two layers of meaning and this allows for the intrusion of imagination. Therefore we must proceed with care and check the play of our imagination. To do otherwise is to obscure the word of God.

E. Kinds of Types

We may note six kinds of types in Scripture:

(1). *Persons* may be typical. Adam is a type of Christ as the head of a race (Romans 5:14, "who is the figure of him that was to come"). Abraham is the father and type of all who believe by faith. Elijah is the prefigurement of John the Baptist. Joseph is the rejected kinsman, yet future Savior. David is the type of the Great King. Solomon is the type of the Chosen Son. Zerubbabel is the type of the Head of a new society.

(2). *Institutions:* The sacrifices are types of the cross. Creation and the Promised Land are types of salvation rest. The passover prefigures our redemption in Christ. The Old Testament theocracy looks forward to the coming kingdom.

(3). *Offices:* Moses, the prophet, was a type of Christ, as was Aaron the high priest and Melchisedec the priest of the most high God.

(4). *Events:* Paul writes that the things which happened in the Wilderness Wanderings were types for our benefit (1 Cor. 10:6, 11).

(5). *Actions:* The lifting up of the brazen serpent is a type of the crucifixion (John 3:14–16). The ministries of the high priest were typical of the ministries of our Lord.

(6). *Things:* The Tabernacle was a type of the Incarnation —the presence of God with his people. Incense is a type of prayer. The curtains of the Tabernacle express principles of access to God.

F. Symbolism

Properly speaking symbolism is a special study of its own. However, any discussion of typology suggests the study of symbolism. Types differ from symbols in that "while a symbol may represent a thing either past, present, or future, a type is essentially a prefiguring of something future from itself . . . A symbol has in itself no essential reference to time." [33] A type (as previously indicated) is a species of

[33] Terry, *op. cit.*, p. 246. For further studies of symbolism cf. Far-bridge, *Studies in Biblical and Semitic Symbolism;* Wilson, *This Means That;* Pierson, *Knowing the Scriptures* (p. 341 ff.); Harwood, *Handbook of Bible Types and Symbols;* Angus and Green, *Cyclopedic Handbook to the Bible,* p. 221 ff.; Barrows, *Companion to the Bible,* p. 555 ff. All standard Bible dictionaries and encyclopedias contain articles on symbolism. Cf. also the elaborate discussion in Lange, *Revelation* by the American editor, Craven. Pp. 10–41.

prophecy, but a symbol is a timeless figurative representation. A lion as a symbol of strength or of voracious hunger does not predict anything in the future.

Symbolization occurs early in written history and literature, and is deeply rooted in human nature which seeks to represent the abstract by the concrete and pictorial.[34] The presentation of the ideational in pictures and images is also more forceful than mere verbal explication. The Hebrew Scriptures are full of symbols because in addition to these general considerations it is known that the Semitic and Oriental mind of the Hebrews was much more given to symbolism than the Western analytic, philosophical, and scientific mind.

In any symbol there are two elements: (i) the idea which is mental and conceptual, and (ii) the image which represents it. In a given culture these ideas and images are kept close together through the familiarity of constant usage. But when a culture is gone leaving but a segment of its literature it is not always easy to discover the ideas associated with symbols. To interpret the symbolism of a culture when that culture has not left us a convenient handbook to symbols is a difficult task, and for this reason there are some significant gaps in our knowledge of Biblical symbols.

For the interpretation of symbols we suggest the following:

(1). *Those symbols interpreted by the Scriptures are the foundation for all further studies in symbolism.* When the Scripture interprets a symbol then we are on sure ground. These interpretations may be used as *general guides* for all further studies in symbols. Ferocious beasts in the book of Daniel stand for wicked political leaders or nations, and we are not surprised to find them again in the book of Revelation bearing the same general idea. The lamb is a frequent symbol of either sacrifice, or the waywardness of the human heart. The context readily decides which is meant in the passage. Incense stands as a symbol of prayer.

[34] Cf. Farbridge, *op. cit.*, pp. 3–4.

(2). If the symbol is not interpreted we suggest the following:

(i) Investigate the *context* thoroughly. It might be that in what is said before or after, the idea corresponding to the symbol is revealed. (ii) By means of a concordance check other passages which use the same symbol and see if such cross references will give the clue. (iii) Sometimes the nature of the symbol is a clue to its meaning (although the temptation to read the meanings of our culture into these symbols must be resisted). The preservative character of salt is common knowledge, as is the ferocity of lions, the docility of doves, the meekness of lambs, and the filthiness of pigs. (iv) Sometimes comparative studies of Semitic culture[35] reveal the meaning of the symbol. Perchance too in archeological materials the clue will be discovered. If we are not able to turn up any clues to symbols uninterpreted in the text it is wiser to be silent than to speculate.

(3). *Be aware of double imagery in symbols.* There is nothing in the symbolism of the Bible which demands that each symbol have one and only one meaning. This appears to be the presupposition of some works on symbolism, and it is a false presupposition. The lion is at the same time the symbol of Christ ("the Lion of the tribe of Judah") and of Satan (the lion seeking to devour Christians (1 Peter 5:8). The lamb is a symbol of sacrifice and of lost sinners (1 Peter 2:25). Water means "the word" in Ephesians 5:26; the Spirit in 1 Cor. 12:13, and regeneration in Titus 3:5. Oil may mean the Holy Spirit, repentance, or readiness. Further, one entity may be represented by several symbols, e.g., Christ by the lamb, the lion, the branch, and the Holy Spirit by water, oil, wind and the dove.

In general, care and good taste should govern one's interpretation of uninterpreted symbols. An uncritical association of cross references in determining the meaning of symbols may be more harmful than helpful.

[35] Cf. Farbridge, *op. cit.*

There is no question that there is a basic symbolism of numbers in the Bible.[36] A study of the Tabernacle reveals a very even or regular proportion among the various dimensions, and in the articles of furniture themselves. Daniel and Revelation are especially rich in the symbolic use of numbers. Apart from a few basic agreements on some of the numbers, fancy characterizes most studies on the subject.

The parent of all excessive manipulation of Bible numbers is to be found in the Jewish Rabbinical method known as *Gematria*. Examples of such are as follows:[37] The numerical value of the word Branch in Zechariah 3:8 is 138. This has the same value as Consoler in Lam. 1:16 so that it is one of the names of the Messiah. In Genesis 49:10 the Hebrew numerical value of "Shiloh come" is 358, which is in turn equivalent to Meshiach, and so Shiloh is identified with the Messiah. There are never less than 36 righteous in the world because the numerical value of "upon him" of Isaiah 30:18 is 36. Genesis 11:1 says that all the inhabitants of the world were of one language. Both "one" and "holy" equal 409 so Hebrew was the primeval tongue of humanity.

A certain minimum number of judgments may be made on the symbolism of number. For example in the ancient Semitic world *three* stood for "some," a "few," i.e., a small total although in some instances it stood for "many" or "enough." *Four* stood for completeness and was used repeatedly with the diffusion abroad of blessings and cursings. Some have thought *seven* represented the covenant of grace. *Ten* sometimes signifies an indefinite magnitude, and sometimes "perfection." *Forty* represented a generation.

[36] Cf. Farbridge, *op. cit.* (Chapter IV, "Symbolism of Numbers"); Terry, *op. cit.*, pp. 288–98; Chafer, *The Science of Biblical Hermeneutics*, p. 23; Wilson, *op. cit., im passim;* Rogers, *Things That Differ*, p. 23; Harwood, *op. cit., im passim;* Craven, *loc. cit.;* Smith, "Number," *The International Standard Bible Encyclopedia*, IV, 2157–63; Philpott, "Number," *Smith's Bible Dictionary*, III, 2192–94; Zenos, "Numbers, Significance and Symbolic," *A New Standard Bible Dictionary*.

[37] From Farrar, *History of Interpretation*, pp. 98 ff., and 445.

Closely associated with symbolism is the symbolism of metals and colors. In the Tabernacle gold, silver, and brass were used. In Daniel 2 we have another symbolic usage of metals. The gold and silver of the Bible are apparently the same metals we know today, but modern brass is composed of copper and zinc whereas Biblical brass was a combination of copper and tin. It resulted in an alloy almost as hard as steel.

The symbolism of metals has been a matter of considerable debate. P. Fairbairn insists that their only symbolism is in their *value* indicating that God is to be worshipped by our very best. However most writers on symbolism and typology would press for more specific meanings. For example, silver was the universal medium of exchange in Old Testament days and the money for redemption was silver and was called atonement money.[38] Thus silver would stand for redemption.

It is urged that the use of brass in connection with the brazen altar, the blazing feet of Christ (Rev. 1:15), and the brazen serpent lifted up in the wilderness points toward judgment as the symbolic meaning of brass.[39] Gold stands for the highest and holiest ("Pure gold [is] is the light and splendour of God . . . as he dwells in his holy temple").[40]

The acacia wood of the Tabernacle was added to give frame and rigidity to the Tabernacle and its furniture. The wood is hard, close-grained, orange in color with a darker heart, and well-adapted to cabinet making. It is light, fragrant, sheds water, and is not attacked by insects. The Septuagint calls it "wood that does not rot." It was used in the Tabernacle for its lightness, durability, and resistance to insects. Symbolists uniformly identify it with human nature.

The symbolism of colors is far more difficult, for it was not until art was well-established that there was a strict and uniform association of one word with one color. Ancient

[38] Cf. Miller, *The Tabernacle*, p. 52. "The kopher."
[39] *Ibid.*, p. 53 for an excellent discussion.
[40] Terry, *op. cit.*, p. 303.

literature simply does not make the fine color distinctions that are necessary in modern times. For example, the Latin word *purpureous* was used to describe snow, the swan, the foam of the sea, a rose, a beautiful human eye, and purple objects.[41] "Both the Old Testament and the New Testament," writes Pratt, "illustrate the general fact that ancient literature knows little of the modern sensitiveness to color-effects and their subtle gradations." [42]

Blue (Hebrew, *tekeleth*) is a difficult hue to determine. It sometimes means violet or purple. Gesenius derives it from the verb, "to peel, to shell," with reference to a shell-fish from which came a purple blue dye. Bevan advocates violet; [43] Barrows calls it bluish purple.[44] It is apparent that there is some red in the blue of the ancients giving it a violet tinge, but the bluish cast predominated. For practical purposes blue is an adequate translation.

Scarlet (Hebrew, *tola'ath shani*) is derived from the scarlet worm. The Greek and Latin versions mistook the "shani" for the similar word meaning *two*, and so translated it *twice-dipped*.

White (Hebrew, *shesh*) is identical with the word for white linen, and usually stands for holiness or purity or righteousness.

Like metals the symbolism of colors has been a matter of debate. Some interpreters believe that colors represent only such a general notion that a king's presence is indicated by rich tapestry or drapery. Likewise the rich colors of the Tabernacle indicate that it is the dwelling place of God. Others attempt to give the colors specific symbolic meaning. With reference to blue Terry writes that "blue, as the color of heaven, reflected in the sea, would naturally suggest what is heavenly, holy, divine." [45] Delitzsch calls blue "the maj-

[41] *Exodus (The Holy Bible Commentary)*, p. 366.
[42] Pratt, "Colors," *The New Standard Bible Dictionary*, p. 142.
[43] Bevan, "Colors," *Smith Bible Dictionary*, I, 480.
[44] *Sacred Geography and Antiquities*, p. 546.
[45] *Op. cit.*, p. 301.

esty of God in condescension." [46] Purple is usually acknowl-
edged as the color of royalty having been worn by kings,
great officials, officers, the wealthy, and the highest in priestcraft. The meaning of scarlet is more difficult to determine
though most commentators favor sacrifice as its idea. Interpretations vary from associating the word with red-earth and
thus suggesting sacrificial humility to those who take it to
mean a full, free, joyous life. In such a case our interpretations must be tentative.

There is at least one general principle to guide in such
matters of symbolism. Careful investigation must be made
of the meaning of the terms in the original, of their deriva-
tions etymologically or culturally, and a close examination
of their associations to see what the natural symbolism
might be.

BIBLIOGRAPHY

Terry, *Biblical Hermeneutics* (revised edition).

Miller, *The Tabernacle*.

Davidson, *Old Testament Prophecy*.

Fairbairn, *The Typology of Scripture* (2 vols.).

Moorehead, "Typology," *The International Standard Bible Encyclopedia*, V, 3029.

Wilson, *This Means That*.

Pierson, *Knowing the Scriptures*.

Harwood, *Handbook of Bible Types and Symbols*.

Angus and Green, *Cyclopedic Handbook to the Bible*.

Torm, *Das Hermeneutik des Neuen Testaments*.

Darbyshire, "Typology," *Hastings Encyclopedia of Religion and
Ethics*, XII, 501 ff.

[46] Delitzsch, "Colors," *Schaff-Herzog Encyclopedia of Religious Knowledge*, I, 514 (third edition).

Chapter X

THE INTERPRETATION OF PROPHECY

A. Confusion of Terminology

A STUDY of hermeneutical literature pertaining to prophecy reveals that there is no uniformity of meaning with reference to the terms employed. Progress among evangelical scholars in attempting to settle hermeneutical differences can but be greatly hindered as long as this terminological confusion exists. We must first do some spade work and attempt to clear up the confusion that exists at this point.

First, note the ambiguous character of the word *literal*. In what we shall call Meaning A it refers to grammatical or literal exegesis. The expression "the literal meaning of the passage" means the grammatical exegesis of the passage. But if a man states that he believes in a literal kingdom he means to state something about the nature of the kingdom. He means that he accepts an *actual* kingdom. In Meaning B the word literal then means *actual* in contrast to fictional, or abstract, or ephemeral. There is something else implied in Meaning B, and that is that by actual we mean earthly, visible, concrete.[1] If the word did not have this overtone then the amillennialist could claim to believe in a literal (actual or real) kingdom and do so with propriety. Literal exegesis frequently leads to belief in literal (actual, real) entities but this is not a rigid relationship. We may have a

[1] In contemporary philosophical literature *literal* is frequently used to mean "referable to sense data." A concept has a literal meaning when it can be demonstrated that it has sensory rootage or counterparts. Cf. Ayer's *Language, Truth, and Logic* for a repeated use of literal in this sense.

literal exegesis about heavenly or spiritual matters, and conversely, we may have poetic or imaginative descriptions of earthly matters. The great inward world of religion is described by the Psalms in much language capable of literal interpretation, and the millennial kingdom which shall be is set forth by the prophets under many figures of speech, poetic pictures, and ideal visions.

We must then be careful in hermeneutics to note whether a writer is using literal in the sense of Meaning A or Meaning B, and we must further keep in mind that although literal exegesis may lead to belief in the existence of actual entities, nevertheless spiritual matters may be literally exegeted and earthly affairs may be described in figurative and poetic language.

Much more ambiguity surrounds the word *spiritual*. In Meaning A spiritual may mean something about piety, morality, or spirituality. In this sense the premillenarians certainly believe that the kingdom of God is spiritual. They do not think for a minute it is secular. In Meaning B spiritual may refer to a mode of interpretation. The spiritual interpretation of the Old Testament would refer to a method of discovering another meaning in addition to the literal one. But there are different versions of the spiritual interpretation of the Bible.

Let us call the Catholic method Meaning C. Catholic scholars use the expression "spiritual interpretation" to mean the methods of discovering the deeper meanings of Scripture which go beyond the literal meaning. The spiritual interpretation of the Bible is subdivided by them into the *allegorical* (by which is meant typological interpretation); the *tropological* (the application of the Bible to moral and spiritual life); and the *anagogical* (which deals with the manner in which the Church on earth prefigures the Church in glory).

In Meaning D spiritual interpretation is employed by Protestant scholars to indicate the method of discovering New Testament truth in the Old Testament. It thus means the combined study of prophecy and typology. Meaning D among these scholars corresponds to what Catholic hermeneutics calls allegorical interpretation, incidentally adding to the terminological confusion.

In Meaning E spiritual interpretation means to refine to ideas or principles, or to read into the document extraneous ideas. Examples of this sort of spiritualizing would be such as finding Greek philosophy in Moses, or taking the Tabernacle as a diagram of the soul, or calling Abraham *faith* or Joseph *virtue*. This is the sort of spiritual interpretation carried on among mystics, metaphysical cults, Christian Science, and the like.

A word as ambiguous as *spiritual* must be used with care and with a sense of fair play. For example, it is not unusual to find a strict literalist putting some interpreters in Meaning E to embarrass them whereas in truth they belong to Meaning D.

Further involved in this terminological hodge-podge are the words *mystical, allegorical,* and *typological.* Many scholars use the expression mystical interpretation as synonymous with spiritual Meaning D (i.e., the study of the types and prophecies of the Old Testament which refer to the New). Further these scholars may use the word mystical in one line and allegorical in the next for they consider the terms as equivalent.

To some allegorical interpretation (Meaning A) refers to the sort of speculation found among many of the Fathers and equivalent to spiritual Meaning E. To others (Meaning B) allegorical interpretation is the same as spiritual Meaning D, and still others (Meaning C) the term is equivalent to typological exegesis. Here again the expression "allegorical interpretation" must be used with care. For example some ardent literalists accuse their fellow exegetes as being allegorists with the definite slurring implication of following Meaning A, whereas these exegetes may actually state in µ.int that they renounce Meaning A² and follow Meaning B.

Finally, in *typological* interpretation we have two meanings. Meaning A refers to what is specifically denoted as the study of types, and Meaning B denotes the general prophetic and typological interpretation of the Old Testament and is equivalent to spiritual Meaning D.

We may summarize our discussion as follows:

Literal Meaning A—grammatical exegesis.

Literal Meaning B—the assertion that the words used have actual or real or earthly referents.

Spiritual Meaning A—piety, spirituality, religious.

Spiritual Meaning B—any meaning of a document beyond the literal meaning.

Spiritual Meaning C—Catholic division of the spiritual meaning of Scripture into allegorical, tropological, and anagogical.

Spiritual Meaning D—the prophetic and typological interpretation of the Old Testament finding in the Old the New Testament realities.

Spiritual Meaning E—either thinning meanings out to ideas or principles, or the importation of strange and foreign meanings to a passage.

Mystical Meaning—generally equivalent to spiritual Meaning D.

Allegorical Meaning A—importation of strange meanings to scripture equivalent to spiritual Meaning E.

Allegorical Meaning B—equivalent to Spiritual Meaning D.

Allegorical Meaning C—equivalent to typological exegesis.

Typological Meaning A—typology in strict sense.

Typological Meaning B—equivalent to spiritual Meaning D.

Much misunderstanding and misrepresentation among evangelical interpreters would be eliminated if some sort of

² We shall illustrate this later.

code of well-defined meanings of words could be followed, but until then the terminological confusion will continue to abet the hermeneutical differences.

The issue among evangelical interpreters is not over the general validity of grammatical or literal exegesis. For most of the didactic parts of the Old Testament, and practically the complete New Testament there is agreement that we follow the grammatical method. In fundamental theory there is no difference between Berkhof's *Principles of Biblical Hermeneutics* (amillennial) and Chafer's *The Science of Biblical Hermeneutics* (dispensational). Both agree that the grammatical, historical method is basic to understanding the Bible.

Nor is the issue one of the figurative or non-figurative language of the prophets. The literalist in prophetic interpretation admits the presence of poetic and figurative elements, and the amillennialists who think they deny this are wrong. Some amillennialists think that the figurative and poetic elements weaken the case of the literalists, but their difference from the literalist at this point is not as great as they imagine.

If we may provisionally define the spiritual as the non-literal method of the exegesis of the Old Testament we may further state that the issue is not between a completely literal or a completely spiritual system of interpretation. Amillennial writers admit that many prophecies have been literally fulfilled, and literalists admit a spiritual element to Old Testament interpretation when they find a moral application in a passage, when they find a typical meaning, or when they find a deeper meaning (such as finding Satan and his career in Isaiah 14 and Ezekiel 28 with reference to the kings of Babylon and Tyre). Nobody is a strict literalist or a complete spiritualist.

Further, some Old Testament passages present *idealized* pictures. For example, in Zechariah 14 Jerusalem is exalted to the top of a mountain, the surrounding mountainous country is made a plain, and two great rivers pour out of Jerusalem one going east and the other west. A strict literal interpretation of this passage fails to catch the spirit and vision of it. And indeed a very strict literalism would also call for a recreation of iron age culture and iron age peoples of that ancient world. One way of escape from this return to the iron age is to insist that the items mentioned are real,' but they will appear in their modern counterparts at the time of the millennium. Prophecies involving horses or chariots or camels are dealing with *transportation;* prophecies speaking of spears and shields are about *armaments;* and prophecies about surrounding nations are about *God's enemies.* A strict literalism would hardly be appropriate in such matters and Davidson says that to call for the complete restoration of all these ancient peoples on the basis of strict literal interpretation *"may not unjustly be called the insanity of literalism."* [3]

The real issue in prophetic interpretation among evangelicals is this: *can prophetic literature be interpreted by the general method of grammatical exegesis, or is some special principle necessary?*

B. Principles for the Interpretation of Prophecy

There can be no question that Girdlestone's judgment that "there is no royal road to the scientific study of prophecy" is correct.[4] Many royal roads have been advocated but none has been so obvious as to compel the total assent of interested scholars. We have not lacked for advocates of various royal roads and this has led to the hopeless division of evangelical Christianity in prophetic and eschatological matters.

There are two reasons why there is no royal road to prophetic interpretation (and thereby accounting for such wide divergences of prophetic interpretation). First, the prophetic language itself partakes of a measure of ambiguity. It is

[3] Davidson, *Old Testament Prophecy*, p. 476. Italics are ours.
[4] *The Grammar of Prophecy*, p. 104.

visionary in that it is speaking of the future and painting it in word pictures. We are not in the position in most instances to compare the picture painted by the prophet and the fulfilment of it. If we could the ambiguity of the passage would drop away, but in that we cannot it remains. The richness of the Christological elements in Psalm 22 and Isaiah 53 are noticed by Christians because they read these passages in the light of the historical existence of Jesus Christ. We should not be surprised if these passages are puzzling to Jewish scholars who do not share this insight. If the language of prophecy were unambiguous the differences among interpreters could be assigned to the superior intelligence of one group and the inferior intelligence of another. But the source of this ambiguity is not in the interpreters but in the visionary character of a record which is speaking of future historical events.

The second reason why interpreters differ so widely is the extent of the prophetic Scriptures. The prophetic material of Scripture is to be found from Genesis to Revelation. To assemble each passage, to thoroughly digest its meaning, to arrange the passages in a prophetic harmony, would involve a prodigious memory, years of exacting work, a masterful knowledge of Biblical languages, an exhaustive reading of prophetic literature, a keen exegetical sense, a thorough knowledge of the histories of many peoples and a knowledge of all relevant archaeological materials. And yet some claim that prophetic Scripture is as easy to interpret as the prose passages of the New Testament! With such a great body of Scripture to keep in focus all at once, with its inherent complexity, and with the requisite learning to interpret it, it is not surprising that there is such a variety of schools of prophetic interpretation.

(1). *Fundamentals in the interpretation of any passage of prophetic Scripture.* Regardless of our millennial views (the *crux interpretum* of prophetic interpretation) certain principles must be followed by all exegetes of the prophetic Word.

(i) We must, to begin with, *give careful attention to the language of the prophetic passage*. We must determine the meaning and significance of all proper names, events, references to geography, references to customs, references to material culture, references to flora and fauna, and references to climate.

A proper noun whose meaning or significance is not known stands enigmatical in the text. For example in Hosea 11 these nouns occur: Israel, Egypt, Ephraim, Assyrian, Admah, Zeboim, and in Isaiah 21 we find: Elam, Media, Babylon, Dumah, Seir, Arabia, Dedanim, and Kedar. We must not presume we know the meaning of a term because it is familiar. The word Arabia, by way of illustration, is used in Scripture to indicate different territories than the word signifies to us. The meaning of proper nouns may be ascertained by referring to Bible dictionaries, Bible encyclopedias, or commentaries.

In Daniel 11 numerous historical events are referred to and no interpretation of this chapter is adequate which is not familiar with the necessary historical information. Joel mentions the locust, canker-worm and the caterpillar and the careful interpreter will acquaint himself with requisite information about these matters of natural life. A knowledge of the history of Jerusalem and Edom is necessary to properly interpret Obadiah 10–14, and we need to understand some of the geography of Jerusalem's environs to understand the reference to the *crossway* (v. 14).

With further regard to the language of a prophetic passage the interpreter should note the *figurative, poetic*, and *symbolic* elements. We do not debate here the issue between the amillennialists (who claim dispensationalists underplay the significance of the figurative elements in prophecy) and the dispensationalists. We refer to matters which *all* interpreters must recognize. Figures of speech recur repeatedly in the prophets and the Psalms. Certainly much of the prophetic literature is poetic, and none can deny the numerous symbolic passages in Daniel, Ezekiel, and Zechariah. It was a convinced premillennialist who wrote:

That which makes the language of prophecy so vivid and yet so difficult is that it is always more or less figurative. It is poetry rather than prose. It abounds in peculiar words and expressions which are not usually to be found in prose writings of the same date. It is rich with allusions to contemporary life and to past history, some of which are decidedly obscure. The actions recorded in it are sometimes symbolical, sometimes typical. The present, the past, and the future, the declaratory and the predictive, are all combined and fused into one. The course of individuals, the rise and fall of nations, the prospects of the world at large, are all rapidly portrayed in realistic language.[5]

Girdlestone buttresses this by making a Scriptural study showing the different meanings of such terms as: earth, earthquake, sea and river, sand, stars of heaven, the darkening of the sun and moon, and the falling of stars. Sometimes the prophets use these terms literally and sometimes figuratively. Whether the usage in a given passage is literal or figurative must be a matter of careful attention.

Further, as Girdlestone[6] explains, *much of the prophetic description of the future is in the language of past, historical events.* The new creation is the analogue of original creation; the blessedness to come is in terms of paradise past; future judgment is likened to the flood of the past; destructive judgment finds its type in the destruction of Sodom and Gomorrah; great deliverance is paralleled after the deliverance of the exodus. Girdlestone notes that besides past events being used as forms for future events, past persons and past natural events are used as forms for future persons and future events.

The strict literalist would *ex hypothesi* have to call for not only the restitution of Israel, but all the nations which surrounded Israel. The going is rough, no doubt, and one of the ways out suggested by Girdlestone is to make these ancient enemies representative of Israel's future enemies.

(ii). *We must determine the historical background of the*

---

[5] Girdlestone, *op. cit.*, p. 48.
[6] *Ibid.*, Chapter IX.

prophet and the prophecy. This establishes the universe of discourse in which the prophet writes. Much of Isaiah is illuminated by a knowledge of the political maneuvers in Israel and among the surrounding nations. A knowledge of the captivities is indispensable for the interpretation of Jeremiah and Ezekiel. To understand Obadiah the history of Edom must be studied and to know Jonah properly a history of Syria must be examined. The so-called automobile prophecy of Nahum 2:4 is not defensible because a study of the prophecy and its historical background reveals that the prophecy alluded to has been fulfilled in ancient times.

Habakkuk 1:5 ff. has been interpreted as a dispersion of the Jews ("behold ye among the nations"), yet if the historical situation is carefully recovered it will be discovered that no such interpretation is possible. The prophet is complaining of the sin and evil unpunished in Israel. God tells the prophet that the wicked will be punished. He invites the prophet to look among the nations. What the prophet beholds among the nations is not Israel in dispersion, but the *avenger* of the ungodly in Israel—the Chaldeans ("For, lo, I raise up the Chaldeans"). The one thing which Israel could not bring himself to believe was that God would ever use a Gentile nation for his punishment. Yet God did precisely this very thing, and so it parallels that day when God shall save the Gentile to the bewilderment of Israel (Acts 13:37 ff.).

If all the examples were given to prove the importance of a thorough study of the prophet's background almost the entire body of prophetic literature would have to be cited. The importance of this principle cannot be underestimated especially when it is a frequent charge that premillennialism too easily passes by historical considerations.[7]

A further observation is that although history is necessary to understand the prophet, and that some historical event occasioned the giving of the prophecy, prophecy is not to be

[7] Cf. the strong words against premillennialism with reference to this spoken by Berry (*Premillennialism and Old Testament Prediction*, p. 8).

limited by purely historical considerations. Radical criticism has tried to eviscerate the supernatural character of prophesy by means of historical interpretation.[8]

(iii). Although it is a principle of general hermeneutics it needs to be reëmphasized here that *diligent attention must be paid to the context and flow of the discussion in the interpretation of prophecy*. Chapter and verse divisions are man-made and frequently arbitrary and misleading. The interpreter will look beyond these divisions and discover the natural divisions and connections of the Scripture. For example, to understand Malachi 3:1 properly the interpreter must go back at least to 2:17 to pick up the proper context, and the context necessary to understand Malachi 4 is deep in chapter 3.

(iv). *The interpreter must be mindful of the nonsystematic character of prophetic writings.* The prophets were preachers and visionaries and not academic lecturers. Prophetic writings are not organized like lecture notes but bear a peculiar impress. The prophets are not systematic in their presentation of sequences. The future may appear present, or nearby, or indefinitely remote. Widely separated events on the actual calendar of history may appear together in the prophetic sequence. The Jewish scholars unable to decipher pictures of Messianic suffering and Messianic glory were not properly prepared for the advent of humiliation of our Lord. Only in the pages of the New Testament are these two pictures properly related in terms of *two* advents of the Messiah (cf. 1 Peter 1:10–12 and Hebrews 9:28).

(v). *Every interpreter of prophetic Scripture should search the entire body of prophetic Scripture to find what passages parallel each other.* Such concepts as the day of the Lord, the remnant, the shaking of the nations, the outpouring of the Spirit, the regathering of Israel, and the millennial blessings occur repeatedly in the prophetic writings. Similar images

---

[8] A good statement in this regard is made by Wace (*Prophecy: Jewish and Christian*, p. 144 ff.). Fairbairn said that "History is the *occasion* of prophecy, but not its *measure*." (*Prophecy*, p. 40, italics are his.)

and symbols also occur. All of this must be reckoned with carefully and intelligently in the interpretation of prophecy.

(2). *The interpreter must determine the distinct essence of the passage of prophetic Scripture.* The essence or genius of a passage means its very nature, its innermost characteristic.

(i). The interpreter must determine whether the passage is *predictive* or *didactic*. Not all prophecy is foretelling the future. It is necessary to determine whether the passage is predictive or if it deals with moral, ethical, or theological truth. The opening verses of Zechariah (1:1–6) are didactic but the following vision is prophetic (1:7–21). Most of Zechariah 7 is didactic but the preceding and following materials are prophetic.

(ii). The interpreter must determine whether the passage is *conditional* or *unconditional*.[9] The Scriptures may or may not state if the passage is conditional.[10] The great promises of a Saviour and his salvation are certainly unconditional. On the other hand it is not difficult to suggest some conditional prophecies (Jer. 18:8, 10 and 26:12–13 and 3:12. Jonah 3:4. Ezekiel 33:13–15 and 18:30–32). Another class of passages is that which sets forth two possible destinies of which only one can be realized, such as the curses and blessings of Deut. 28.

The statement of Girdlestone is a remarkably strong one: "It is probable that hundreds of prophecies, which look absolute as we read them were not fulfilled in their completeness because the words of warning from the prophet produced some result, even though slight and temporary, on the hearts of the hearers. God does not quench the smoking flax."[11]

(iii). If the passage is prophetic determine further if it is

[9] An excellent treatment of the subject is Girdlestone's (*op. cit.*, chapter IV).

[10] "A prophet may set down a prophecy in his book without indicating whether it was fulfilled or set aside." Sutcliffe, "Prophetical Literature," *A Catholic Commentary on the Holy Scripture*, p. 536. Cf. also Girdlestone, *op. cit.*, p. 25, and Fairbairn, *op. cit.*, Chapter IV.

[11] *Op. cit.*, p. 28.

fulfilled or *unfulfilled*. A prophecy that is conditional and unfulfilled is at the end of the line, so to speak. The interpreter must search the New Testament to see whether the passage is cited there as fulfilled. If the passage is cited in the New Testament then a careful study must be made of both the Old and New Testament passages. It may turn out that the prophecy was made in the Old Testament and fulfilled in Old Testament times such as the prophecy of Genesis 15 fulfilled in the latter chapters of Genesis and the book of Exodus or the captivity-restoration prophecies of Isaiah and Jeremiah as fulfilled in the books of Daniel, Ezra and Nehemiah.

This problem pushes us to the next major consideration, namely, (3) *the problem of fulfilment in prophecy*. If the prophecy is fulfilled (i) then a study of the text with the historical materials which contains the fulfilment must be made. Most students will not have such materials available and must rely on good commentaries to supply it. From a study of fulfilled prophecy we gain some valuable insights. We have already noted that in the prophetic language things which are widely separated in time appear close together, and that orders of events are somewhat obscure. Fulfilment of prophecy brings these matters to the surface. But most important is that the fulfilled prophecies indicate how careful we must proceed from the prophecy to its *manner* of fulfilment. Sometimes the prophecy is very obviously fulfilled as was the case with Elijah's prediction of a drought (1 Kings 17:1) or his prediction of Ahab's death (1 Kings 21:17 ff.). Other times the prophecy is very cryptic (e.g., Gen. 3:15) or symbolic (Zech. 5:5–11). Interpreters should be cautious in the interpretations proposed for unfulfilled prophecy, for these examples demonstrate that in some instances little can be gained about the manner of fulfilment from the prophecy itself.

(ii). If the prophecy is *unfulfilled* we must take the lesson gleaned from the previous point—proceed with caution. The essence of the prophecy must be ascertained. Is it about

Israel? or Judah? or the Messiah? or the inter-Biblical events?

Determine whether the prophecy is expected to be fulfilled before or after the advent of Christ. Some of the restoration prophecies certainly refer to the return of the Jewish people from Babylon and not to some future period. If the prophecy is pre-Christian, then pre-Christian history must be searched for materials of its fulfilment. If it is apparently to be fulfilled after the first Advent of Christ then we must proceed on considerations we shall subsequently discuss.

Determine what is local, temporal, cultural in the prophecy and what is its fundamental idea awaiting fulfilment. Not every detail of Psalm 22 is about the Messiah, and some scholars have asserted that not all the particulars of Isaiah 53 are about Christ. In the famous prophecy of 2 Samuel 7 where Christ is prefigured in terms of Solomon, the expression "if he commit iniquity" cannot refer to Christ. In Isaiah 7:14–15 Christ is immediately in the foreground, but verse 16 ("for before the child shall know how to refuse evil, and choose the good, the land that thou abhorest will be forsaken of both her kings") is a local reference. In Psalm 16 David's sweet meditation does not become Messianic until verse 8.

(iii). There is the possibility of *multiple fulfilment*. There is a difference between "multiple sense" and "multiple fulfilment." [12] Misunderstanding has arisen due to the failure to distinguish double sense from double fulfilment. Beecher speaks of *generic prophecy* which he defines as "one which regards an event as occurring in a series of parts separated by intervals, and expresses itself in language that may apply indifferently to the nearest part, or to the remoter parts, or to the whole—in other words a prediction which, in applying to the whole of a complex of event, also applies to some of the parts." [13] To be sure, Beecher affirms, if the Scriptures had many meanings interpretation would be equivocal, but

---

[12] Cf. Beecher, *The Prophets and the Promises*, p. 129 ff., and Johnson, *The Quotations of the New Testament from the Old*, p. 197 and 231 ff.

[13] Beecher, *op. cit.*, p. 130.

manifold fulfilment of a generic prophecy preserves the one sense of Scripture. Both promises and threats work themselves out over a period of time and therefore may pass through several fulfilments. Or one may view the same event from more than one perspective. The destruction of Jerusalem is prophesied by our Lord and through it we have a perspective through which to envision the end of the world.

Johnson has an extended discussion of *double reference*. Double reference is characteristic of all great literature, and the Bible being great literature contains it. Hence deeply buried in the events, persons, and words of the Old Testament are references to events, persons, and words of the New Testament. An Old Testament prophecy may find a fulfilment in a pre-Christian event and later in the Christian period, such as the astonishment of the Jews (Habakkuk 1:5–6), which was fulfilled in the Old Testament with the destructive armies of the Chaldeans and in the New Testament with the salvation of the Gentiles.

The presupposition, and a valid one certainly, that the Old is profoundly typical of the New intrudes itself all the way through Johnson's excellent discussion. This is somewhat similar to what Catholics call *compenetration*.[14] In an Old Testament passage the near meaning and the remote meaning for the New Testament so *compenetrate* that the passage at the same time and in the same words refers to the near and the remote New Testament meaning.

(3). The interpreter should take *the literal meaning of a prophetic passage as his limiting or controlling guide*. How else can he proceed? This is the footing for the interpretation of any passage of Scripture. Davidson makes this point with great force and although he later adds a qualification he insists that prophetic interpretation commence with literal interpretation. To the Jew Zion meant Zion and Canaan Canaan. "This I consider the first principle in prophetic interpretation," writes Davidson, "to assume that the literal

[14] Sutcliffe, *op. cit.*, p. 537.

meaning is *his* meaning—that he is moving among realities, not symbols, among concrete things like people, not among abstractions like *our* Church, world, etc." [15] Davidson treats with a measure of scorn those interpreters who blithely make Zion or Jerusalem the Church, and the Canaanite the enemy of the Church, and the land the promises to the Church, etc., as if the prophet moved in a world of symbols and abstractions.[16]

But Davidson is just as much opposed to a forced literalism. He objects to the millennial restitution of the Old Testament worship system, and to press for the restoration of Israel's ancient enemies is the insanity of literalism.[17]

The balance in prophetic interpretation is not easy to attain. The strict literalist attempts to embarrass the "spiritualizer" by asking him how he stops spiritualizing once he starts. Bales puts the shoe on the other foot and asks how the literalist stops "literalizing" once he gets started (i.e., the literalist does not plow through all figures of speech and symbols with a mechanical, literal exegesis). Further, Bales argues, in that the literalist also accepts Biblical symbolism and typology he must state how he limits his symbolic and typological interpretation. If the literalist states that it is the nature of the passage with the attendant considerations

[15] *Old Testament Prophecy*, p. 168. Italics are his.

[16] Cf., "Certainly the extreme anti-literal interpretation which considers the names Zion, Jerusalem, Israel, and the like to be mere names for the Christian Church, without reference to the people of Israel, does no justice either to the spirit of the Old Testament and its principle, or to the principles on which the apostle reasons." *Ibid.*, p. 490. The essay of Neale and Littledale (*A Commentary on the Psalms*, Vol. I, Dissertation III, "On the Mystical and Literal Interpretation of Scripture," pp. 426–470) is a perfect illustration of this sort of exegesis Davidson refers to, and also constitutes a very stout defense of the traditional mystical system of interpretation. For a more recent defense of mystical interpretation see Darwell Stone, "The Mystical Interpretation of the Old Testament," *A New Commentary on Holy Scripture*, pp. 688–697.

[17] Insufficient attention has been payed to the *idealized pictures* in the Old Testament which are not properly interpreted either by a strict literalism or a vapid spiritualizing.

which tells him when to stop "literalizing" or to limit symbolic and typological interpretation, then Bales replies these are the considerations which guide the spiritualizer.[18]

If one maintained a strict literalism he would require that David sit on the millennial throne and not Christ, yet most literalists would say at this point that David is a type of Christ. However, in so doing, his literalism is modulated and all we are arguing at this point is that literalism requires a measure of modulation.

The measure to which literal interpretation is to be followed in Old Testament interpretation is directly related to the problem of the restoration of Israel. Davidson lists four opinions in this regard: (i) those who assert that God's dealings in Christianity are completely personal so a restored national Israel is unthinkable; (ii) those who believe in Israel's conversion but not restoration; (iii) those who believe in a conversion and restoration but with no special prominence for Israel; and (iv) those who believe in a conversion of Israel, a restoration of Israel, and the millennial preëminence of Israel.[19] Mention should be made too of the almost dramatic record that we have of Fairbairn. As a young man he defended the conversion and restoration of national Israel with great ability and persuasiveness; and then as a mature scholar he takes a non-chiliast view of the problem and denies the restoration of Israel.[20]

In general, the premillennialists concur with Girdlestone when he says that: "Israel has a great future is clear from Scripture as a whole. There is a large unfulfilled element in the Old Testament which demands it, unless we spiritualize it away or relinquish it as Oriental hyperbole." [21] A literal

[18] Bales, *New Testament Interpretations of Old Testament Prophecies of the Kingdom*, p. 21.

[19] *Op. cit.*, Chapter XXIV, "The Restoration of the Jews."

[20] These two essays are contained in one volume with their story entitled *Fairbairn versus Fairbairn*.

[21] *Op. cit.*, p. 138.

interpretation calls for the fulfillment of many Old Testament passages in a future millennial age.

The premillenarians are not all in one camp, being divided into the dispensational premillenarians and the non-dispensational premillenarians. The former are insistent that the promises made to Israel be fulfilled in Israel; and the latter build their doctrine of the millennium on the progression of the kingdom of God through several stages including an earthly, glorious manifestation as the prelude to eternity. They would approve a measure of sentiment in the words of Frost:

> We are a generation of Christians who have learned the dangers of 'liberal protestantism' [whose entire eschatology was that we die and go to heaven]. What he [the liberal protestant] is to make of this world—both literally and figuratively—he does not know. In this situation, I venture to suggest that perhaps millenarianism which also finds a place in Revelation, was too readily scorned by the Alexandrians and evaded by Augustine. There are values attaching—in so sacramental and incarnational religion as Christianity—to the material and the temporal which must be conserved for the Age to come; it may be that a return to the entire eschatology of the Bible, that is, the eschatological 'form' which we have called the 'double-eschaton,' would provide a means whereby the preservation of those values could be presented to our minds.[22]

Hermeneutically the premillenarians are then divided between the strict and the moderate literalists.

The postmillenarians are convinced of the spread of the Christian Church by the power of the Spirit until it brings the millennial conditions upon the earth. Some postmillenarians accept the conversion of Israel and some do not. Among those who accept the conversion of Israel some accept the

[22] *Old Testament Apocalyptic*, p. 246. Note also Quistorp's sharp criticism against Calvin because Calvin failed to understand the eschatological character of the millennium of Rev. 20, and did not therefore fit it into the necessary events by which time is ended and eternity commenced. *Calvin's Doctrine of the Last Things*, pp. 161–162.

238 PROTESTANT BIBLICAL INTERPRETATION

national restoration and some do not. But a measure of literalism pervades postmillennial hermeneutics. To be sure some of the promises made to Israel are transferred to the Church and thereby postmillennialists cross with the dispensationalists, but yet the promises are interpreted as fulfilled here on the earth.[23]

The amillenarians believe that the prophecies made to Israel are fulfilled in the church. If these prophecies are so fulfilled no millennium on earth is necessary. The hermeneutical method of the amillennialists (by which they accomplish this claim) is variously called allegorical, mystical, or spiritual.

It must be strongly reiterated here that amillenarians are just as strong in rejecting baseless allegorical speculations as are the ardent literalists. Wyngaarden rejects it as the work of man. Acceptable "spiritualization" is the interpretation of a passage in which the interpreter finds a broadened or figurative or typical meaning *given to it by the Holy Spirit*.[24] To accuse the amillenarians of being allegorists and implying that their allegorizations are of the same species as that of Philo or Origen is simply not being accurate with or fair to the amillenarians. In speaking of the hermeneutics of amillennialism Chafer wrote: "In sheer fantastical imagination this method surpasses Russellism, Eddyism, and Seventh Day Adventism since the plain, grammatical meaning of the language is abandoned, and simple terms are diverted in their course and end in anything the interpreter wishes." [25]

[23] To equate the postmillennialism of godly, devout, Bible-believing men with the kingdom speculations of religious liberalism is (to say the very least) tragic and lamentable.

[24] Wyngaarden, *The Future of the Kingdom in Prophecy and Fulfilment*, pp. 85–86. This could be extensively documented in hermeneutical literature.

[25] *Systematic Theology*, IV, 281–282. A similar comment with reference to postmillennialism is made by Blackstone: "Why! the same process of *spiritualizing* away the literal sense of these plain texts of Scripture will sap the foundation of every Christian doctrine and leave us to drift into absolute infidelity, or the vagaries of Swedenborgianism." *Jesus is Coming*, p. 22.

Equally contestable is the frequent allegation that the amillenarians are Romish. This allegation must be made with a weather eye to the counter-charge. Are there not millennial cults? Millerism? Seventh Day Adventism? Millennial Dawnism? British Israelism? If similarity of the millennial doctrine of premillennialism with some millennial cults does not constitute a refutation of premillennialism, neither does similarity with Catholic doctrine refute amillennialism. It is true that Augustine marks a definite shift in eschatological thought. Augustine (and Calvin after him)[26] made the kingdom of God the spiritual rule of Christ in the church. It was, however, a subsequent development which identified the visible Roman Catholic Church with the kingdom of God. The Romish doctrine is that the visible Catholic Church is the kingdom of God. This to our knowledge was not the claim of Augustine.[27]

However, it is also to be most certainly noted that it is not unusual for the amillenarians to misrepresent both dispensationalism and premillennialism. Feinberg has caught them with their foot considerably off base at more than one point.[28]

If it be granted that the literal interpretation is the point of departure for prophetic interpretation the question to be asked is: *does the Old Testament prophetic Scripture admit of any additional principle besides the strict, literal principle?* Such a principle would of necessity exclude the sort of exegesis characteristic of Philo, Patristic allegorizing and Christian Science spiritualizing. It must also exclude that sort of fanciful typological exegesis which can find New Testament truth in the Old Testament anywhere it wishes. Is there, then, an *expanded typological principle* employed in Old

[26] Calvin calls Ezekiel's temple "the spiritual kingdom of Christ" (*Institutes*, IV, 20, 13). The same term is used in IV, 20, 12. He also speaks of the "spiritual and internal reign of Christ" (IV, 20, 21).

[27] Robertson, *Regnum Dei*, Lectures **V** and VI.

[28] Feinberg, *Premillennialism or Amillennialism?* This material will be found in the appendix to the second edition which is really a treatise in itself containing a rebuttal of the amillennial and anti-dispensational literature which appeared since his first edition.

Testament prophetic exegesis? The answer to this must be that there is.

(i). The conviction of the early Church was that the Old Testament was a Christian book. It recognized its inspiration no doubt. But a sheer appeal to the inspiration of the Old Testament without the profound conviction that it was a Christian book would not have made its case. The heresy of Marcion—that the Old Testament was not a Christian book—has been vigorously contested in the Christian Church wherever and whenever it has appeared and in whatever form it has appeared. The entire Patristic period is uniform in its testimony that the Old Testament belongs to the Church because it is a Christian book.

There is absolutely no doubt that this conviction stemmed from the manner in which our Lord and his apostles used the Old Testament. Our Lord said that the Old Testament was his witness (John 5:39), and that he fulfilled it (Matt. 5:17, Luke 4:21). Paul found Christ in many places in the Old Testament; he found justification by faith; he found moral instruction for Christians. The Christian Church has concurred with Vischer's verdict that "The Christian Church stands and falls with the recognition of the unity of the two Testaments." [29] Without too much sense of guidance, and without too much understanding of principles of hermeneutics, the Fathers found Christianity and its doctrines in the Old Testament by improper methods. But regardless of their hermeneutical ineptitude we must recognize their inspiration, namely, *that they were seeking the Christian faith in what they deemed to be a Christian book.* In short, an expanded typological interpretation (to distinguish it from typology proper) was characteristic of the interpretations of the Old Testament by our Lord, by his apostles, and by the early Church although in the latter it suffered from malpractice.

Such typological exegesis (as previously defined) is no return to Philonian or Alexandrian exegesis, nor can it by one

[29] *The Witness of the Old Testament to Christ*, I, 27 (E.T.).

hair's breadth go beyond the implicit and explicit teaching of the New Testament. For example, it would be very improper on the basis of this principle to state that Aaron is a type of the pope because he was the chief of the priests (as the Catholic interpreters insist) because not a line from the New Testament can be found to support it, and the entire tenor of New Testament typology is against such an identification. Further, we must agree with Davidson that a thin spiritualizing of the Old Testament with no proper recognition of the literal meaning of the passages is not to be permitted. And we must further agree with Davidson when he argues that "any hermeneutic which goes so far as to eliminate from the prophecies of the Old Testament which refer to the New Testament times, *the natural race of Abraham, seems to go against the methods of interpretation applied by the apostles.*" [30]

(ii). Again we must agree with Davidson that the coming of Jesus Christ gives us a new perspective for interpreting the Old Testament. The Old Testament was given in a specific *dispensational* form and if Old Testament truth carries over into the New Testament some of the dispensational form must be dropped as it most certainly is in typology proper. That is to say, the fulfilment of the prophecy is not to be expected to be in the exact form of the prophecy. The amillennialist makes the greatest divorce between the form and the fulfilment of prophecy and that is why the more literal-minded postmillenarians and premillenarians are restive with it. The dispensationalists judge that the distinction between the form and the idea of prophecy is spurious, and therefore they look for the fulfilment of prophecy to be very similar to the precise form in which it was given in the Old Testament.

Davidson's point is that with the advent of Christ *some change in the form of fulfilment* must be expected. With Davidson's strong insistence on the primacy of the literal

[30] *Op. cit.*, p. 477. Italics are ours.

meaning of the Scripture this does not at all prejudice the case for amillennialism, although it does prejudice the case against an extreme and indefensible literalism.

(iii). Contemporary scholars like Hebert and Vischer are advocating a return to a typological (Vischer) or mystical in-terpretation (Hebert) as the only means of counter-attacking the prophetic negativism use of the grammatico-historical method of exegesis in the hands of the religious liberals. In a very real sense radical criticism was a return of Marcionism, and an unusually narrow use of the grammatical principle in Old Testament exegesis spelled the death of any predictive element in it. This exegetical negativism is to be escaped by a return to an expanded typological exegesis (although Vischer has been accused of being too free in his use of it).[31] Again the inspiration for a return to the typological exegesis of the Old Testament is the firm belief that in some significant sense the *Old Testament is a Christian book*.

We have now come to the issue which can be delayed no longer: *what hermeneutical method does the New Testament use in employing the Old?* Certainly this should be decisive if it could be unequivocally settled. This does not mean that we cannot garner some hermeneutical insights by a study of the Old Testament. The literal fulfilment of some of the prophe-cies within the Old Testament period indicates the validity

---

[31] Cf. Vischer, *op. cit.*, I, Chapter I; and Hebert, *The Throne of David* ("Clearly, in this general sense the mystical interpretation of the Old Testament is for Christians a matter of obligation." P. 256). Hebert's mystical interpretation is similar to Vischer's typological, and Hebert makes it clear he is advocating no return to previous excesses of this method. Ludwig Koehler has brought four major criticisms against the revived typological exegesis of Vischer ("Christus im Alten und im Neuen Testament," *Theologische Zeitschrift*, 4:253, July–August, 1953). (i) Vischer robs the Old Testament of its own individuality by making its function exclusively that of a pointer to the New; (ii) all the promises within the Old Testament for its own time period have no meaning to Vischer until related to the New; (iii) his typological exegesis is too much an appeal to the understanding and not enough to the heart and conscience; (iv) and he judges interpretations by their effectiveness not their truthfulness.

of that principle, and Wyngaarden has pointed out a measure of typological interpretation within the Old Testament itself of such terms as Zion, Israel, and Jerusalem (to mention a few). But if the New Testament contains an inspired interpretation of the Old Testament then we ought to be able to settle the basic issue at least. Wace properly writes that "no interpretation of prophecy can be compatible with the claims of the Christian faith which is not in harmony with that of our Lord, and of the Evangelists and Apostles." [32] How does the New Testament use the Old?

(i) Sometimes it is cited to *prove* a point (John 6:45) or a doctrine (Mat. 22:32, 43–44). (ii) Sometimes it is cited to *explain* a point such as bringing out the fearsomeness of Mt. Sinai (Hebrews 12:20). (iii) Sometimes it is cited to *illustrate* some New Testament truth (Rom. 10:18) or to illustrate forcibly by using the language of the Old Testament when some other thought is intended. (iv) Sometimes it is cited as being *literally fulfilled* in the New Testament as with our Lord's birth in Bethlehem (Mat. 2:5–6). Sometimes the New Testament cites the Old Testament *in an expanded typological sense.*

First, the New Testament contains typological interpretations of the Old Testament with reference to its moral teachings and spiritual teachings. The evidence of 1 Cor. 10:6, 11 and Rom. 15:4 is simply incontrovertible at this point. Whenever we draw out an ethical principle, a spiritual rule, or a devotional from the Old Testament which is not a matter of its literal expression we have made a typological interpretation. No doubt all caution and hermeneutical care is to be followed in such instances, but much of the use of the Old Testament in the preaching and teaching ministry would be lost if we denied this use of the Old Testament.

Second, the New Testament contains typological interpretations of theological elements in the Old Testament. This is the province primarily of typology proper but its extended

[32] *Prophecy: Jewish and Christian*, p. 131.

usage cannot be denied. Creation is a type of new creation in Christ (2 Cor. 4:6), as it is of the complete salvation in Christ (Hebrews 4:4). Further, all that has been said previously of *multiple fulfilment* (and compenetration) applies here. Multiple fulfilment is possible only if a much deeper and pervasive typical element is recognized in the Old Testament than typology proper.

Third, the Greek word *epouranios* ("heavenly") is approximately equivalent to typological. The earthly calling of the Hebrew people is typical of the heavenly calling of the Christian (Hebrews 3:1), and the earthly blessing of Israel is typical of the heavenly gift in Christianity (Hebrews 6:4), and the earthly land of Palestine is typical of the heavenly country of Christian promise (Hebrews 11:6), and the earthly Jerusalem of the coming heavenly Jerusalem (Hebrews 12:22). The typical character of much of the Old Testament economy therefore cannot be denied.

Fourth, the deep-seated typical character of the Old Testament economy (and thereby requiring typological exegesis) is noted in those instances where Israel and the Church are spoken of interchangeably. Paul's use of the Israel of God in Galatians 6:16 bears this out. What avails in Christ, Paul argues, is the cross and the new creation, not circumcision. Upon those who walk according to *this rule* (that which counts is the cross and the new creation in Christ) Paul invokes a blessing. Then he adds: "and upon the Israel of God." If this expression meant the Jewish people, or even Jewish Christians he would be directly contradicting himself. The true people of God are not the Judaizers who wish to circumcize their converts, but those who glory in the cross and are new creations in Christ. Further, the peace and mercy invoked in this passage *on the basis of this rule* is invoked upon those who walk according to it (and as the parallel Greek construction demands) upon the Israel of God. It is inescapable that the *Israel of God* means the true people of God (in contrast to the Judaizers) who glory in the cross and count the new birth as that saving act of God and not circumcision.

In Hebrews 8:8 the new covenant is made with the house of Israel and Judah. The strict literalists insist that this means Israel and Judah and not the Church for if it meant the Church we would have an unequivocal instance in which Israel is spoken to when the Church is meant and the essential distinction between Israel and the Church would be obliterated. The following is to be noted: (i) The New Covenant is one of the several items discussed in Hebrews all of which are now realized in the Church and the present age. That Christ is our Moses, our Aaron, our Sacrifice the strict literalists readily admit. To isolate the New Covenant and forward it to the millennium is to disrupt the entire structure of Hebrews. (ii) The writer of Hebrews applies the New Covenant to Christian experience in Hebrews 10:15-17. Bales makes a sharp but accurate observation here. If the New Covenant belongs to Israel alone and that during the millennium, then the writer of Hebrews has erred in applying it to present Christian experience.[33] To say that we are under the benefits of the Covenant without actually being under the covenant is to clandestinely admit what is boldly denied. (iii) The multiplication of covenants becomes confusing. When our Lord initiated the Lord's Table he mentioned the new covenant. Dispensationalists observe the Lord's Table and must so admit that some new covenant is now in effect, but deny that the New Covenant of the Lord's Table is the same as the New Covenant of Hebrews 8. We thus have two new covenants. (iv) The terms of the New Covenant are distinctly Christian and that is why they are applied to Christians in Hebrews 10. Yet to strict literalists the millennial age is an age of the restitution of the law.[34] But the very

[33] *Op. cit.*, pp. 110-111.

[34] The Sermon on the Mount is called the constitution of the millennial kingdom (*Scofield Reference Bible*, p. 999) and is labeled as *pure law* (p. 1000). So much so that even the petition for forgiveness of sins in the Lord's Prayer is called *legal ground* (p. 1002).

wording of the New Covenant is so clear at this point. It is declared that it will not be like the Covenant made at Mount Sinai (Hebrews 8:9).

Fifth, the context of the passage associates the mediatorial office of Christ with the New Covenant. Christ is the *mediator* of a new covenant and this is speaking of his *present work as mediator*. If his mediatorship is *present*, the covenant which he founded and upon which his mediatorship is based is *present*. To remove the covenant from its present operation is thereby to remove the grounds of the mediatorship of Christ. Strict literalists who would push the New Covenant on to the millennium have not calculated properly with the implications of such an interpretation upon Hebrews 8:6.

In short, the only consistency in Hebrews is to admit either that *all* items refer to the Jews during the millennium or that *all* pertain to the Christian dispensation. But no interpreter would dare remove the precious truths of Hebrews *en toto* from the Christian Church and make them valid only for the millennium. We are compelled to believe that the New Covenant spoken of in Jeremiah spoke of Israel and Judah as typical of the New Testament people.

Finally, we have some examples of typological exegesis in Paul's use of the Old Testament. Physical circumcision is typical of spiritual purification (Col. 2:11, Romans 2:29, Phil. 3:3, and Eph. 2:11). The care given the treading oxen of the Old Testament is typical of the care to be given the servants of Christ (1 Cor. 9:9). The veil covering the face of Moses is typical of the spiritual darkness of present unbelieving Israel (2 Cor. 3:13–16). The law written on tablets of stone is typical of the gospel written on the human heart (2 Cor. 3:1). The darkness and light of creation are typical of the darkness of human sin and the truth of the gospel in illumination (2 Cor. 4:6). The passover lamb is typical of the saving death of Christ (1 Cor. 5:7).

Supplementary to this is similar treatment of the Old Testament in the closing chapter of Hebrews. The altar of the

Old Testament is typical of the cross of Christ (13:10–12). The burning of the sacrifice without the camp is typical of the rejection of Christ, and so we too ought to go without the boundaries of "official religion" and fellowship with the sufferings of Jesus (13:13). The city of Jerusalem is typical of the city to come (13:14). The Old Testament sacrifices are typical of the spiritual sacrifices of Christians (13:15).

As Girdlestone put it, "Israel is thus a representative or typical nation, in its origin, its history, its bondage, and its deliverance. Its story is prophetic, inasmuch as it is the key to the philosophy of all history. It is also provisional and there is an anticipation running through it which is fulfilled in Christ." [35]

An extreme literalism or an extreme typological approach is equally contrary to the method by which the New Testament interprets the Old. But just as the ellipses of the planets have two foci while the sun is only at one of them, so there must be a controlling principle between the typological and the literal interpretation of prophecy. One must be the point of departure, and in keeping with the system of hermeneutics proposed earlier in this volume we make the literal the control over the typological. Therefore, *interpret prophecy literally unless the implicit or explicit teaching of the New Testament suggests typological interpretation.*

Obviously this does not immediately settle the millennial question, the *crux interpretum* of Old Testament prophetic interpretation, and it is not the function of hermeneutics as a science that it should. A particular belief is the product of an applied hermeneutical theory. However the position here stated favors a millennial interpretation of the kingdom of God.

In some passages of Old Testament prophecy it is difficult to determine whether the deliverance spoken of refers to the return from the Babylonian captivity or to millennial deliverance. Further, passages of great salvation and joy usually

[35] *Op. cit.*, p. 85.

referred to the millennium could refer to the future state in glory. Further, the *raison d'être* of the millennium must most assuredly be (as John Gill so forcibly points out in his great *Body of Divinity*) the manifestation of the glory of Christ.

(4). *The centrality of Jesus Christ must be kept in mind in all prophetic interpretation.* Millennialism degenerates into cultism whenever prophetic interpretation ceases to be dominantly Christological. Some premillennialism has been branded as excessively Jewish and perhaps those premillennialists are misunderstood because they have failed to be sufficiently Christological in their interpretation. Girdlestone's advice can be well taken in this connection: "To study the prophets without reference to Christ seems as unscientific as to study the body without reference to the head. The Spirit of Christ was in the Prophets all the way through (1 Pet. 1:11), and each book is to be read as part of a great whole." [36] The Roman Catholic exegetes have erred at this point, finding far too much Catholicism in the Old Testament rather than Jesus Christ.

The finest statement of the Christological principle in Old Testament interpretation is that of Francis Roberts who lived in the seventeenth century:

Now that we may more successfully and clearly understand Scripture by Scripture, these ensuing particulars are to be observed: (I) *That Jesus Christ is our mediator and the salvation of sinners by Him is the very substance, marrow, soul and scope of the whole Scriptures.* What are the whole Scriptures, but as it were the spiritual swadling clothes of the Holy child Jesus. (1) Christ is the truth and substance of all types and shadows. (2) Christ is the matter and substance of the Covenant of Grace under all administrations thereof; under the Old Testament Christ is *veyled*, under the New Covenant *revealed*. (3) Christ is the centre and meetingplace of all the promises, for in him all the promises of God are yea, and they are Amen. (4) Christ is the thing signified, sealed, and exhibited in all the sacraments of the Old and New Testaments, whether

[36] *Ibid.*, p. 107.

ordinary or extraordinary. (5) Scripture genealogies are to lead us on to the true line of Christ. (6) Scripture chronologies are to discover to us the times and seasons of Christ. (7) Scripture laws are our schoolmaster to bring us to Christ; the moral by correcting, the ceremonial by directing. And (8) Scripture gospel is Christ's *light*, whereby we know him; Christ's voice whereby we hear and follow him; Christ's cords of love, whereby we are drawn into sweet union and communion with him; yea, it is the power of God unto salvation unto all them that believe in Christ Jesus. Keep therefore still Jesus Christ in your eye, in the perusal of the Scripture, as the end, scope, and substance thereof. For as the sun gives light to all the heavenly bodies, so Jesus Christ the sun of righteousness gives light to all the Holy Scriptures.[37]

The *apocalypse* is one of the modes of prophetic communication. Religious liberalism and radical critics have had some very harsh things to say about the Biblical apocalypses but recent scholarship has more properly assessed them and taken a far more wholesome attitude toward them.[38] Apocalyptic language is *prophetic*, *historical*, and *symbolic*. The rules are easy; the interpretation difficult. (1) In interpreting apocalyptic literature all that has been said of the rules and praxis for general interpretation applies at this point. (2) In the interpretation of apocalyptic imagery a complete literalistic method is impossible. Those who claim to be complete literalists with reference to Revelation cannot consistently follow their program out. The issue is not between spiritualization and literalism but between lesser and greater degrees of spiritualization. To be thoroughly literal we would have to insist that a literal (actual) woman sat literally upon seven literal hills! that Jesus Christ has a literal sword coming out of his

[37] *Clavis Bibliorum* (1675), p. 10, cited by Briggs, *Biblical Study*, p. 363. Italics are his.

[38] Cf. H. H. Rowley, "The Voice of God in Apocalyptic," *Interpretation*, 2:403–429, October, 1948; E. F. Scott, "The Natural Language of Religion," *Interpretation*, 2:420–429, October, 1948; Raymond Calkins, "Militant Message," *Interpretation*, 2:430–443, October, 1948; and Charles T. Fritsch, "The Message of Apocalyptic for Today," *Theology Today*, 10:357–366, October, 1953.

mouth! and that beasts can act and talk like men! To be literalistic in interpreting Revelation really means that the symbols of Revelation pertain to real, visible occurrences here on earth in contrast to some sort of gradual or historical fulfilment of the symbols in a thinner form. (3) Every effort must be made to discover whether the symbol had any meaning in the culture of the writer. This demands a very careful and exacting historical research by the exegete. (4) The passage in which the apocalyptic symbol appears must be carefully examined to see whether the meaning of the symbol is there revealed. (5) An examination must be made of history if the apocalypse is fulfilled in history. Fortunately, with reference to much of Daniel and Zechariah this is possible. (6) With reference to New Testament books, inter-Biblical apocryphal literature must be examined to see whether it contributed any of the symbols. (7) With special reference to the book of Revelation the Old Testament must be searched thoroughly for every possible clue to the symbols there used.[39]

C. The Meaning of 2 Peter 1:20

This verse of Scripture has been given three major interpretations. The first is that the Catholics use it to prove that

---

[39] Once again it must be said that if the student works with the genuinely scholarly works, commentaries and other reference works, he will find much of these details already settled. A comprehensive survey of all the types of apocalyptic symbols used in the book of Revelation will be found in J. P. Lange, *Revelation* (E. R. Craven, American editor), pp. 1–41. Another substantial list of apocalyptic symbols is in *The Holy Bible Commentary*, IV (New Testament), pp. 468–86. A sensible set of rules for interpreting Revelation, which could be applied to all apocalyptic literature is in Henry Cowles, *The Revelation of John*, p. 39 ff. Terry, *Biblical Hermeneutics*, gives two chapters to the interpretation of apocalypsis, but merely for illustration. He says that "the hermeneutical principles to be observed in the interpretation of apocalyptics are, in the main, the same as those which we apply to all predictive prophecy," p. 340. There is no rule of thumb method to unlock the mysteries and perplexities of apocalyptic imagery. Hermeneutics is an art and a science, and the specific interpretations of the interpreter reveal to what degree he is an artist and scientist.

the church, not the individual, is to interpret the Bible. Some Protestants use it to prove that no prophetic passage is to be interpreted in isolation from other passages. And the third, and that which appears to be the correct one, is that it has nothing to do with prophetic interpretation at all, but with the divine origin of prophecy.

The theme that Peter is discussing is the divine origin and nature of prophecy. He is talking about the sure word of prophecy, that it is well for all of us to reckon with, for it is a shining light in a dark place. Having said this, he then tells us that the reason for these remarks is that the prophetic utterances come not from man but from the Holy Spirit. Thus the *context* has nothing to do with the interpretation of prophecy, but its inspiration, and verse 20 should be so interpreted.

In justification of this is the most evident parallelism of thought between verses 20 and 21. (a). *Private inspiration* of verse 20 is apposite to the *will of man* in verse 21. (b). The *origination* of prophecy is denied to man in verse 20, but affirmed of the Holy Ghost in verse 21. (c). Personal, private, self-inspiration of verse 20 stands opposite to the holy men of God in verse 21.

Moreover, a careful study of the Greek text of verse 20 seems to bear the interpretation we give it. The King James Version translates the Greek *ginetai* very weakly with an "is." If it were translated more accurately, it would have been rendered *came*, or *came into existence*, anticipating the *were moved* of verse 21. The word translated by *interpretation* is not the customary word for such but is from the verb meaning "to loose." There is a sense in which *to loose* means to interpret, in that the meaning of a passage is explained releasing its sense, and it is so used in Mark 4:34. Rendering the expression painfully literally, it would read "private unloosing." That is, no Scriptural prophecy originated through personal, individual, inspiration (loosing or releasing) but by the unloosing, releasing, or inspiration of the Holy Spirit.

Robertson[40] translates *epiluseos* as *disclosure*. As such it makes the verse speak of inspiration, not of interpretation. In his *Word Pictures in loco*, he says: "It is the prophet's grasp of the prophecy, not that of the readers that is here presented, as the next verse shows." [41] Fronmüller, in Lange's *Commentary*, says: "The reference is to the origin, not to the interpretation of the prophecy, as is evident from v. 21." [42] The American editor of the same cites Alford and Bengel as agreeing with this view. Williams, in the *American Commentary on the New Testament*, shows how the Catholics take the usual interpretation of this verse much to their own advantage and then says: ". . . but the best view seems to be this: 'That no prophecy of the Scripture is a matter of one's own explanation'—that is, the prophets do not originate their own prophecies; they receive them entire from above as is clear from the fact given in the next verse. Peter, therefore, must be understood as saying nothing whatever relative to interpreting the Scriptures." [43]

Alford gives quite an extended note in his *Greek Testament* substantiating the interpretation we are defending. Others interpreting the verse this way are Huther in Meyer's *Commentary*, and Lumby in *The Holy Bible Commentary*. Fairbairn also takes this to be the meaning of the passage and brings out the same point we have about *ginetai*.[44] However, Bigg[45] makes *ginetai* simply equivalent to "is," and says that the text does not state who the authoritative interpreters are. Bigg says the important question is: what is the opposite of private interpretation? It can only be that (a) no prophetic

[40] *A Grammar of the Greek New Testament in the Light of Historical Research* (fifth edition), p. 514.

[41] Vol. VI, p. 159.

[42] Vol. IX (second German edition), p. 21.

[43] *Peter*, vol. VII, p. 91.

[44] P. Fairbairn, *Prophecy*, p. 497.

[45] C. Bigg, *The Epistles of St. Peter and St. Jude* (The International Critical Commentary), p. 269 ff. Bigg does not even mention this alternative interpretation suggested here and defended by a number of scholars.

passage can be interpreted by itself since all prophecy is by the same author and must be therefore correlated, or (b) that there must be a "public" authority to interpret Scripture. But Peter is not talking of possibilities of misinterpreting Scripture, but of the divine origin of prophecy and its usefulness to the Christian.

BIBLIOGRAPHY

Bales, *New Testament Interpretations of Old Testament Prophecies.*
Davidson, *Old Testament Prophecy.*
Girdlestone, *The Grammar of Prophecy.*
Berry, *Premillennialism and Old Testament Prediction.*
Wace, *Prophecy: Jewish and Christian.*
Fairbairn, *Prophecy.*
———, *Fairbairn versus Fairbairn.*
A Catholic Commentary on the Holy Scripture.
Beecher, *The Prophets and the Promises.*
Johnson, *The Quotations of the New Testament from the Old.*
Feinberg, *Premillennialism or Amillennialism?* (second edition).
Wyngaarden, *The Future of the Kingdom in Prophecy and Fulfilment.*
Robertson, *Regnum Dei.*
Vischer, *The Witness of the Old Testament to Christ.*
Hebert, *The Throne of David.*
Briggs, *Biblical Study.*
Zenos, "Prophecy," *A New Standard Bible Dictionary*, p. 742.
Oehler, *Old Testament Theology.*
von Orelli, "Prophecy, Prophets," *The International Standard Bible Encyclopedia*, IV, 2459–66.
Meyrick, "Prophet," *Smith's Dictionary of the Bible*, III, 2590–2602.
Chafer, *The Science of Biblical Hermeneutics.*
Angus and Green, *Cyclopedic Handbook to the Bible.*
Murray, *Millennial Studies.*
Rutgers, *Premillennialism in America.*
Reese, *The Approaching Advent of Christ.*
Mauro, *God's Present Kingdom.*
Rall, *Modern Premillennialism and the Christian Hope.*
Snowden, *The Coming of the Lord.*
Allis, *Prophecy and the Church.*

CHAPTER XI

THE INTERPRETATION OF PARABLES

A. THE NATURE OF PARABLES

THE etymological meaning of the word *parable* is "a placing alongside of" for the purpose of comparison. It thus represents a method of illustration so that it could be said: "The kingdom of heaven is illustrated by the following situation." However, historical studies have revealed that the word is really not capable of simple definition, but has been used in many senses.[1] Besides the word *parabolē*, the word *paroimia* is used which means "a saying by the wayside, a proverb, a maxim." The use of *paroimia* is restricted to John's gospel.

Dodd's definition is that a parable "at its simplest . . . is a metaphor or simile drawn from nature or common life, arresting the hearer by its vividness or strangeness, and leaving the mind in sufficient doubt about its precise application to rouse it into active thought." [2] As such a parable differs from a *fable* in that it is neither trivial nor fantastic; from the *myth* in that the parable is not a creation of popular folklore; from the *allegory* which finds meaning at many points in the narrative; and from such *figures of speech* as simile or metaphor although in a qualified sense as Dodd has indicated the parable is a sort of metaphor or simile. At times too it is difficult to separate the parable from the allegory, especially in the longer parable where several elements have symbolic meaning.

Scholars differ widely in their count of the number of par-

[1] B. T. D. Smith, *The Parables of the Synoptic Gospels*, Chapters I and II.

[2] *The Parables of the Kingdom* (third edition), p. 16.

ables in the Gospels,[3] and this is due to the difficulty of decid-
ing what is parabolic and what is not. Smith has indicated
the different forms that parables may take, and also notes
the types of introductions which usually preface parables.[4]
The argument that the account of Lazarus and Dives is not
a parable because it is not introduced as a parable is not valid
because Oesterly has demonstrated that parables may be
given with no typical introduction.[5] Generally scholars divide
the parables into simple utterances, parables, and extended
parables.[6] It is the extended parable which has similarities
to the allegory.

There are about thirty parables usually treated in works
on the parables. Luke has the most and John the least. The
importance of the study of the parables is to be found in their
sheer number representing a large part of the text of the
Gospels, and thereby embodying considerable material of a
didactic nature. They give us information as to the progress
of the gospel in the world, the results of its propagation, about
the end of the age, the dealings of God with the Jewish people
and the Gentiles, and the nature of the kingdom of God. Any
doctrine of the kingdom or eschatology which ignores a careful study of the parables cannot be adequate.

The intention of parabolic teaching is given by Christ in
Matthew 13:11-17, Mark 4:10-12, and Luke 8:8-10. First,
it is a method of teaching the *responsive* disciple. At the end
of the first parable our Lord said, "He that hath ears to hear,
let him hear" (Luke 8:8). When the disciples asked him why

[3] Moulton notes that by different countings scholars have suggested
79, 71, 59, 39, 37 and 33 parables. "Parables," *Dictionary of Christ and
the Gospels*, II, 313. This is a most valuable article for the study of
parables as is Nourse, "Parable," *Hastings Encyclopedia of Religion and
Ethics*, IX, 628.

[4] Smith, *op. cit.*, p. 30 ff.

[5] Oesterly, *The Gospel Parables in the Light of Their Jewish Background*, p. 11.

[6] Dodd gives *Gleichnis, Parabel*, and *Novellen (op. cit.*, pp. 17-18),
and cites Bultmann's division of *Bildwörter, Gleichnisse*, and *Parabel*
(p. 18 fn.).

he said this and taught in parables our Lord answered that it was given unto the disciples to know the mysteries (disclosures) of the kingdom of God. Hence, parables were used by our Lord as instruments of his revelation to those who had ears to hear. Parables contain much that every Christian servant needs to know about the kingdom of God. Some parables teach him not to be depressed at the apparent failure of the gospel or the corruption of the gospel; others tell him not to be ambitious beyond which the gospel promises; and still others tell him not to be discouraged because the success of God is secure. Thus the parables stand as *sine qua non* material for intelligent Christian service.

The second intent of parabolic teaching was to hide the truth from the *unresponsive* and so aid in the hardening of their heart as they continuously rebelled against God. This is the special import of the citation from Isaiah 6. The truth taught in a parable is veiled and so is a test of a person's spiritual responsiveness, of whether he has the spiritual intention to follow through and learn its meaning.

The origin of parabolic teaching has been traced by Smith from Old Testament references, to rabbinical teaching, to New Testament usage.[7] The method was copiously used among the rabbis. The Greek word *parabolē* is equivalent to the Hebrew word *mashal*. One of the current rabbinic sayings was, "I will parable to thee a parable." Among the Greeks a parable stood for an argument from analogy.

There are four elements to a parable: (i) A parable is some commonly known *earthly* thing, event, custom, or possible occurrence. The emphasis is on the word *earthly*. Parables are about farming, marriages, kings, feasts, household relationships, business arrangements, or customs of the peoples. It is this concrete and pictorial grounding which makes them such remarkable instruments for instruction.

[7] Smith, *op. cit.*, p. 3 ff. Also, Oesterly, *op. cit.*, p. 3 ff. Cf. also the work of Feldman, *The Parables and Similes of the Rabbis*.

(ii). Beyond the earthly element is the spiritual lesson, or theological truth which the parable *intends* to teach.

(iii). This *earthly* element bears an *analogical* relationship to the spiritual element. It is this analogical relationship which gives the parable its illustrative, or argumentative force.

(iv). Because a parable has two levels of meaning every parable stands in need of interpretation. The actors, elements, and actions need to be identified. One of the tributes paid to Jülicher's famous work on the parables is that he freed the interpretation of parables from allegorization. Whenever any interpreter seeks an elaboration of meaning in a parable, and commences to find meaning in far more points than the parable can hope to make, that interpreter has returned to the reprehensible method of allegorizing the parables.

B. RULES FOR THE INTERPRETATION OF PARABLES

A study of the literature of the parables reveals that the parables are not as easy to interpret as their simple nature would seem to indicate. We propose to discuss the interpretation of parables from the viewpoint of four principles: perspective, cultural, exegetical, and doctrinal.

(1). The *perspective principles* inform us that to adequately interpret the parables we need to understand them in their relationship to Christology and the kingdom of God.

One of the factors in which recent studies differ somewhat from older studies in the parables is that the recent studies indicate the *Christological nature* of parabolic teaching.[8] In these studies it is indicated that we have more than the *mashal* teaching of the rabbis, more than apt illustrations of moral or spiritual truths. In the Gospels it is the Christ who

---

[8] Cf. Hoskyns and Davey, *The Riddle of the New Testament*, p. 132, and, Wallace, "The Parables and the Preacher," *The Scottish Journal of Theology*, 2:13–28, March, 1949.

is teaching about *his* kingdom, and in some measure is reflectively teaching truth about *himself*. In some parables Christ is the leading figure, or the parable has meaning only as related directly to Christ or his word. Thus in approaching any parable we must ask ourselves this: *how does this parable relate to Christ?* Are any of the persons in the parable Christ? Does the parable concern the word or teaching or mission of Christ? Only when we thus approach each parable Christologically do we obtain the correct perspective.

The second perspective principle is *the kingdom principle*. Christ came preaching a gospel of the kingdom and announcing that a kingdom was at hand. Many of the parables directly state that they are about the kingdom, and others not specifically stated cannot be divorced from the kingdom. Adequate interpretation of the parables must now be based upon an understanding of the kingdom of God and the relationship of Jesus Christ and His gospel to that kingdom. This Hope stated when he wrote that "it must be borne in mind that all of [the parables] deal with one great subject, and one great subject only, namely, the kingdom of God." [9]

(i). First of all, *the kingdom has come*. In some sense it is in existence from Christ's first preaching, and men are entering it. This is the kingdom in its *actualized* sense. It is entered by the new birth (John 3:3) and our Lord stated that the tax collectors and harlots were entering the kingdom (Matt. 21:31).[10] And whatever be the interpretation of Luke

[9] Hope, "The Interpretation of Christ's Parables," *Interpretation*, 6:303, July, 1952.

[10] Modern scholarship on purely lexical grounds has asserted that there is no difference between the kingdom of God and the kingdom of heaven. Concentration on these two terms has obscured the fact that there are *several* terms used interchangeably as a study of the harmony of the Gospels in the Greek will reveal. Cf. Oesterly, *op. cit.*, pp. 19–20; Dodd, *op. cit.*, p. 34; Berkhof, *The Kingdom of God*, p. 166; Ladd, *Crucial Questions about the Kingdom of God*, p. 106 f. For a stout defense of the dispensational interpretation cf. Feinberg, *Premillennialism or Amillennialism?* (second edition), p. 286 ff., and p. 297 ff.

17:20–21, the passage indicates that in some sense the kingdom is *here*.[11]

Being *here* the kingdom continues through this age. The parables of the kingdom were also *prophecies* of the kingdom. They describe the fortunes of the kingdom through the centuries. They tell of the sowing and the reaping of the word of the kingdom; they tell of the great net let down into the sea and not pulled in until the end of the age; they tell of the grain growing until it is ripe. There can be no clear understanding of many of the parables unless we understand the continuing character of the kingdom.

(ii). The kingdom is *eschatological* in character. There is a harvest at the end of the age. The final issues are not settled until the angels of God separate the true from the false. The rightful Heir of the kingdom must come in the power and the glory of his kingdom. Certainly the eschatological element looms large in any parable which mentions the end in the form of a harvest or separation. The parables of the talents (Matt. 25:14 ff.) and the virgins (Matt. 25:1 ff.) are certainly eschatological. This eschatological element is a real and necessary element in understanding the parables and the liberals who pruned it off obscured this depth of meaning in the parable.

In summary, the interpreter must keep in mind that the kingdom in some sense has come; it is continuing; and it will come, and with this in mind he must understand whether the parable under consideration is concerned with one or all of these aspects.

(2). *The cultural principles.* To understand the parables we need not only to see them from the standpoint of the

---

[11] Those holding that the expression *entos hymōn* means "within you" are Oesterly, *op. cit.*, p. 32 and Dodd, *op. cit.*, pp. 84–85, fn. 1. To the contrary is Fuller, *The Mission and Achievement of Jesus*, p. 28 ff.; Dinkler, *The Idea of History in Near East*, p. 176; Kümmel, *Verheissung und Erfüllung*, p. 27. I am indebted to Dr. Ladd of Fuller Seminary for these *per contra* references.

kingdom of God and Christology, but also from the cultural background. Our Lord lived in ancient Palestine amidst the Jewish people, and the parables are drawn from that cultural backdrop.

In general, the parables are drawn from material familiar to a poor, agricultural peasant. The manners, customs, and material culture exhibited in the parables amply substantiate this. Further, the parables were spoken in Aramaic and some helpful information can be gleaned by translating the parables back into Aramaic.[12]

Studies in the local color of the parables have turned up a rich store of information and one is tempted to say that one should never preach again on any parable until he has made himself familiar with this material. Jeremias' book, *The Parables of Jesus*, is filled with the local color which so clearly lights up the parables. *In the interpretation of every parable it is necessary to recover as much as possible the local color employed in it.*

For example, farmers sowed their fields and then plowed them up thus making the parable of the sower much clearer. Harvest, wedding, and wine were Jewish symbols of the end of the age. The fig tree is a symbol of the people of God. Lamps were put under baskets to extinguish them, hence to light a lamp and put it under a basket is to light it and immediately put it out. The lamb which strays from the fold lies down and will not move, so he must be carried back. Mustard trees grew from small seeds to trees eight to ten feet tall. One speck of leaven penetrated enough dough to feed 162 persons. What Jeremias is able to deduce about the life of the prodigal from knowledge of Jewish customs is remarkable.[13]

---

[12] Part of the value of the work of Jeremias (*op. cit.*) is that he has the requisite learning to make this retranslation, and his work is very valuable from this standpoint. It was the necessity of knowing the cultural background for the understanding of the parables which inspired Osterly to write his work (*op. cit.*).

[13] Jeremias, *op. cit.*, pp. 103–104.

(3). *Exegetical principles.* We have tried to close in on the parables from two sides. Coming from theology we have noted the Christological and kingdom setting of the parables, and coming from background considerations we have noted the necessity of understanding the general cultural background of the parables and the specific matters of local color and customs which figure in each parable. We now come directly to the parable and consider the direct exegetical principles for the interpretation of parables.

(i). *Determine the one central truth the parable is attempting to teach.* This might be called the golden rule of parabolic' interpretation for practically all writers on the subject mention it with stress. "The typical parable presents one single point of comparison," writes Dodd. "The details are not intended to have independent significance." [14] Others have put the rule this way: *Don't make a parable walk on all fours.*

A parable is not like an allegory, for in the latter most of the elements of the narrative have meaning. To be sure, some parables are more elaborate than others and in this regard approach an allegory. But as a general or guiding rule, look for the one central thesis of the parable.

A parable is a truth carried in a vehicle. Therefore there is the inevitable presence of *accessories* which are necessary for the drapery of the parable, but are not part of the meaning. The danger in parabolic teaching at this point is to interpret as meaningful what is drapery.

(ii). *Determine how much of the parable is interpreted by the Lord Himself.* After reciting the parable of the Sower (Mat. 13:18 ff.) our Lord interprets it. After stating the parable of the enemy's sowing darnel among the wheat, our Lord interprets it later in the house. After setting forth the parable of the virgins he says, "Watch therefore, for ye know neither the day nor the hour wherein the Son of man cometh," (Matt. 25:13). In such instances we have the definite word of Christ concerning the meaning of the parable, which further conveys

[14] *Op. cit.*, p. 18.

to us the spirit of his teaching for help in parables that are not interpreted.[15]

(iii). *Determine whether there are any clues in the context concerning the parable's meaning.* The context may include what follows as well as what precedes. In Luke 15 occurs the triadic parable of the lost sheep, lost coin, and lost son. The interpretative context is Luke 15:1–2, "Then drew near unto him all the publicans and sinners for to hear him. And the Pharisees and scribes murmured saying 'This man receiveth sinners, and eateth with them.' " The parables that follow are a justification for eating with sinners and publicans. Therefore, the shepherd, the woman, and the father represent the attitude of love, forgiveness, and redemption in Christ; the lost sheep, lost coin, and lost son represent the publicans and sinners who gathered round our Lord.

The parable of the Tower and the King (Luke 14:25 ff.) is a parable of Christian service, not of salvation as indicated by the context (note v. 33, "He cannot be my disciple"). After giving the parable of the unjust steward Luke adds: "And the Pharisees also, who were covetous, heard all these things and derided him" (Luke 16:14). Therefore, the point of the parable must be taken as aimed at them.

(iv). *The comparative rule*—compare the parable with any possible Old Testament association, and with the parable as recited in one or more other of the Gospels. Both our Lord and his listeners were familiar with much of the content of the Old Testament. We must attune our thinking to be sensitive to possible Old Testament references in the parables.[16] Dodd [17] notes that such things as vineyards, fig trees, harvests, and feasts have Old Testament referents, and the Old Testament referent must be understood if we are to better understand the parable.

[15] Williams has written specifically on this point of noting how our Lord interpreted his own parables. "Jesus' Method of Interpreting Parables," *Review and Expositor*, 14:210–222, April, 1917.

[16] Cf. Wallace, *op. cit.*, p. 25.

[17] *Op. cit.*, p. 32.

Further, the interpreter must take a harmony of the Gospels in hand and study every version of each parable if it occurs in more than one Gospel. He must note concurrences and divergences, parallels and synonyms. The truest interpretation will arise out of such a comparative study.[18]

(4). *Doctrinal principles.* Any use of a parable for doctrinal purposes must observe historical sense. We ought not to read our theological debates back into the parables. Primary consideration should be given to what we judge to be the meaning which the immediate listeners garnered from the parable. There could well be more in the parable than was evident at that time but we must lay that bare with great care. We must not unceremoniously intrude into parabolic interpretation arguments about Calvinism, Arminianism, or millennialism.

Parables do teach doctrine, and the claim that they may not be used at all in doctrinal writing is improper. But in gleaning our doctrine from the parables we must be strict in our interpretation; we must check our results with the plain, evident teaching of our Lord, and with the rest of the New Testament.[19] Parables with proper cautions may be used to illustrate doctrine, illumine Christian experience, and to teach practical lessons.

The modern debates on the millennial question have frequently centered around the interpretation of some of the parables. In general, amillennialists and postmillennialists have interpreted certain parables optimistically whereas premillenarians and dispensationalists have interpreted the same parables pessimistically. For example, the growth of the mus-

[18] The thesis of Dodd (*op. cit.*) and Jeremias (*op. cit.*) is that the Church has elaborated and altered the parables. A summary of Jeremias' seven laws of transformation will be found on page 88 of his work. Needless to say this view does not reflect a substantial doctrine of inspiration by either Dodd or Jeremias.

[19] Dodd, *op. cit.*, p. 32. Wallace, *op. cit.*, p. 306. Kirk (*Lectures on the Parables*) gives more attention than most writers on parables to the matter of doctrinal teaching. Cf. pp. v-vi.

tard seed to a tree, and the permeation of the meal by the leaven is taken by the former to be a teaching of the powerful growth and spread of Christianity, and by the latter of the corruption of the professing Church. Further, some premillennial expositors interpret the pearl to be the Church, and the treasure, Israel, whereas previous interpreters took these parables as teaching how men found the Saviour.

With reference to the present status of affairs in parabolic interpretation the following may be said: (i) constant check must be made with students of rabbinics to see whether anything in their studies reveals beliefs about controversial matters in parabolic interpretation.[20] (ii) Convictions about the nature of the kingdom must certainly be built on a broader basis than two or three parables. The parables may be used to bolster millennial convictions, but the entire edifice cannot be made to rest on them. (iii) Millennial views must certainly contain the balance of optimism and pessimism as contained in the parables, as well as the teaching of the parables that the kingdom is established, is progressing, and is eschatological. A completely futuristic view of the kingdom (that in no sense does the kingdom now exist) and a completely spiritualized view of the kingdom (that the kingdom is solely the rule of God in the heart) are not true to the doctrinal teaching of the parables. The premillennialist must not be blind to the optimism of some parables, e.g., that the corn will ripen in the ear (i.e., God's purposes in this age *will be done*), nor can the postmillennialist be blind to the pessimism of other parables, e.g., the Enemy who sows darnel. Premillennialism does not require *ex hypothesi* that leaven means evil (though most premillennialists interpret it that way),[21] nor that the Hid Treasure is Israel, nor that the

[20] For example, with reference to leaven note the remarks of Findlay, *Jesus and His Parables*, p. 24; Smith, *op. cit.*, p. 121, and Oesterly, *op. cit.*, pp. 78–79.

[21] Oesterly notes that this parable really shocked the listeners, as to them leaven was uniformly associated with evil. Hence to compare the kingdom of God to leaven would be most improper. *Op. cit.*, p. 78.

Pearl is the Church. Millennial views are established on broader grounds than these.

BIBLIOGRAPHY

Angus and Green, *Cyclopedic Handbook to the Bible*, p. 220 ff.

Arndt, *The Parables of our Lord Interpreted and Illustrated.*

Bowie, "The Parables," *The Interpreter's Bible*, 7:165–175.

Barry, "Parables," *The Catholic Encyclopedia*, XI, 460–467.

Cadoux, *The Parables of Jesus, Their Art and Use.*

Dodd, *The Parables of the Kingdom* (third edition).

Findlay, *Jesus and His Parables.*

Godet, "Parables," *The New Schaff-Herzog Encyclopedia of Religious Knowledge*, III, 1739.

Habershon, *The Study of Parables.*

Hope, "The Interpretation of Christ's Parables," *Interpretation*, 6:301–307, July, 1952.

Horne, *Introduction to the Critical Study and Knowledge of the Holy Scriptures* (eighth edition), I, 366 ff.

Jeremias, *The Parables of Jesus.*

Jülicher, *Die Gleichnisreden Jesu* (1899–1910).

Kirk, *Lectures on the Parables.*

Manson (William), *Jesus the Messiah.*

Morgan, *The Parables and Metaphors of our Lord.*

Moule, "J. Jeremias 'The Parables of Jesus' and 'The Eucharistic Words of Jesus,'" *The Expository Times*, 66:46–50, November, 1954.

Moulton, "Parables," *Dictionary of Christ and the Gospels*, II, 313.

Nourse, "Parables," *Hastings Encyclopedia of Religion and Ethics*, IX, 628.

Oesterly, *The Gospel Parables in the Light of Their Jewish Background.*

Plumptre, "Parables," *Smith's Bible Dictionary*, III, 2327.

Schodde, "Parable," *The International Standard Bible Encyclopedia*, IV, 2243.

Smith (B.T.D.), *The Parables of the Synoptic Gospels.*

Cf. Allis, "The Parable of the Leaven," *The Evangelical Quarterly*, 19:254–273, October, 1947 for a thorough examination of the Old Testament usage of the word *leaven.*

Taylor, *The Parables of Our Savior.*

Terry, *Biblical Hermeneutics*, p, 188 ff.

Trench, *Notes on the Parables of Our Lord* (twelfth edition).

Wallace, "The Parables and the Preacher," *The Scottish Journal of Theology*, 2:13–28, March, 1949.

Westphal, "Some Notes on the Parables," *Crozer Quarterly*, 5:184–199, April, 1928.

Williams, "Jesus Method of Interpreting Parables," *Review and Expositor*, 14:210–222, April, 1917.

Zenos, "Parables," *A New Standard Bible Dictionary*, p. 697.

Feldman, *The Parables and Similes of the Rabbis.*

EPILOGUE

THE whole system of Conservative Protestant Christianity rests unreservedly on special revelation and the divine inspiration of Scripture. In that the message of God has meaning only when interpreted, it is ever incumbent upon the church to reflect and inquire if she has rightly interpreted the Word of God. A system of hermeneutics is crucial to our theology.

It has been the spirit of this work to endeavor to present a system of hermeneutics that would most faithfully uncover the native meaning of the Sacred Scripture. We have surveyed both the fields of general and special hermeneutics, and have given lists of many principles. Such lists are as good only as the training, intelligence, and ability of the interpreter, and the tools he uses. It is the solemn duty of every interpreter to see if these rules are correct and to equip himself with training and tools to do adequately the task of a faithful interpreter.

There is a prevailing danger to let differences in interpretation interrupt the unity of the Spirit. When differences are sharp, feelings are apt to run high. With foreboding storm clouds of oppression billowing on the distant horizon, it is well for conservative Protestantism to discover bases of fellowship rather than of divergence. If we stand together in the great truths of the Trinity, of Jesus Christ, and of Salvation, let us then work out our interpretative differences in the bounds of Christian love and endeavor to *preserve* the unity of the Spirit. A hermeneutical victory at the expense of Christian graciousness is hardly worth winning.

Finally, we all need a new sense of respect for Holy

Scripture. Believing it to be the veritable word of God, we must exercise all the human pains possible to keep from overlaying it with a gossamer pattern of our own spinning. In each of those cases where human error enters, divine truth is obscured. Let us then steer a straight course through the Holy Bible, neither turning to the left side of heresy nor to the right side of unbridled imagination.

Every interpreter, from the professional philologist to the Sunday school teacher, can well take to heart the following words of Barrows:

Foremost among the qualities that belong to the interpreter is *a supreme regard for truth.* . . . He will need a constant and vivid apprehension of the sacredness of all truth, more especially of scriptural truth, which God has revealed for the sanctification and salvation of men. "Sanctify them through thy truth: thy word is truth." These words of the Savior he will do well to ponder night and day, till they become a part of his spiritual life; and to remember always that, if such be the divine origin and high office of scriptural truth, God will not hold guiltless any who tamper with it in the interest of preconceived human opinions, thus substituting the folly of man for the wisdom of God.[1]

[1] *Companion to the Bible,* p. 522. Italics are his.

INDEX OF NAMES

INDEX OF SCRIPTURE

INDEX OF TOPICS